60 Hikes within 60 Miles: Cleveland
(including Akron and Canton)

Dedication

For Dawn—May you find joy on every trail, especially those you blaze yourself.

60 Hikes within 60 Miles:

CLEVELAND
(including Akron and Canton)

DIANE STRESING   **1st Edition**

MENASHA RIDGE PRESS
Birmingham, Alabama

Library of Congress Cataloging-in-Publication Data

Stresing, Diane, 1966–
    60 Hikes within 60 Miles, Cleveland/Diane Stresing—1st ed.
       p. cm.
    Includes index
    ISBN 0-89732-531-1
    1. Hiking—Ohio—Cleveland Region—Guidebooks. 2. Cleveland Region
(Ohio)—Guidebooks. I. Title: Sixty hikes within sixty miles, Cleveland. II. Title

    GV199.42.O32 C547 2003
    796.52'09771'32—dc21

                                                            2002037958
                                                                  CIP

Cover and text design by Grant M. Tatum
Cover photo by Diane Stresing
Maps by Steve Jones and Diane Stresing
Author photo by Dawn Ceccardi
All other photos by Diane Stresing

Menasha Ridge Press
P.O. Box 43673
Birmingham, AL 35243
www.menasharidge.com

Table of Contents

Table of Contents (cont.)

MAP LEGEND

Main Trail

Alternate Trail

Interstate Highway

U.S. Highway

State Highway

County Road

Forest Service Road

Local Road

Unpaved Road

Direction of Travel

Boardwalk or Stairs

State Border

County Border

Power Line

NATIONAL OR STATE
FOREST/PARK

Park-Forest Boundary
and Label

Trailhead
Locator Map

Water Features
Lake/Pond, Creek/River,
and Waterfall

capitol, city, and town

Peaks and Mountains

Footbridge/Dam,
Footbridge, and Dam

Tunnel

Swamp/Marsh

35: Name of Hike

Compass, Map Number,
Name and Scale

Off map or pinpoint
indication arrow

Caution/Warning

Trailhead
for specific Maps

Ranger Station/
Rest Room Facilities

Ranger Station

Rest Room Facilities

Shelter

Structure
or Feature

Monument/
Sculpture

Parking

Recreation Area

Metro Rail

Shuttle
Dropoff

Campgrounds

Picnic Area

Gate

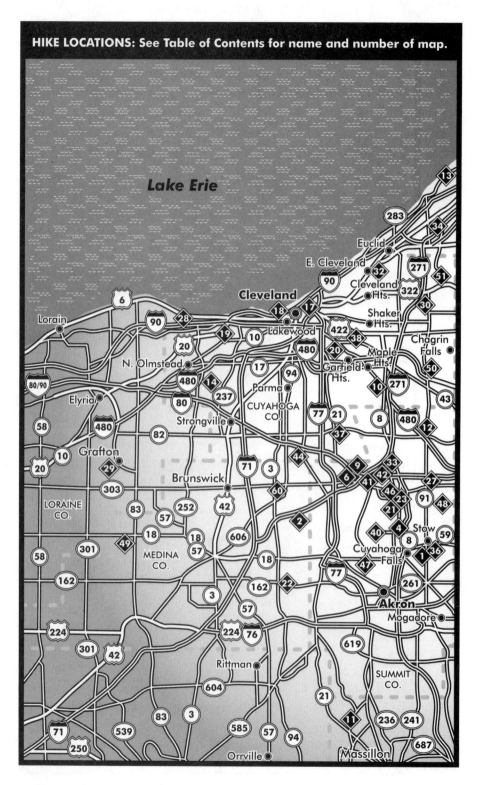

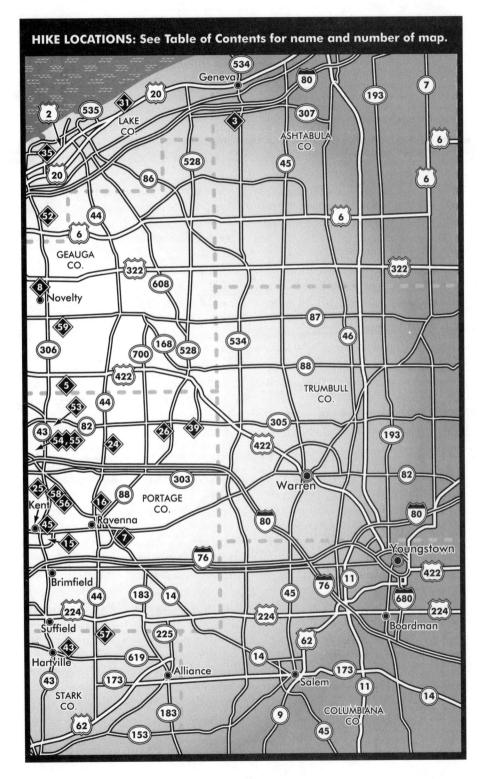

HIKE LOCATIONS: See Table of Contents for name and number of map.

Acknowledgments

Every book is the result of collaboration, and I feel very fortunate to have collaborated with some great people on this one.

It seems appropriate to start by thanking Bud Zehmer, at Menasha Ridge Press, who in giving me this project offered me my greatest assignment yet. Russell Helms took the bits and pieces I sent and turned them into a real book—amazing work! (Thanks, Russell.) Tricia Parks handled things behind the scenes I can only imagine. In fact, everyone at Menasha Ridge Press made working on this book a pleasant experience.

Here at home, my family and friends were terrifically supportive of this project. My husband Dave hiked many trails with me (when he'd rather have been on his bike!), and my daughter pointed out a thousand beetles, butterflies, and snails I'd have missed had I been alone on the trail. She also took quite a few pictures for this project and was my chief cheerleader as I worked toward various deadlines. My father drove up from Columbus on several occasions to hike with me. He is also responsible, I suppose, for giving me the hiking gene. Although it may be a few years before scientists discover it, I'm certain that some of us are predisposed to the sport—and I am grateful for the inclination to hit the trail. (Thanks, Dad!) I am also grateful for years of motherly advice.

Because of it, I was careful, wore sunscreen and good shoes, carried quarters for phone calls, took a light snack, and drank plenty of water along the way. (Thanks, Mom. See, I was listening.) Gary and Michelle Schultz were encouraging to a fault—and as a result, were subjected to countless details of countless trails. (Thank you both!)

I am also indebted to dozens of people "in the field," so to speak, who shared with me their time, enthusiasm, and incredible knowledge as I worked on this book. They include: Sue Allen, Charlie Beckwith, Sally Beckwith, Dan Best, Judy Bradt-Barnhart, Judy Casey (we had fun at Babb Run, didn't we?), Chris Craycroft, Debra-Lynn Hook, Matt Hutter, Chip Gross, Jennifer Hillmer, Paige Hosier, Debbie Laveck, Carol Marik, Sam Marshall, Sue Mottl, Keith Kessler, Mary Krohmer, Dan Kunz, Dave Roberts, Brad Stemen, Eva Stephans, Stephanie Thomas, Carol Ward, and members of Portage Trail Walkers and the Cuyahoga Valley National Park Trailblazers. Finally, though it may seem odd in this context, I also wish to acknowledge the Portage County Animal Protective League. The weak and frightened puppy they rescued (ironically, from a park) grew into a great hiking buddy. Always eager to hit the trail, he never complained about revisiting a section or an entire hike. Now, if I could just get him to carry my camera …

Foreword

Welcome to Menasha Ridge Press's *60 Hikes within 60 Miles,* a series designed to provide hikers with information needed to find and hike the very best trails surrounding cities usually underserved by good guidebooks.

Our strategy was simple: First, find a hiker who knows the area and loves to hike. Second, ask that person to spend a year researching the most popular and very best trails around. And third, have that person describe each trail in terms of difficulty, scenery, condition, elevation change, and all other categories of information that are important to hikers. "Pretend you've just completed a hike and met up with other hikers at the trailhead," we told each author. "Imagine their questions, be clear in your answers."

An experienced hiker and writer, author Diane Stresing has selected 60 of the best hikes in and around the Cleveland metropolitan area, ranging from the rail trails and urban hikes that make use of parklands to flora- and fauna-rich treks along the numerous area lakes and hills in the hinterlands. From urban hikes that make use of parklands and streets to aerobic outings in the Cuyahoga Valley, Stresing provides hikers (and walkers) with a great variety of hikes—and all within roughly 60 miles of Cleveland.

You'll get more out of this book if you take a moment to read the Introduction explaining how to read the trail listings. The "Topographic Maps" section will help you understand how useful topos will be on a hike, and will also tell you where to get them. And though this is a "where-to," not a "how-to" guide, those of you who have not hiked extensively will find the Introduction of particular value.

As much for the opportunity to free the spirit as well as to free the body, let Diane Stresing's hikes elevate you above the urban hurry.

All the best.

—*The editors at Menasha Ridge Press*

What's the difference between a hike and a walk? I fielded this question often while I was writing this book. Sure there's a difference, I thought. But what? In my dictionary, "hike" comes right after "hijack," begging a word-association game. Is a hike just a walk, hijacked by wanderlust? Perhaps.

The folks at Merriam-Webster define *hike* as "a long walk especially for pleasure or exercise," and also "to travel by any means." But walking is a mode of transportation, too. Again, I wondered, what *is* the difference?

With all due respect to Merriam and Webster, walking is *primarily* a means of transportation, a point-A-to-point-B kind of thing. Hiking is more a means of *exploration*—even when the ground you're exploring lies between point A and point B. When you define hiking as a means of exploration, you can turn a walk into a hike by altering your perspective. Your perspective will be different than mine, even on the same trail. That's part of the fun of hiking—finding out where the trail takes you.

Land of Plenty (of Variety)

Every hiker has a favorite topography. When I began this book, I was a hill-lover —the steeper and rockier the better. A view from on high was a bonus, but I was really there for the climb. I recognize that lake loops have a serene quality, and forests offer a comfort of their own. But to my surprise, as I gathered a variety of hikes for this book, I developed a genuine appreciation—a love, really—for wetlands. The sticky goo of a bog and the temporary squishiness of a vernal pool feel like the bottom of a giant petri dish, growing the strangest stuff!

Whatever land type is your favorite, you can probably find it here in northeastern Ohio. Between the gluey bogs and slippery marshes and the edge of Lake Erie, you'll find pretty waterfalls, steep outcroppings of shale and Sharon conglomerate, and glacial formations, including kames and kettle lakes.

Most of these hikes travel over Ohio's glaciated Western Allegheny Plateau, and a few tread along the Great Lakes eco-region. When you consider an eco-region, you must take into account both land and water systems. The land in the Western Allegheny Plateau is dotted with short, gravelly, dome-shaped hills called kames. These bumps in the landscape were formed by converging glacial lobes. Some of the cool, cave-like spots, like those in Nelson's Ledges and Gorge Metropark, even support species native to Canada. The Western Allegheny Plateau also hosts numerous wetlands. Those that remain are generally under protection as State Nature Preserves, such as the Kent-Cooperrider Bog and Herrick Fen.

In considering our water systems, certainly the first to come to mind is the Cuyahoga River. But Grand River and Tinker's

Creek watersheds are of equal importance. Each one hosts a significant number of rare and endangered plants and animals.

To learn more about Ohio's eco-regions and the unique species they shelter, spend some time at The Nature Conservancy's website, www.nature.org, or call the Ohio chapter office at (614) 717-2770.

History Underfoot:
From Terrible Fish to Trains

About 360 million years before the glaciers made their mark on Ohio's landscape, there was no landscape. All of Ohio was under water. When you visit the Rocky River Reservation, you'll see *Dunkleosteus,* the "terrible fish" that was considerably larger than a shark—and probably ate sharks for breakfast! The nature center at Rocky River is a great place to learn about Ohio's ancient history and more recent events as well.

The first white settlers in northeast Ohio came here to create the Connecticut Land Company's Western Reserve. Those hardy easterners built homes, churches, colleges, roads, and railroads when they arrived, and many of these original structures can be seen along the trails in this book. These settlers also built stations on the "invisible" Underground Railroad—you can take a glimpse into the lives of the abolitionists when you visit Austinburg (see p. 14).

The folks who settled here made their mark in other ways, too. Lifesaver candies were invented in Garrettsville, for example, and artist Henry Church of Chagrin Falls left his "signature" on Squaw Rock (see p. 173). Many famous Ohioans are buried at Lake View Cemetery and in dozens of smaller, but equally historic, burial sites in the area. In traipsing and researching these trails, I learned more about Ohio's history than I did in all of my school days. What's more, I found these lessons fascinating. I hope you do too.

You can find solitude within a few miles of the city limits

Seasons on the Trail

"Winter hiking? Are you crazy?"

I thought maybe I was crazy when I signed up for a January/February hiking series a few years ago. But it was great! All four seasons offer scenic sights on northeast Ohio trails. Don't let a little number (like "minus 4") keep you inside. Properly outfitted, you can be comfortable, have fun, and enjoy something that's hard to find in the summer months: solitude.

Hike the same trail in each season and you'll discover it has multiple personalities. What was a serene lake view in June is probably a raucous party of migrating waterfowl in November. If you think the woods look dead and drab in the winter, look again. As soon as the leaves fall off the trees, they already have their spring buds. Look closely and you'll see how much tree bud structures differ from each other. And you don't have to look closely in the winter months to spot other features: bird, squirrel, and insect nests (galls) are easily noticed on bare limbs. So are the unusual shapes of many branches.

Before spring officially arrives, many wildflowers have poked through the snow to reach for the sun. Get out and see if you can identify them by their leaves, before they bloom.

In the summer, poison ivy, black flies, and mosquitoes may make you think twice before you leave home. Don't let them keep you off the trail. The proper repellent will ward off their bites. And here's more good news: Poison ivy is just about the only plant you have to fear. Poison oak usually isn't a problem in Ohio, and if you stay away from the mushiest parts of a bog, you're almost certainly safe from poison sumac as well.

People, unfortunately, are far more dangerous to plants than plants are to us. As tempting as it may be, never pick anything along the trail. Even the seemingly innocent action of picking a wildflower on one part of a trail and leaving it on another can hasten the progression of a hostile species. Many non-native species are aggressive (purple loosestrife in the Cuyahoga Valley National Park, for example) even though they are also pretty. Leave them where they are. In some places, wildlife management experts have decided to control or eradicate the aggressive plants; in others, they remain under observation. In any case, the hiker is bound to follow the trail mantra: "Take only pictures, leave only footprints."

What Do Timberdoodles Do, and are Nuthatches Really Nutty?

You don't have to be a bird guru to find bird-watching fascinating. The common robin has one of the most beautiful songs of all North American birds. The often-heard catbird can imitate the songs of more than 200 other birds. It can also do impressions of other noises, like a rusty

Medina's Green Leaf Park

gate hinge or a crying baby. At Tinker's Creek State Park, I had a rather eerie feeling as I listened to a repeated call: "Wah! Wah!" I watched the catbird as he called; otherwise, I would never have believed that it wasn't a human infant! Another time, walking along a city sidewalk, I spotted a backyard-variety blue jay flying very low. He was weighted down by his catch: a fat mole. (Imagine the feast in that nest!)

Birds, both common and rare, offer great entertainment. If you want to learn about them, but are overwhelmed by the volumes of bird-watching books, I recommend picking up a chart that identifies a few local varieties for starters. Better still, visit the children's section of your local bookstore, where you'll find the thinner books an easy starting point. (Several examples are listed in Appendix D. It was from one of these children's books that I learned nuthatches, unlike other birds, can walk

West branch of the Rocky River

both up *and down* tree trunks and branches. Now, I'm always on the lookout for a bird walking the "wrong" way down a tree.) It doesn't take much effort—or much information—to get hooked on birds.

Another great way to learn about our feathered friends is to attend a naturalist-led outing. The rangers and naturalists I met over the course of this project were all great sources of information and not the least bit stuffy. Watch your local park programs for events and go. Then ask questions! You'll get delightful answers!

I had the good luck to meet Christine Craycroft of the Portage Park system this way. Craycroft led an educational program on the American woodcock, also called the timberdoodle, at Towner's Woods (see p. 193). During the short, enjoyable presentation and walk, I learned more about birds—and frogs, and a few other things— than I had in the previous year. So if you

are able to attend any similar programs, by all means, go! And don't worry that you'll be surrounded by ornithologists—chances are, you won't be the only new bird-watcher in the group.

"Bearly" Mentioned Mammals

Are bears coming back to Ohio? Well, maybe if we're lucky. Are coyotes really common in the Cleveland Metroparks? Probably more so than you think.

Most likely, even if you hike each of these trails more than once, you won't see a bear or a coyote. On the other hand, you are quite likely to spot deer, raccoon, and even fox along these trails. You can also see beaver at work and watch bats zigzag in the early evenings.

For more information about the history of bear in our neck of the woods, see Beartown Lakes Reservation on p. 23. For more information about the coyote population around us, visit the Cleveland Metroparks website. And try to avoid making snap judgments about either of these "ferocious" animals. After all, if Floridians reside with alligators and crocodiles, it seems we should be able to live in harmony with our native species.

Here a Park System, There a Park System, Everywhere . . .

In northeast Ohio, we are fortunate to reap the benefits of many park systems and conservation-minded organizations. Most of the hike descriptions in this book include contact information so you can learn more about the area and the park system that manages it. But if you're really interested in learning about a particular area, the BEST way is to volunteer in it.

Volunteers in parks (often called "VIPs") have increasingly important positions. There's a role for every person and personality, too. You can lead a hike, ring up sales in a nature shop, create posters, build a trail, or file paperwork in the office. I have volunteered in city and county park systems and also in the Cuyahoga Valley National Park. Each experience has proven extremely rewarding. The resources in our parks—both in terms of natural beauty and human resources—are outstanding.

Volunteers have the opportunity to learn from those resources firsthand, and then share their knowledge with others. What a deal! Whether you have 1 hour or 200 hours to offer, a creative volunteer coordinator can help you find your niche. You may start by calling your local parks and recreation office or any of these organizations:

Ashtabula County Parks
www.ashtabulacountyparks.org
(440) 576-0717

Buckeye Trail Association
www.buckeyetrail.org
(800) 881-3062

Cleveland Metroparks
www.clemetparks.com
(216) 351-6300

Cuyahoga Valley National Park
www.dayinthevalley.org
Volunteers in the Park office:
(440) 546-5996

Geauga Park District
www.geaugaparkdistrict.org
(440) 285-2222

Lake Metroparks
www.lakemetroparks.com
(440) 358-7275

Lorain County Metroparks
www.loraincountymetroparks.com
(800) 526-7275

Portage Park District
www.portageparkdistrict.org
(330) 673-9404

Stark Parks
(encourage youth volunteers age 14 and up)
www.starkparks.com
(330) 477-3552

Metroparks Serving Summit County
www.neo.rr.com/metroparks
(330) 867-5511

The Nature Conservancy
www.nature.org
(614) 717-2770

Tinker's Creek Land Conservancy
(330) 425-4159

Finally, even if don't wish to volunteer in a park system, take the time to learn where you are, and to learn the rules that govern that particular trail. Rules vary. State Nature Preserves, for example, prohibit pets and anything with wheels, while most State Parks welcome pets (on leash) and even bikes (on some trails). Stow's city parks do not allow pets; those in other cities welcome canine visitors. The rules of the trail are created for a reason; following them makes outings more pleasant for everyone.

Take a Hike
In assembling a variety of hikes for this book, I walked through parks and labyrinths, up a riverbed, and around the zoo. No matter where I hiked, I discovered something. In the hike profiles, I've tried to convey some of the wonder I felt in those discoveries. Now it's your turn. I hope that this book serves as a list of good suggestions, a set of starting points from which you'll discover many pleasures of your own. *Happy trails.*

Hike Recommendations

Hikes Good for Wildlife Viewing

(continued)

Hikes with Steep Sections

Historic Trails

Lake Hikes

Scenic Hikes

Hikes 1 to 3 miles

(continued)

Hikes 3 to 6 miles

Hikes Longer than 6 miles

Introduction

Welcome to *60 Hikes within 60 Miles: Cleveland!* If you're new to hiking or even if you're a seasoned trail-smith, take a few minutes to read the following introduction. We'll explain how this book is organized and how to get the best use of it.

Hike Descriptions

Each hike contains six key items: a locator map, an In Brief description of the trail, an At-a-Glance information box, directions to the trail, a trail map, and a hike narrative. Combined, the maps and information provide a clear method to assess each trail from the comfort of your favorite chair.

Locator Map

After narrowing down the general area of the hike on the overview map (see pages viii–ix), the locator map, along with driving directions given in the narrative, enables you to find the trailhead. Once at the trailhead, park only in designated areas.

In Brief

A "taste of the trail." Think of this section as a snapshot focused on the historical landmarks, beautiful vistas, and other interesting sights you may encounter on the trail.

At-a-Glance Information

The At-a-Glance information boxes give you a quick idea of the specifics of each hike. There are 13 basic elements covered.

Length The length of the trail from start to finish. There may be options to

shorten or extend the hikes, but the mileage corresponds to the described hike. Consult the hike description to help decide how to customize the hike for your ability or time constraints.

Configuration A description of what the trail might look like from overhead. Trails can be loops, out-and-backs (that is, along the same route), figure eights, or balloons. Sometimes the descriptions might surprise you.

Difficulty The degree of effort an "average" hiker should expect on a given hike. For simplicity, difficulty is described as "easy," "moderate," or "difficult."

Scenery Rates the overall environs of the hike and what to expect in terms of plant life, wildlife, streams, and historic buildings.

Exposure A quick check of how much sun you can expect on your shoulders during the hike. Descriptors used are self-explanatory and include terms such as shady, exposed, and sunny.

Traffic Indicates how busy the trail might be on an average day, and if you might be able to find solitude out there. Trail traffic, of course, varies from day to day and season to season.

Trail surface Indicates whether the trail is paved, rocky, smooth dirt, or a mixture of elements.

Hiking time How long it took the author to hike the trail. She is a fast hiker who stops frequently to take in unusual sights, to take pictures, and to take a sip of water. Her average hiking speed is 2.5 miles per hour.

Access   Notes fees or permits needed to access the trail. In most cases no fees or permits are required. Always check if in doubt.

Maps   Which map is the best, or easiest (in the author's opinion) for this hike and where to get it.

Facilities   what to expect in terms of rest rooms, phones, water and other niceties available at the trailhead or nearby.

Special comments   Provides you with those little extra details that don't fit into any of the above categories. Here you'll find information on trail hiking options and facts such as whether or not to expect a lifeguard at a nearby swimming beach.

Directions   Used with the locator map, the directions will help you locate each trailhead.

Descriptions

The trail description is the heart of each hike. Here, the author provides a summary of the trail's essence as well as highlighting any special traits the hike offers. Ultimately, the hike description will help you choose which hikes are best for you.

Nearby Activities

Not every hike will have this listing. For those that do, look here for information on nearby sights of interest.

Weather

Spring, summer, and fall have obvious allure for northeastern Ohio hikers. On average, August has the clearest days, followed closely by July, September, and October. If there is a "best" month to hike around here, it might be October. Most of the summer bugs are gone, but some of the late summer and fall wildflowers remain. Temperatures tend to be quite nice in the afternoons, and the trees are at their colorful best. But this is no reason to stay inside

during any other month. Consider your destination in terms of the day's weather. A wetland trail may be impassable on a wet spring day, yet stunningly beautiful in December. Black flies bite hard (really hard!) in August; you may want to hit an urban trail then. Wear mosquito repellent when you're on the trail afternoons and evenings, from April through October.

Average Daily Temperatures by Month
Cleveland, Ohio (degrees Fahrenheit)

Jan	Feb	Mar	Apr
24.8	27.2	37.3	47.6
May	**Jun**	**Jul**	**Aug**
58.0	67.6	71.9	70.4
Sep	**Oct**	**Nov**	**Dec**
63.9	52.8	42.6	30.9

Maps

The maps in this book have been produced with great care and, used with the hiking directions, will help you stay on course. But as any experienced hiker knows, things can get tricky off the beaten path.

The maps in this book, when used with the route directions present in each chapter, are sufficient to get you to the trail and keep you on it. However, you will find superior detail and valuable information in the United States Geological Survey's 7.5 minute series topographic maps. Recognizing how indispensable these are to hikers and bikers alike, many outdoor shops and bike shops now carry topos of the local area.

If you're new to hiking you might be wondering, "What's a topographic map?" In short, they indicate not only linear distance but elevation as well. One glance at a topo will show you the difference: Contour lines spread across the map like dozens of intricate spider webs. Each contour line represents a particular elevation, and at the base of each topo a contour's interval designation is given. It may sound confusing if you're new to the lingo, but it's truly a simple and helpful system. Assume that the 7.5 minute series topo reads "Contour Interval 40 feet," that the short trail you'll be hiking is two inches in length on the map, and that it crosses five contour lines from its beginning to end. Because the linear scale of this series is 2,000 feet to the inch (roughly two and three-quarters inches representing one mile), the trail is approximately four-fifths of a mile long (2 inches are 2,000 feet). You'll also be climbing or descending 200 vertical feet (5 contour lines are 40 feet each) over that distance. The elevation designations written on occasional contour lines will tell you if you're heading up or down.

In addition to outdoor shops and bike shops, you'll find topos at major universities and some public libraries, where you might try photocopying the ones you need to avoid the cost of buying them. But if you want your own and can't find them locally, contact USGS Map Sales at Box 25286, Denver, CO 80225; (888) ASK-USGS (275-8747); or www.mapping.usgs.gov. Visa and MasterCard are accepted. Ask for an index while you're at it, plus a price list and a copy of the booklet *Topographic Maps*. In minutes you'll be reading them like a pro.

Trail Etiquette

Whether you're on a city, county, state or National Park trail, always remember that great care and resources (from Nature as well as from your tax dollars) have gone into creating these trails. Treat the trail, wildlife, and fellow hikers with respect.

Here are a few general ideas to keep in mind while on the trail.

1. Hike on open trails only. Respect trail and road closures (ask if not sure); avoid possible trespass on private land; obtain all permits and authorization as required. Also, leave gates as you found them or as marked.

2. Leave no trace of your visit other than footprints. Be sensitive to the dirt beneath you. This also means staying on the trail and not creating any new ones. Be sure to pack out what you pack in. No one likes to see the trash someone else has left behind.

3. Never spook animals. An unannounced approach, a sudden movement, or a loud noise startles most animals. A surprised snake or skunk can be dangerous for you, for others, and to themselves. Give animals extra room and time to adjust to your presence.

4. Plan ahead. Know your equipment, your ability, and the area in which you are hiking—and prepare accordingly. Be self-sufficient at all times; carry necessary supplies for changes in weather or other conditions. A well-executed trip is a satisfaction to you and to others.

5. Be courteous to other hikers, or bikers, you meet on the trails.

Water

"How much is enough? One bottle? Two? Three?! But think of all that extra weight!" Well, one simple physiological fact should convince you to err on the side of excess when it comes to deciding how much water to pack: A human working hard in 90° heat needs approximately ten quarts of fluid every day. That's two and a half gallons—12 large water bottles or 16 small ones. In other words, pack along one or two bottles even for short hikes.

Serious backpackers hit the trail prepared to purify water found along the route. This method, while less dangerous than drinking it untreated, comes with risks. Many hikers pack along the slightly distasteful tetraglycine hydroperiodide tablets (sold under the names Potable Aqua, Coughlan's, and others). Some invest in portable, lightweight purifiers that filter out the crud. Unfortunately, both iodine and filtering are now required to be absolutely sure you've killed all the nasties you can't see. *Giardia,* for example, may hit one to four weeks after ingestion. It will have you bloated, vomiting, shivering with

3

chills, and living in the bathroom. But there are other parasites to worry about, including *E. coli* and *cryptosporidium* (affectionately known as "Crypto," and even harder to kill than *Giardia*).

For most people, the pleasures of hiking make carrying water a relatively minor price to pay to remain healthy. If you're tempted to drink "found water," do so only once you thoroughly understand the method, and the risks involved.

First-Aid Kit

A typical kit may contain more items than you might think necessary. But these are just the basics:

Sunscreen

Aspirin or acetaminophen

Butterfly-closure bandages

Band-Aids

Snakebite kit

Gauze (one roll)

Gauze compress pads (a half-dozen 4 in. x 4 in.)

Ace bandages or Spenco joint wraps

Benadryl or the generic equivalent—diphenhydramine (an antihistamine, in case of allergic reactions)

A prefilled syringe of epinephrine (for those known to have severe allergic reactions to such things as bee stings)

Water purification tablets or water filter (see note above)

Moleskin/Spenco "Second Skin"

Hydrogen peroxide or iodine

Antibiotic ointment (Neosporin or the generic equivalent)

Matches or pocket lighter

Whistle (more effective in signaling rescuers than your voice)

Pack the items in a waterproof bag such as a Ziploc bag or a similar product. You will also want to include a snack for hikes longer than a couple of miles. A bag full of GORP (Good Ol' Raisins and Peanuts) will kick up your energy level fast.

Hiking with Children

No one is too young for a hike in the woods or through a city park. Be careful, though. Flat, short trails are probably best with an infant. Toddlers who have not quite mastered walking can still tag along, riding on an adult's back in a child carrier. Use common sense to judge a child's capacity to hike a particular trail, and always rely on the possibility that the child will tire quickly and need to be carried.

When packing for the hike, remember the needs of the child as well as your own. Make sure children are adequately clothed for the weather, have proper shoes, and are protected from the sun with sunscreen. Kids dehydrate quickly, so make sure you have plenty of fluid for everyone.

To assist an adult with determining which trails are suitable for children, a list of hike recommendations for children is provided on page xix.

Finally, when hiking with children, remember the trip will be a compromise. A child's energy and enthusiasm alternates between bursts of speed and long stops to examine snails, sticks, dirt, and other attractions.

The Business Hiker

Whether in the Cleveland area on business as a resident or visitor, these 60 hikes offer perfect, quick getaways from the busy demands of commerce. Many of the hikes are classified as urban and are easily accessible from downtown areas. Instead of eating inside, pack a lunch and head out to one of the many links in the Emerald Necklace (Cleveland Metroparks) for a relaxing break from the office or convention. Or plan ahead and take a small group of your business comrades on a nearby hike in Cleveland Lakefront State Park or along the canal. A well planned, half-day getaway is the perfect complement to a business stay in Northeast Ohio.

60 Hikes within 60 Miles:

CLEVELAND
(including Akron and Canton)

#1
Adell Durbin Park
and Arboretum

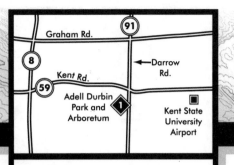

IN BRIEF

This beautifully maintained arboretum and trail sits on a surprisingly rugged 34 acres in the heart of Stow. Hundreds of cars on Route 91 pass by the park entrance every day. Many of those drivers might be surprised to learn what lies beyond the meeting lodges, tennis courts, and kiddie playground. You'll have to pull off the road and put on your hiking boots to find out.

DIRECTIONS

Head south on State Route 8, and exit Graham Road heading east, toward Silver Lake. Turn right, heading south on Darrow Road (State Route 91). After you cross Route 59 (Kent Road) the park is about 0.3 miles south, on the right (west) side of Route 91.

DESCRIPTION

This hike follows the park's three trails: The Hiker's Trail (marked in red), Cliff Trail (blue), and Tree & Shrub Trail (yellow). If you're short on time, take the 0.6-mile Cliff Trail. Any hike you choose, though, be sure to take along the self-guiding brochure that identifies dozens of trees and shrubs in the park. The trees are marked with round numbered tags; their names are listed numerically on the brochure.

To start, step onto the Yellow Trail (also called the "Tree and Shrub" Trail)

KEY AT-A-GLANCE INFORMATION

Length: 2.6 miles

Configuration: Three intersecting loops

Difficulty: Easy

Scenery: Over 80 identified species of trees and shrubs; ravine overlook and creek-crossing opportunity

Exposure: Mostly shaded when trees have leaves

Traffic: Moderately busy, especially on weekends

Trail surface: Dirt and grass

Season: Open year-round

Access: Park open daily until dark; nature center open only on weekend afternoons

Maps: Check box on trailhead sign for map and self-guided tour brochures identifying trees, shrubs, and various natural occurrences

Facilities: Rest rooms, water, vending machines, and pay phone in main parking lot

Special comments: Dogs and other pets are not allowed. For information about educational programs at the Harold Welch Nature Center, call (330) 689-2759.

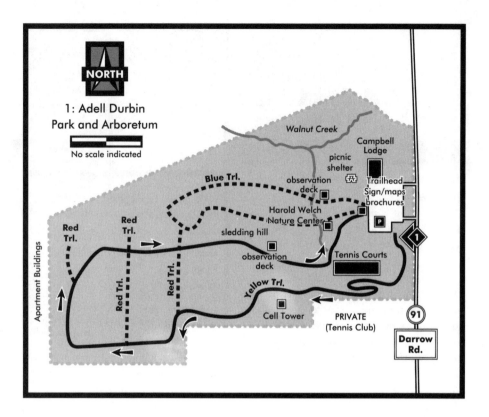

1: Adell Durbin
Park and Arboretum

No scale indicated

by Denning Lodge, at the southern end of the parking lot. Take the concrete steps down from Denning Lodge, and follow the mulched path in a clockwise direction. You will briefly walk parallel to Route 91, and when you reach the end of the tennis courts, you'll notice quarter-sized silver tags on some of the trees. After you've logged a third of a mile, you should have spotted at least 25 tree-identifying tags.

As the path veers right, you'll skirt the western edge of the park to find a wide variety of grasses, wildflowers, and the birds and insects that are attracted to them. Look north to enjoy a lovely panorama—a diverse ring of deciduous trees. In the fall, of course, the panorama is at its boldest, brightest best; even the

poison ivy vines that wrap around the tree trunks turn bright orange-red, like ribbons tying up the season. In the spring, the beauty is subtler, but worth contemplation. As the various trees awake in slow progression, each buds in its own time. It's visible proof that while winter slows us all down, at the same time, it leads to renewed growth.

Continuing west, you'll pass a sign for the Red, or "Hiker's" Trail. The sign marks one of several spots where the park's trails intermingle. This can cause some confusion if you attempt to follow the trails without a map. There's little danger of getting lost (the park is relatively small at 34 acres), but you could miss a significant, and pretty, section of the trail and the park. Swallow your

Heading down to the observation deck

pride, grab a map, and refer to it as needed.

Where the Red Trail crosses your path, turn left (south) following the Yellow Trail through the thick forest. A number of tall, old pines grow along here, and the forest floor is strewn with pine needles and rotting logs of all sizes. In various states of decay, they provide both food and shelter for a host of animals, birds, and insects.

As you walk near the park's southern border, you'll pass the short and pretty balsam fir (its tag is no. 93) and a few hardy strands of goldenrod poke up though the forest floor looking for the sun. The path veers right, heading north and a bit east as you pass near some apartment buildings. Here you'll see English ivy that has escaped domesticity for the relative wilds of this little park—score one for houseplants! Red-bellied woodpeckers like to dart about here, 10

to 20 feet above, tapping on dead branches to scare out a snack. (*Note to novice birders:* The name "red-bellied" is a bit misleading, as its head is dark red, but its belly is actually rather light—a pinkish white. Don't let this discourage you from developing a bird-watching habit; it's a hobby that develops keen observation skills and patience, too!)

A sign at about 0.6 miles confirms that you have been following the yellow and red paths. A few steps later, on your right, you'll see tree no. 87. Old number 87 is the rigid hornbeam; its gray, taut bark gives it a face as distinguished as its name. Its pretty bark is almost too smooth, as if it had a facelift that pulled too tight. Not surprisingly, it is also commonly referred to as muscle wood.

Before you cross the Red Trail again, you'll go up a small hill, past a small wooden observation deck, and pass beneath a row of chestnut trees, to reach a persimmon tree. In the late summer and early fall, the fruits reach the size of cherry tomatoes. In the fall, this section of the trail might be considered a "hard hat" area, as it is full of shedding oak, beechnut, and chestnut trees. When the winds or squirrels are very active, nuts literally rain down from the trees along here. You'll hit the bottom of a short hill at about 0.9 miles, trek uphill a few steps to pass the Nature Center, and then return to the parking lot. Long before you reach this point, you'll probably realize you've followed the Yellow Trail backwards, according to the Tree and Shrub Guide provided by the park. Of course, you are free to follow it in any direction you like. One argument for taking the path south to north is that when you reach the "end" (or the beginning?) you come to the heart of the park, the deep gorge that cradles Walnut Creek.

In the parking lot, look for the Blue Trail trailhead, and follow the 83 steps (give or take a couple) down into the ravine. The Blue Trail is also known as the "Cliff Trail," and you'll see why about halfway down the steps. A large wooden deck there overlooks the creek, which is clean, shallow, and in most places, about seven feet wide. If you follow the Blue Trail, you'll cross the creek and have a choice of veering left to join up with the Red Trail, or turning sharply back to the north, and then venturing east again, through the thick of the forest. However, you don't have to follow the Blue Trail to enjoy the creek and ravine.

NEARBY ACTIVITIES

Adell-Durbin is small, but it's packed with options. When the Harold Welch Nature Center is open (Saturday and Sunday afternoons) you'll find fascinating displays of bugs, butterflies, and other wild things . . . like a stuffed coyote. Outside the nature center, you'll find a small fenced-in play area, volleyball and tennis courts, and a sledding hill.

Special thanks to Dave Roberts, naturalist for the City of Stow Parks and Recreation Department, for reviewing this section—forwards, backwards, and sideways.

#2
Allardale Loops

IN BRIEF

When Stan and Ester Allard donated 336 acres of their farm to the Medina County Park District in 1992, they guaranteed that at least some of the rolling landscape would remain beautifully undeveloped. What they did with the land before they gave it away is as impressive as their generosity.

DIRECTIONS

From I-271, exit onto Route 94 (Ridge Road) and follow it south 0.5 miles to Remsen Road. Turn left and follow Remsen east approximately 3 miles. Allardale is on the north side of Remsen, less than 1 mile west of Medina Line Road.

DESCRIPTION

The best advice about hiking Allardale is this: Walk the outer loop counterclockwise. That way, you're treated to the marvelous overlook view at the end of your hike. It is a deserved reward for your effort; to reach it early on makes the rest of the trip almost anticlimactic. Walking the trail clockwise isn't wrong, exactly; it's just sort of like having dessert first.

The 1-mile outer loop of dirt and grass winds through a valley and through former farmland. Along the way you'll find many examples of the careful planning and maintenance this land enjoyed under the Allards' ownership. When you reach the dedication overlook, you may

KEY AT-A-GLANCE INFORMATION

Length: 1.5 miles

Configuration: Two nested loops

Difficulty: Easy

Scenery: Forest, farmland, wide variety of identified trees, and one incredible view

Exposure: About half shaded

Traffic: Moderate

Trail surface: Inner loop trail, paved; outer loop, hard-packed gravel/dirt

Hiking time: 1 hour

Season: Open year-round

Access: Park closes at dark

Maps: Large relief map posted on a signboard at the trailhead

Facilities: Water and flush toilets at main parking lot; a sheltered picnic area is also available

Special comments: The nearest pay phone is at Granger Township Hall, 0.5 miles south of intersection of Remsen Road and SR 94

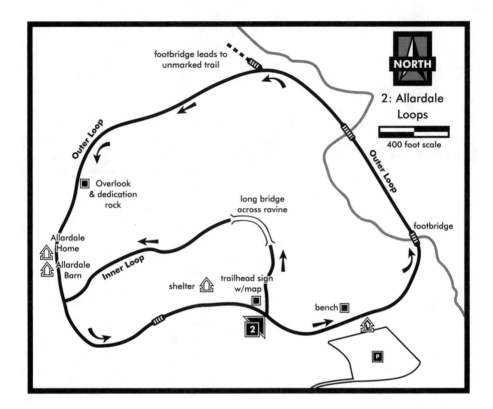

2: Allardale Loops

400 foot scale

NORTH

footbridge leads to unmarked trail

Outer Loop

Overlook & dedication rock

long bridge across ravine

footbridge

Outer Loop

Allardale Home

Allardale Barn

Inner Loop

shelter

trailhead sign w/map

bench

2

P

be overwhelmed at the generosity they demonstrated in giving it away.

From the trailhead sign, turn right and head down a paved hill. As the trail curves to the left, the pavement ends and you'll follow a dirt-and-gravel path down a few more feet. Here, the wind rushes across the wide-open trough to meet you head-on. You'll cross a short footbridge into the prairie meadow. Tall pines rise on the west of the hill; young beech trees on the eastern side of the path shade you as you cross over a second footbridge.

At about the half-mile point, you'll pass the remnants of an old sawmill dam. It is marked with a hand-lettered sign, perhaps written by Mr. Allard himself. Several other items, like an old wagon wheel, are also signed; they dot the trail like snapshots decorate a

refrigerator. "Hey, remember this," they seem to say. Just past the sawmill sign, turn left heading uphill toward the barn. (*Note:* This turn will go against your natural desire to continue west, across an inviting and relatively new footbridge. If you give in and cross the bridge, you'll soon find yourself off the path and on private property.)

Allardale has been recognized, several times, as an outstanding example of forestry and land conservation. In the 1930s, this farm was among the first to practice soil-saving techniques such as contour strip farming and erosion control using pines and spruces planted along steep hillsides. Since then, at least 100,000 trees have been planted—today you'll walk through established collections of black walnut, red and white oak, white pine, and a variety of other trees. Allardale has received awards from the Ohio Department of Natural Resources Division of Forestry and is considered one of the finest tree farms in Ohio. Perhaps no one appreciates it more than the myriad moths and butterflies that dance happily in the diverse and crowded woods.

You'll enjoy their antics as you climb uphill, around a bend, and up another 50 feet or so through the woods, emerging into an open field via a wide, mown path. Look north (to your left) over the tall grass and take in a view that stretches for miles. From this point you'll get a glimpse of the rolling hills, farms, and dales that long ago were all that comprised Medina County.

A few more feet up, at the highest point on the hill, a bench sits under a tree. A large rock directly in front of it doesn't obscure your view; it adds to your overall appreciation. It is inscribed:

"Allardale, a gift from Stan and Ester Allard, so others can enjoy the open spaces, the blue sky, the trees, the flowers, the birds, and the hills and valleys that they have loved so much."

If you can tear yourself away from the beautiful vista, take a few more steps to east, so you can see the Allards' red barn, standing on the hillside just south of the trails. Until it was given to Medina County, this farm had been in the Allard family since 1877. That being the case, it has a lot of history to relate. A plaque near the shelter explains a bit of the history of the farm and of Medina County.

Just past the plaque, on your left, you'll walk by the western end of the inner loop. Pass by the trail here and enter the shorter loop just east of the shelter, so you can follow it counter-clockwise, too. The entire half-mile trail is paved. Turn left onto the path, and descend a moderately steep hill to a long wooden bridge. As you approach the bridge, your feet will grind over rusty pine needles, releasing a piney fragrance, regardless of the season. You'll have a good look at the ravine from the bridge, which spans about 50 feet. As the loop turns to head west, it leaves the woods and affords another view of the valley, this time from the middle of the hill. When you reach the southwestern end of this short loop, you can turn left to return to the parking lot. More likely, though, you'll turn right—for one more look at the view the Allards left behind.

NEARBY ACTIVITIES

The picnic shelter here, adjacent to the inner loop trail, can be reserved by calling the Medina Park District at (330) 722-9364. While you're in the area, visit Green Leaf Park a few miles south on Medina Line Road (see p. 78).

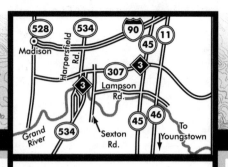

#3
Ashtabula:
Underground Railroad/
Covered Bridges

IN BRIEF

Ohio's largest county has a lot of secrets. Consider these two short hikes a teaser: the first introduces you to Austinburg's most notable Underground Railroad sites; the second takes you across Ohio's longest covered bridge.

DIRECTIONS

Take I-90 east from Cleveland, then go south on Route 45 (Exit 223). Follow Route 45 south about 1 mile to Route 307. Turn left to park at Town Hall, at the corner of 307 (River Road) and Miller Street; additional parking may be available off Miller near the Western Reserve Greenway Trail entrance. *Note:* Directions from Austinburg to Harpersfield in text below.

DESCRIPTION

Travel light. On foot. At night. Leave behind your family, friends, and all that is familiar. Depend on the kindness of strangers to hide you from those who would capture you, beat you, and return you to a life of slavery. Would you trust your life to an invisible thing called the Underground Railroad? The Underground Railroad (UGRR) operated from about 1816 until 1865. During that time, an estimated 40,000 freedom-seeking slaves passed through Ohio. Many were spirited through Austinburg along the UGRR, courtesy of the fervent

KEY AT-A-GLANCE INFORMATION

Length: 1.5–4 miles (Austinburg), plus 2 miles (Harpersfield)

Configuration: Austinburg is a loop; Harpersfield is an "h".

Difficulty: Easy

Scenery: Three historic Underground Railroad sites, two cemeteries from the 1800s, one Grand River, and one long covered bridge

Exposure: Austinburg mostly exposed; Harpersfield shaded

Traffic: Both moderately busy

Trail surface: City sidewalks and dirt paths

Hiking time: 50 minutes in Austinburg; 30 minutes (plus water play time) at Harpersfield

Season: Harpersfield main parking area, concessions, and rest rooms are closed November 1–April 1

Access: Austinburg, bridge always open

Maps: None available

Facilities: Pay phone and rest rooms at I-90/Route 45 exit; rest rooms, concession stand, and picnic shelters open seasonally at park

Special comments: To learn more, start at the Friends of Freedom Society website at www.ohio undergroundrailroad.org.

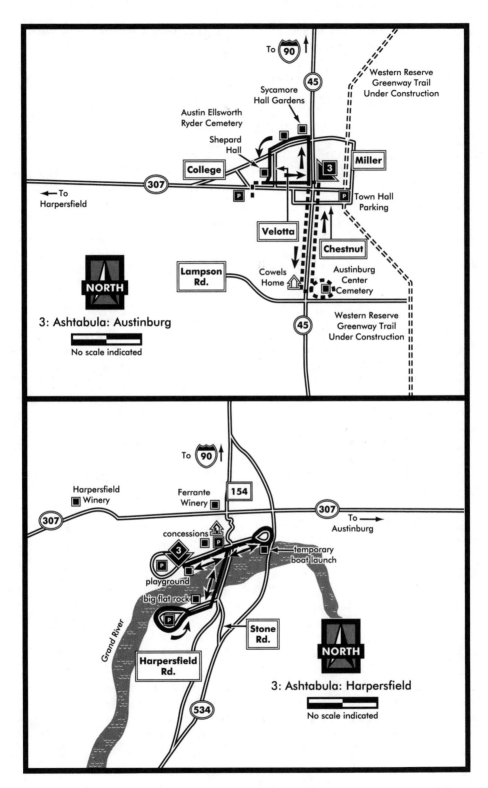

To **90** ↑

45

Western Reserve
Greenway Trail
Under Construction

Sycamore
Hall Gardens

Austin Ellsworth
Ryder Cemetery

Shepard
Hall

College

Miller

3

← To
Harpersfield

307

P

P

Town Hall
Parking

Velotta

Chestnut

**Lampson
Rd.**

Cowels
Home

Austinburg
Center
Cemetery

NORTH

3: Ashtabula: Austinburg

No scale indicated

Western Reserve
Greenway Trail
Under Construction

45

To **90** ↑

Harpersfield
■ Winery

Ferrante
Winery ■

154

307

307

To →
Austinburg

concessions

3

P

temporary
boat launch

P

playground

big flat rock ■

P

Grand River

**Stone
Rd.**

NORTH

**Harpersfield
Rd.**

3: Ashtabula: Harpersfield

No scale indicated

534

abolitionists who lived here. This hike gives you a small taste of what they experienced.

From the Austinburg Town Hall, follow Route 307 west, cross route 45, and turn right. Head north about 0.25 miles, then turn left onto College Street, where you'll find Sycamore Hall Gardens on the right. According to Debbie Laveck, northeast regional coordinator for the Friends of Freedom Society, Sycamore Hall was built by Eliphalet Austin in 1810. The Austin family was very active in the UGRR and built a secret compartment in the house to hide fugitive slaves. Laveck tells the story of a slave master who pursued his "property" all the way to the Austin home. When Mr. Austin gave in to the master's demands to search the home, he combed every room of the house, even opening the door to Mrs. Austin's bedroom. Finding her in bed, he apologized for the intrusion. The master left, empty-handed and disappointed. When he was gone, the slave slid out from under Mrs. Austin's bed and continued on his way north. Behind Sycamore Hall and just off College Street is Austin Ellsworth Ryder Cemetery, dating to 1803. It is open to the public during daylight hours; walk around and note the many famous abolitionists buried there.

Follow College Street west as it slopes downhill. Continue about 0.5 miles and turn left at Velotta Street and onto the campus of Grand River Academy. Founded in 1831 as the Grand River Institute, today Grand River Academy is a private boarding high school for boys. Shepard Hall, on Velotta, was known at the time of the UGRR as "Main Hall," and many abolitionist meetings were held there. It was also used as a safehouse for fugitive slaves until they could be moved to the next station.

Continue through the campus until you reach Route 307. Turn left (east) and follow the sidewalk back to Route 45. From here, you can turn right and walk about 1.5 miles south along the wide, grassy berm of Route 45. You will pass the entrance to Coffee Creek Industrial Park and, just before the corner of Lampson Road, you'll see signs for the Austinburg Little League Ticknor Memorial Ballfield. (*Note:* As there is no path here, you may prefer to return to your car and drive the 1.5 miles along Route 45, from Route 307, to Lampson Road.) Three homes sit in front of the ball fields. Laveck points out that the northernmost house was the home of Betsey Mix Cowles. Betsey's father, Giles Hooker, raised Betsey and her seven siblings with values that were rather unusual for the time. They valued women, education, and freedom for all people. Betsey's life epitomizes those values: she taught both black and white children in Austinburg's Sabbath schools, served as the first dean of women at Grand River Institute, graduated from Oberlin College, and became one of the first female public school superintendents in Ohio. She was an advocate for women's rights, participating in several women's rights conventions in the 1850s, as well as serving on the Executive Committee for the Ohio Women's Rights Association. She also served as an agent of the Underground Railroad.

Betsey Cowles left more than a few marks on history, and she encouraged her family and community to preserve the past. In fact, her will calls for the home to stay in the family in perpetuity. To this day it has, and Betsey's great-great-great-grandniece occasionally gives tours of the parlor.

Cross Route 45 to the east at Lampson Road, and explore the small and

The Grand River runs beneath Ohio's longest covered bridge

pretty Austin Center Cemetery, also known as Cowles Cemetery. Many of the stones here under the shade of old pines date to the 1800s; quite a few are from the 1820s and 1830s.

As you return to the center of Austinburg, by foot or by car, it is inspiring to realize what a tremendous impact the actions of a few, in a small and unassuming town, had on the lives of so many.

UGRR history lesson complete, leave the center of Austinburg and find Harpersfield Covered Bridge MetroPark just about 4 miles west on route 307. Drive past State Route 534, then turn left onto Harpersfield Road (County Road 154). Harpersfield Road winds down a steep hill and bottoms out at the small but popular County Park.

Park in the lot at the bottom of the hill, and wander along the banks of the Grand River. The river—designated both "wild" and "scenic" by the state of Ohio, bisects the small park and runs under the longest covered bridge in the

state. It is one of 16 covered bridges in the county, and Ashtabula celebrates them all during the annual Covered Bridge Festival, held the second weekend of October.

From the parking lot on the north side of the park, you can walk east on a dirt-and-gravel path to the riverbanks and a temporary boat launch, or walk west to find play equipment and picnic shelters. Cross the bridge on the cantilevered walkway, and, when you emerge, read the historical marker detail the bridge's history.

Originally built in 1868, a 1913 flood washed away the northern section of the bridge. Later that year, a 140-foot steel extension was added; in 1992 the bridge was rehabilitated (the walkway was added at that time) and eventually added to the National Register of historic places.

The bridge is popular with photographers and artists, so bring your favorite tools to capture its likeness. Picnic tables abound, but perhaps the best spot from which to contemplate the bridge is a giant, flat rock planted on the riverbank, just southwest of the bridge. It's not the driest spot, but it offers great ambience.

Although the park's concessions and main parking lots are closed from November through March, the river (and the park) is a popular year-round destination. It is also a good fishing spot; anglers here lure bass, trout, crappie, and bluegill onto their hooks.

NEARBY ACTIVITIES

In July 2002, the first stretch of the Western Reserve Greenway Trail opened. It is a paved, mixed-use trail running from Austinburg (just east of route 45/Miller Road) 8 miles north. You can learn more about the Greenway Trail and other Ashtabula MetroPark projects at www.ashtabulacounty parks.org or by calling (440) 992-0717. The Grand River offers good canoeing and kayaking, and nearby Raccoon Run Canoe Rental (a private operation) rents boats and organizes canoe trips. Call (440) 466-7414 for more information. For directions to all of Ashtabula's covered bridges (and many award-winning wineries, too), visit the county visitors bureau website at www.accvb.org.

In addition to her work with the Friends of Freedom Society, Debbie Laveck is the former director of the Hubbard House Underground Railroad Museum in Ashtabula and is a walking encyclopedia of information about the Underground Railroad in Ohio. I am grateful for her suggestions and help as I researched this area and for her careful review of this section.

#4
Babb Run Bird and Wildlife Sanctuary

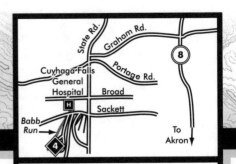

IN BRIEF

You'll have to find your own way through here, as Babb Run's sandy paths are unmarked and trodden only by the passing deer and occasional hiker. About 3 miles of trails are fairly easy to find; negotiating them requires a sense of adventure and a good pair of hiking boots. Tread lightly, and your rewards will be close encounters with wildlife and a symphony of sounds—from Babb Run's low babble to the boisterous blare of the river's rapids.

DIRECTIONS

Take State Route 8 south to Graham Road exit. Follow Graham west about 2.5 miles; turn left (south) onto State Road. Turn right onto Sackett Avenue, and continue west about 0.75 miles. Enter Babb Run on the south side of Sackett, where it intersects with West 26th.

DESCRIPTION

Step onto the paved path from the northwest edge of the small parking lot, marked by a large sign that explains the park's erosion problems. To find evidence of those problems, follow the paved path to the left, heading south down a steep hill. The pavement ends abruptly 0.2 miles later at the bottom of the hill where the path splits. For a short detour, follow the right path straight to the banks of the Cuyahoga River; here, look

KEY AT-A-GLANCE INFORMATION

Length: 3 miles

Configuration: One loop and one out-and-back

Difficulty: Moderate

Scenery: The Cuyahoga River and a tributary, sandstone cliffs, a wide variety of ferns, trees, small animals, and birds

Exposure: Shady

Traffic: Moderate to heavy in the picnic areas; light on the river's edge

Trail surface: Varies from paved to pebbles, dirt, rocks, and roots

Hiking time: 2 hours

Season: Open year-round, dawn–dusk

Access: No permits required

Maps: Not available

Facilities: Portable rest room at parking lot

Special comments: Because Babb Run is designed to preserve wildlife and native plants, pets are not permitted here

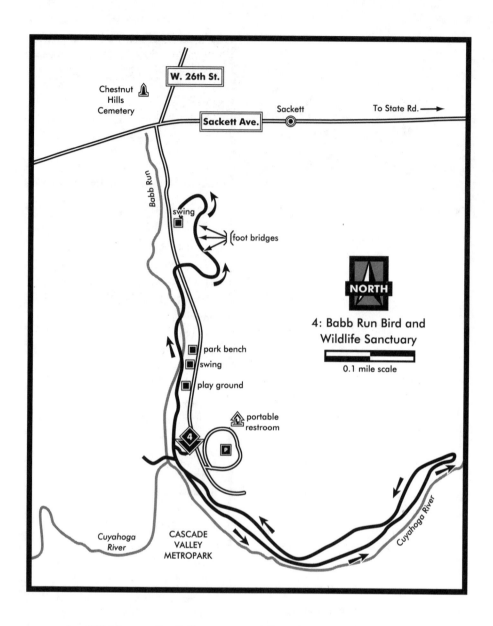

NORTH

4: Babb Run Bird and Wildlife Sanctuary

0.1 mile scale

west at the cliff rising nearly 40 feet above the river. Sit still for a while and listen as the birds and the water converse. When you're done eavesdropping, retrace your steps to the fork in the path and turn right, heading east.

Soon the path forks again. Take the southernmost trail, veering slightly to the right to follow the river. As you

follow along the banks of the Cuyahoga, you'll find that even in a half-mile stretch, the river has multiple personalities. At each turn it is different—sometimes wide and quiet, other times narrow and noisy. The trail also provides a variety of sights and sounds.

As you bump along on the rooty, sandy soil, 30-foot banks rise up to your

left. In places they are signed, "no climbing," but in other spots, they beckon.
Ignore their calls. The banks are deterio-
rating quickly; your feet would only hasten their demise.

About 0.5 miles into the trail, you can
look across the river to a park bench on
the north end of the Cascade Valley
(Metroparks, serving Summit County).
This is a popular fishing spot; don't be
surprised if you see anglers knee-deep
in the river here. Where the river is less-
easily accessed by humans, you're likely
to spot a great blue heron fishing for a
meal. Kingfishers fly by often, too; the
nests of both birds are scattered among
the tops of the tall trees on the riverbank. A few steps south of the beaten
path, you can peer into the shallow, still
edges of the river and see minnows
lolling about. You may also spot the
small white shells of freshwater clams
nearby.

Across the river is Cascade Valley Metropark

About 0.75 miles into the trail, you'll
have to turn back. Your only other
options are to climb the steep banks to
your left (unwise) or to cross the large,
slippery sandstone boulders to reach the
other side of the river and the residential
street immediately east of it. Turning
back, though, doesn't mean you'll have
to exactly retrace your steps.

As you head back upstream, you'll soon
see that the path you followed along the
river splits. Follow the trail to the right. At
times it will take you 50 feet or further
north of the path you first followed. In
fact, at points along this path you can
barely hear—and cannot see—the river at
all. Under a canopy of tall oak, maple, and
beech trees, you'll encounter a few fallen,
decaying limbs and other obstacles across
the path. Keep your eyes open (so you
don't trip!) and you'll also see a host of
ferns, fungus, and moss taking advantage
of the cool ravine climate.

In warm months, you will catch colorful glimpses of the butterflies and
moths that flourish here in the cool
woods. At least three times, the northern
path joins up with its southern sister;
then it wanders off again, as siblings
often do. The two finally meet up and
return, together, to the paved trail.

Now follow the paved path uphill to a
small playground area with swings. About
0.2 miles north of the swings you'll follow a dirt path to two footbridges that
crisscross Babb Run. The beauty of the
ravine is only marginally interrupted by
the drainage pipes inserted here. They are
necessary to minimize erosion in the area.
(In time, the tributary will overcome the
drainpipes' efforts, so enjoy the walkway
while it lasts.) As you continue north
along Babb Run, the path veers east and
rises up about 20 feet to meet the park's
roadway. Alongside the roadway you'll

find a 10-foot-long wooden bridge, stuck rather precariously into the steep bank. It is secured by three mature trees, but walking along without the benefit of a railing is slightly unnerving. A few paces further north, cross the road and continue climbing 15 feet up and to the east.

Turn left at the top of the rise to find three footbridges set close together. At the end of the last bridge, the path bends sharply to the left, twisting downhill to another bench swing, which faces east. Sit for a spell and wonder what the now-closed path to your left once revealed. The path, blocked by a wooden fence, is overgrown with mayapples, poison ivy, and other vines. Return the way you came, up and down the twisting path, heading south over the bridges. Along the way, you'll notice several patches of English ivy creeping down the hill from the east. Most likely, these vines have escaped from the residential yards high above. One can hardly blame them. Babb Run is indeed a sanctuary from urban life.

NEARBY ACTIVITIES

Chestnut Hills Memorial Park, a small but lovely cemetery, is across the street from Babb Run. At its entrance, a stone path leads to a bench overlooking a fountain. With several bird boxes set in and around the water, it serves to continue the sanctuary for the birds and other wildlife that venture north. Babb Run is situated within a couple of miles of Cascade Valley Metropark and Gorge Metro Park (see p. 75).

#5
Beartown Lakes Reservation

IN BRIEF

Mature beech and maple forests, a small pine grove, and 3 lakes comprise this 149-acre park in southern Geauga County. Beaver, herons, hawks, and deer are prevalent. But will you see a bear?

DIRECTIONS

From I-271 take Route 422 east to Route 306. Turn right, following Route 306 south about 1.5 miles. Turn left (east) onto Taylor May Road; then turn right onto Quinn Road. Follow it south 1.4 miles to the park entrance, at 18870 Quinn Road.

DESCRIPTION

Bainbridge Township was settled in the early 1800s. At the time, the area was simply awash in bear. Local lore tells of a time when one of the McConoughey boys killed five bears in a single day. Not surprisingly, residents began calling the area "Beartown."

In the 1960s and 1970s, three interconnecting lakes were constructed, and the surrounding land was operated as a private fishing club. In 1993, Geauga Park District purchased the land; Beartown Lakes Reservation was dedicated in 1996.

The park is a mixture of water (22 acres), wetlands (40 acres), and forest (70 acres). Three trails encircle the park. Each has distinct characteristics, and yet,

KEY AT-A-GLANCE INFORMATION

Length: 3 miles

Configuration: Three interconnecting loops

Difficulty: Easy

Scenery: Tall beech forests, three lakes, fish, and wildlife; bear sightings unlikely

Exposure: Whitetail and Beechnut trails are mostly shaded; exposed by the lakes

Traffic: Moderately busy, especially on warm weekend afternoons

Trail surface: Lake Trail is paved, Whitetail and Beechnut are packed gravel.

Hiking time: 1 hour

Season: Open year-round

Access: 6 a.m.–11 p.m.

Maps: Usually available at park welcome sign

Facilities: Rest rooms and water at North Point picnic area in the middle of the park and at Minnow Pond picnic area on the east side of the park

Special comments: Will the Black Bear make a comeback? For more information about black bears, contact the Ohio Division of Wildlife at (330) 644-2293.

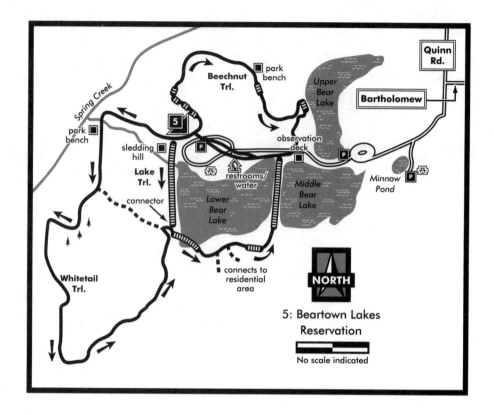

like the wetlands, woods, and water they visit, all three are closely related. The trails also share a common trailhead area, under the shade of tall maples and oaks, just north of the parking lot.

Lake Trail

(a 0.7-mile, paved, all-purpose trail)
Lake Trail heads west from the trailhead, and quickly bends left, crossing a wooden footbridge that overlooks the sledding hill. Lake Trail is exposed on the north-to-south stretch. As you head south, you'll be able to peer into Lower Bear Lake to catch a glimpse of a bluegill. They are easy to catch here, locals say, as long as you use short, live bait. (*Any bait dangling off the end of your hook will be nibbled away; the fish is then free to go, having enjoyed a safe snack. It really is a game, isn't it?*) In addition to the

small bluegills, bass and northern pike are found in Lower Bear Lake. The park district strongly encourages releasing all catches.

Cattails and duckweed are plentiful at the south end of the lake. A boardwalk bridge runs across the corner of the lake; from it you'll head east through the woods. Avoid the unmarked paths that wander off from the south side of the Lake Trail, which lead to private residential areas.

Continue east until you reach the southeastern edge of Lower Bear Lake where the woods open to reveal a boardwalk that spans the dam separating Middle and Lower Bear Lakes. Turn left, crossing the boardwalk where in the summertime you'll enjoy an amazing array of dancing dragonflies. From the north end of the walkway, turn left and follow the shoulder of the park roadway back to the parking lot.

Beechnut Trail (0.6 miles)

The Beechnut and Whitetail Trails are not paved, and they run north together for a few yards before they split.

The Whitetail Trail veers to the left; follow the Beechnut (trail signs are marked by two beech leaves) to the right. The sandy dirt-and-gravel trail is flat, but it winds about as it leads you through the woods. You'll cross four small footbridges in the first quarter-mile.

As you wind your way to the observation point at Upper Bear Lake, you might amuse yourself by watching for, or imagining you see, bear. Or maybe that's not so amusing. A bear seems to have made the rounds (and the local news) in Geauga County each year in recent memory. Black bears, typically young males in search of a territory, can and do wander in from Pennsylvania. Still, your chances of seeing a deer or a rabbit are much greater than of seeing a bear.

Your chances of seeing a turtle, water snake, or frog from the observation deck at Upper Bear Lake are pretty good, too. You can relax and watch on the western side of the little lake, before getting back on the path and heading south.

Before you leave the woods, you'll cross a fifth and final footbridge. The trail curves to the left, then goes up a short incline; its five-foot rise is the only "climb" you'll have on this trail.

The path ends at the park road, directly across from a fishing pier on Middle Bear Lake. Turn right, following the road back to the parking lot (the same return path as you follow for Lake Trail).

Whitetail Trail (1.5 miles)

From the Beechnut/Whitetail Trailhead, head west with the sledding hill on your left, following the trail to the edge of Spring Creek. The water here is quite clear and pretty, but remember: no matter how good a stream looks, the only water safe to drink is the stuff you brought from home, in your own bottle.

Crossing the creek is easy; relatively stable rocks lead the way. Even if you slip in, you'll find yourself in only two to four inches of water. Trudge uphill a few steps from the creek, where you'll come to a park bench, a great place to watch and listen for woodpeckers. Soon, the trail bends to the left. Whitetail Trail is the only one of the three trails designated for horseback riding, and you're likely to encounter a rider or two through here.

About 0.5 miles into the hike, you'll cross a small tributary where you may spot some spring peepers. Enjoy the fragrant pines as you go up a little hill and follow the trail as it bends left again. From here you can see some private farmland. Enjoy it while it lasts. Relatively new subdivisions abut the park on all other sides.

Heading east as you pass the farmland, the trail meanders through an old sugar bush (a narrow strip of sugar maples), then heads northeast. At about 1 mile, Whitetail approaches the southwest corner of Lower Bear Lake. From here, you can follow the trail left, through the prairie, as Whitetail circles back onto itself, or you can jump onto Lake Trail, and finish your hike on its paved path.

NEARBY ACTIVITIES

The park's picnic areas can be reserved through the park office by calling (440) 286-9504. Much of Middle and Lower Bear Lakes are open to fishing, and several piers make it easy to get a line in the deep-water areas.

The small sledding hill north of Lower Bear Lake provides young children a gentle introduction to the downhill sport. (Groaning grown-ups will appreciate the steps on the side of the hill!) Geauga Park District offers year-round educational programming. Call for a schedule of activities or view the calendar online, at www.geaugalink.com /gcpdist.

Special thanks to Naturalist Judy Bradt-Barnhart, Geauga Park District, for reviewing this park description.

#6
Beaver Marsh Boardwalk

IN BRIEF

This area was a garbage dump in the 1970s. Beginning in the early 1980s, beaver (also known as "park engineers") transformed the dump into a viable habitat, and not only for themselves. Today the area is home to more than 65 other animal species. The National Park Service built a wooden boardwalk across the marsh; now humans can enjoy its serene beauty, too.

DIRECTIONS

Go south on I-77 and take the Wheatley Road/Richfield exit (Exit no. 143) east about 4.5 miles to Riverview Road. Turn left, heading north on Riverview. Turn right onto Bolantz Road. Park on the south side of Bolantz Road at the Hunt Farm Trailhead.

DESCRIPTION

Want to see a dramatic makeover? It doesn't get much better than this . . .

As recently as the early 1980s, this stretch of land was a soggy dumping ground, full of junk from a nearby car repair shop and assorted other trash. Even before the National Park Service could reclaim the land, a couple of beaver took matters into their own, um, paws. Park volunteers and employees helped the beaver by clearing out the debris, and in 1993 the National Park Service placed a beautiful 530-foot-long boardwalk across the marsh. From a single dam to a community of beaver,

KEY AT-A-GLANCE INFORMATION

Length: 3.5 miles (with optional 2 miles)

Configuration: Out-and-back

Difficulty: Easy

Scenery: Beaver marsh and pond, and nearly 600 types of plants and animals

Exposure: Almost entirely exposed; the southernmost section of this hike is shaded.

Traffic: Moderate to heavy (expect some bikes)

Trail surface: Paved towpath trail and wooden boardwalk

Hiking time: Allow 90 minutes for walking and watching; add 40 minutes for a side trip to Indigo Lake, and 2 hours if you plan to explore Hale Farm, too.

Season: Open year-round

Access: 7 a.m.–11 p.m.

Maps: Free, inside Cuyahoga Valley National Park visitors centers; a smaller online version is available at www.dayinthevalley.com.

Facilities: Rest rooms at Hunt Farm Visitors Center and Ira Road Trailhead

Special comments: Watch for heavy bike traffic in warm weather.

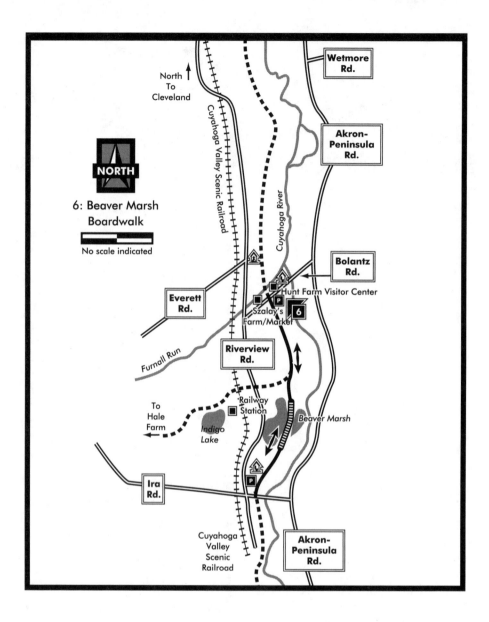

6: Beaver Marsh Boardwalk

No scale indicated

North
To
Cleveland

NORTH

Wetmore Rd.

Akron-Peninsula Rd.

Bolantz Rd.

Everett Rd.

Riverview Rd.

Ira Rd.

Akron-Peninsula Rd.

Cuyahoga Valley Scenic Railroad

Cuyahoga River

Hunt Farm Visitor Center

Szalay's Farm/Market

6

Furnall Run

To Hale Farm

Indigo Lake

Railway Station

Beaver Marsh

Cuyahoga Valley Scenic Railroad

muskrat, mink, and many other animals and birds, the marsh and towpath have grown together, reclaiming the land as habitat for more than 500 types of plants and animals. Pretty impressive, especially for a flat stretch of land less than 2 miles long.

The marsh and its adjacent land constitute one of the most diverse spots in the 33,000-acre National Park. Its diversity and accessibility have earned it a spot on the Ohio Division of Wildlife's list of "Watchable Wildlife" sites.

As you follow the towpath south from Bolantz Road, you'll pass by private farmland, usually sporting cornstalks. During the summer growing season, the loud shots of "corn cannons" sound periodically, in an effort to scare away the crows and other animals that enjoy the corn. You can enjoy the corn without the noise when you purchase it at the nearby farm market. About 0.25 miles south of your starting point, look to your left and try to imagine the field full of wildflowers as a gravel pit. Yes, it was—in the not-so-distant past. Another successful makeover, satisfying thousands of park visitors each year. . .

When you reach the beaver marsh, you're sure to notice the cattails. They are an important food source for many animals, and when this area was first settled, they were also a staple in the diets of the Native Americans and early settlers, who made meal from their long stems. *(Speaking of diets, this might make you grateful for your next salad, hmm?)*

Now that you've reached the beaver marsh, you want to see beaver, right? Here are some basic tips: First, beaver are nocturnal. That means they do most of their home building and repair work in the evening. Visit near dusk and look for them as they swim. Watch for a wake, the V-shaped disturbance in the water created by a beaver's tail as it swims. Keep an eye on the water lilies, and you may see a hungry beaver grab a leaf to eat. He will roll the leaf and hold it in his paw like a green cigar as he nibbles on it. Also look for mink and muskrat that make their homes in and around the water. Muskrat build their homes along the banks of ponds and streams and occasionally on top of beaver lodges.

The boardwalk offers such beautiful scenery, and so much to see, that you may not want to leave at all. But if you head south from the boardwalk, Ira Trailhead (just past Lock 26) makes a natural turn-around point. Of course, if you don't turn around, you can follow the towpath into Akron, south into Zoar, and beyond . . .

On the way back, you can take a pleasant excursion to Indigo Lake and walk around it, adding about 0.5 miles to your hike distance. Indigo Lake is small but lovely; its name was inspired by its deep blue hue. If you follow the trail west another 0.75 miles from Indigo Lake, you'll find yourself at Hale Farm and Village and way, way back in time. The working museum is owned and operated by the Western Reserve Historical Society. It offers an accurate representation of life in the Western Reserve, circa 1826. Candle making, glass blowing, and pottery demonstrations are regular fare; special seasonal events, like the spring sap collection are even more fun. For an events schedule and admission rates, call (800) 589-9703.

As you head north and cross the boardwalk again, it's still hard to imagine this spot was a dump. Clearly, this was a successful makeover. The beautiful result: a safe haven for hundreds of animals and plants, and a great escape for the humans who make their homes on either side of the valley.

NEARBY ACTIVITIES

Hunt Farm, just north of the parking lot along Bolantz Road, is a visitors' center that doubles as a museum. It highlights the role of the small, family farm as a force in the valley's development. Just a long stone's throw from the visitors' center, Szalay's Farm (4563 Riverview Road) sells fresh produce, from spring strawberries and summer sweet corn to fall apples and squash. The Cuyahoga Valley National Park offers hundreds of educational and recreational events throughout the year. Pick up a free calendar of activities at a park visitors' center, or check the online calendar that is updated daily at www.dayinthevalley. com.

#7
Beckwith Orchards

To Streetsboro, Ravenna

14

43 Twin Lakes

Towners Woods

Brady Lake Rd.

Ravenna Rd.

Lake Rockwell Rd.

To Kent

7

RR

To Kent

orchard

IN BRIEF

The best way to appreciate Ohio's family farms is to work hard on one, breaking a sweat while working the soil. If you can't do that, at least visit one for a day. The same family has tended the Beckwith Orchards in Kent since 1878. They welcome walkers, wannabe farmers, gardeners, and those who just love to eat farm-good food.

DIRECTIONS

From Route 14 in Streetsboro, take Route 43 south through the small community of Twin Lakes. Turn left onto Ravenna Road, heading east about 1.5 miles. Turn right onto Lake Rockwell Road; follow it southwest about 0.5 miles where the entrance to Beckwith Orchards & Gift Shop will be on your right, at 1617 Lake Rockwell Road.

DESCRIPTION

This 101-acre farm has been in the Beckwith family since 1878. In this millennium, Charlie and Marilyn Beckwith will hand the farm over to their children.

The orchards produce 24 varieties of apples and 8 peach varieties, and they host quiet a few visitors, too. According to Charlie, about 3,000 elementary school children visit each year. The children and other visitors and shoppers enjoy walking the orchards, where a casual stroll affords glimpses of many

KEY AT-A-GLANCE INFORMATION

Length: 0.5 miles

Configuration: Loop

Difficulty: Very easy

Scenery: Hardy and lovingly tended apple, peach, and chestnut trees; children's and community gardens, bluebirds, geese, and the occasional eagle.

Exposure: Mostly exposed

Traffic: Moderate

Trail surface: Grass and dirt path

Hiking time: 30 minutes

Season: Open Labor Day– December 24

Access: Hours vary by season; generally open noon–6 p.m.

Maps: None; but it's hard to get lost here—if you get turned around, just head for the barn!

Facilities: Rest room inside

Special comments: Technically, the orchard is open only during the fall harvest; each year, however, the Beckwiths invite visitors to bring their mothers (and the rest of the family) out to walk around the grounds on Mother's Day weekend, to enjoy the trees in full bloom.

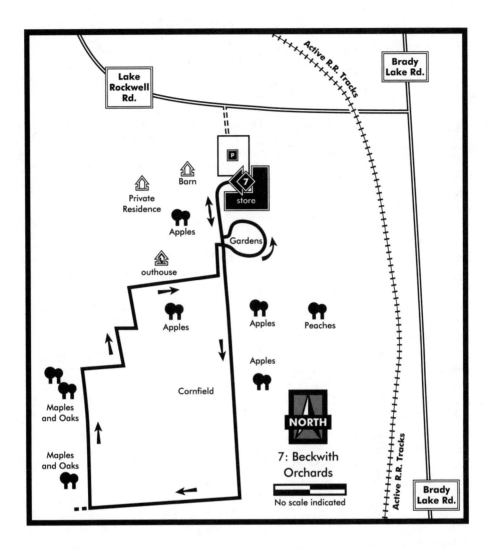

Lake Rockwell Rd.

Brady Lake Rd.

Active R.R. Tracks

P

7 store

Barn

Private Residence

Apples

Gardens

outhouse

Apples

Apples

Peaches

Apples

Cornfield

Maples and Oaks

Maples and Oaks

NORTH

7: Beckwith Orchards

No scale indicated

Active R.R. Tracks

Brady Lake Rd.

birds and other wildlife at work. "Once in a while the Lake Rockwell eagle flies by," Charlie says. There are 18 bluebird boxes scattered throughout the farm that lure the small, cherry-bellied songbirds to the property.

After stopping in the store to see what's just been picked, step off the front porch and turn left, heading down a short hill. Walking south, the community gardens will be on your left and a brisk fall breeze may rise up to meet you. If you visit during the picking season,

you'll probably notice the boughs of the trees literally groaning with the weight of their fruit. Between the chilly breeze and fragrant fruit, you may have to fight the urge to run back inside for a snack. If you prevail, of course, you still can get a snack upon your return.

You'll pass a small planting of corn, and, more often than not, a few Canadian geese pecking around for leftover grains. As you walk up a slight rise, you'll come to a nice vantage point. At the top of this little hill, look around and enjoy a scene as typical of Ohio as any other you could find. Rows of apple trees are to your left; tall deciduous trees in front of you mark the farm's southern boundary. During the harvest season, the barn, fields, and gardens drip fall colors. If you like to hike with a sketchpad, by all means, bring colored pencils on this trip.

Moving along again on the well-worn path, you'll pass the cornfield and turn right. Head west briefly, then turn right again at the tree line. Follow the path north past the corn, and keep your eyes peeled for birdhouses as you walk under the tall oaks and maples. Stop and look into the old outhouse on your left (*"All the kids on the tours are fascinated with that!," Marilyn notes*) As the barn comes back into view, you can turn left, heading back to the store (and inside the snack shop for some homemade pie) or follow the path on to the community gardens. Whether under autumn sun or fall skies, the dark glossy blooms of the plantings in the garden are gorgeous. It's a great place to sketch or snap some bright, colorful photos.

Back inside the store, be sure to step into the back room. It is a veritable nature museum, filled with abandoned nests of paper wasps, honeycombs, and old farming implements. Charlie explains the paper wasps are the apples'

friends, because they eat the insects that would eat the apples. Gives the menacing wasp a nicer image, doesn't it?

Although the orchard has traditionally been open from Labor Day through December 24 each year, the next generation of Beckwiths has taken the reigns of the family business. A new greenhouse has popped up on the western side of the property, and the business just may grow a new branch or two. Call, or check in, to find out about a possibly expanding season.

NEARBY ACTIVITIES

The Annual Harvest Festival is held in October; usually it is scheduled for the second weekend. In recent years, the festival has featured Irish bands, cloggers, strolling poets, and a well-known gourd authority or two. An evening walk in the woods is also slated for an October evening; you never know whoooooo you might see then. Call (330) 673-6433 for more information. If you want to put more mileage on your boots in the same trip, hike Towner's Woods (see p. 193), which is literally around the bend from the orchard.

Special thanks to Sally Beckwith for reviewing this hike.

#8
Bessie Benner Metzenbaum Park

IN BRIEF

This 65-acre park in Chester Township is a beautiful memorial to James Metzenbaum's wife, Bessie. Mature beech-maple woods cover much of the property, while the remains of an old orchard and two pine plantations add greenery year-round. Three trails traverse the park; two of them are accessible to all. The Summit Trail climbs 140 feet up a sandstone knoll, providing a treetop view of the Griswold Creek wetland.

DIRECTIONS

Exit I-271 at Route 322, heading east 4 miles into Chesterland. Turn right onto Route 306. Follow 306 south 1 mile. Turn right onto Cedar Road. Traveling west on Cedar, you'll pass Bessie Benner Metzenbaum Sheltered Industries and Opportunity School before turning right into the park's entrance (1 mile west of Route 306) at 7940 Cedar Road.

DESCRIPTION

James Metzenbaum purchased this pretty parcel of land in the 1940s, intending it to be a tribute to his wife, Bessie, who had died several years earlier. He deeded the land to the Bessie Benner Metzenbaum Foundation, and for years it was used by organizations such as the Girl Scouts and the YMCA. The Metzenbaum School was built in 1965, and in 1991 the foundation donated these 65 acres of wooded land, including a former homestead, to the Geauga Park District.

KEY AT-A-GLANCE INFORMATION

Length: 1.2 miles

Configuration: Two loops and a short out-and-back

Difficulty: Easy; with steep sections along Summit Trail

Scenery: Wildflowers and ore outcropping on Summit Trail; beaver on Griswold Trail

Exposure: Shady

Traffic: Light

Trail surface: The Summit Trail follows a bumpy, hilly, dirt path; the Evergreen and Griswold trails have hard surfaces (asphalt and wooden boardwalk)

Hiking time: 40 minutes

Season: Open all year

Access: 6 a.m.–11 p.m.

Maps: Available at trailhead

Facilities: Rest rooms and water on the eastern side of the parking lot

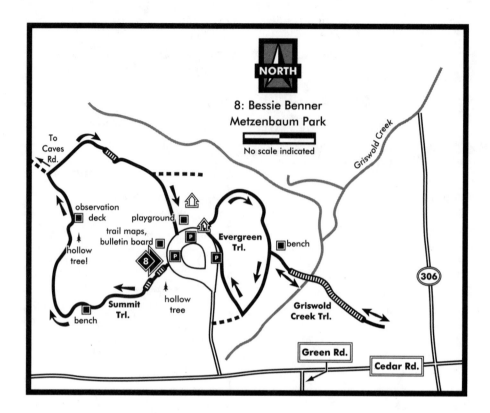

**8: Bessie Benner
Metzenbaum Park**

No scale indicated

NORTH

To Caves Rd.

Griswold Creek

observation deck

playground

trail maps, bulletin board

hollow tree!

8

Summit Trl.

bench

hollow tree

P

P

P

Evergreen Trl.

bench

Griswold Creek Trl.

306

Green Rd.

Cedar Rd.

The homestead is gone, but some apple trees remain on the eastern side of the parking lot, conjuring up memories of an old orchard. A significant portion of the park is wetland, and the Griswold Creek Trail is necessarily a boardwalk trail. It provides an opportunity to view the work of beaver, including an active beaver dam.

The three short trails in this park cover a wide variety of ground. Start on the Summit Trail, the longest at 0.5 miles. Enter the trail on the northwestern side of the parking lot. There are two entry points to the trail; take the one south of the trailhead bulletin board to follow the trail clockwise. You'll cross two footbridges almost immediately. On your left, stop to look through a very hollow tree (as long as it stands!). The trail wiggles a bit before it gets down to

business—climbing business, that is. The ascent will take you to a point nearly 140 feet above Griswold Creek. Along the way, you'll notice at least half-a-dozen other hollow trees. In fact, there's one immediately south of the large observation deck that you'll come to about 0.25 miles into your hike. Whew. Benches built into the deck give you a chance to catch your breath. Almost certainly, you'll enjoy several birds flying by. Summer songbirds include wood thrush, hooded warbler, and scarlet tanager. The trail by the deck is level, but not for long. As you head north and down the hill, you'll see a sign marking an offshoot trail to Caves Road. Stay on Summit Trail as it bends to the right, heading down 17 wooden steps. You'll find several fern varieties here below the observation deck. The path soon curves right and then straightens out to head south for a few dozen steps. At the end of the trail, you'll find a small playground, just north of your starting point.

From here, cross the parking lot toward the rest rooms, and turn left onto the paved Evergreen Trail. Evergreen turns left and right, whipping into the thick of a planting of white pines. In places, the path is entirely covered with their needles. A few steps past a park bench (perfect for bird watching), you'll turn left onto Griswold Creek Trail. The boardwalk takes you across the stream and through the wetlands. Be quiet as you enter the trail, and you may spot some beaver at work here. At the end of the trail (about 0.2 miles) turn around and return to the Evergreen Trail to complete the loop.

Turn left onto the trail, heading south through even more fragrant pines. This is a popular spot for birds, and some have built their nests rather low in the trees, giving you a good look into their homes. You may also notice that the poison ivy here is an equal-opportunity climber, wrapping up the trunks of the few maples as well as the evergreens. As the path curves, heading north as it parallels the parking lot, you'll notice some crabapples and a hollow apple tree. It's as if Evergreen were trying to compete with Summit. There's no contest here, though—all three trails are beautiful, each in a different way than the other.

NEARBY ACTIVITIES

The park's playground is designed to be enjoyed by people of all abilities; the picnic shelter is available for use by families and organizations. Call the Geauga Park District at (440) 286-9504 for details. Bessie Benner Metzenbaum is the smallest park in the Geauga District. About 7 miles south of here, you can visit Beartown Lakes Reservation, with 3 miles of trails (see p. 23).

Special thanks to Dan Best, chief naturalist, Geauga Park District, for reviewing this park description.

#9
Blue Hen Falls

IN BRIEF

"Now I'm a REAL hiker!" my five-year old said, soon after we started out on this trail. Great for young, surefooted trekkers, this trail offers beautiful scenery, climbing, creek jumping, and the opportunity to wade in the shallow waters at the bottom of 20-foot-tall Buttermilk Falls.

DIRECTIONS

From Cleveland, take I-77 south to Brecksville Road (Route 21). Take Route 21 north to Boston Mills Road and turn right (east). Entrance and parking are about 1 mile west of Riverview Road. Enter the small parking lot with the "Blue Hen Falls" sign, on the north side of Boston Mills Road.

DESCRIPTION

Enter the trail at the north end of the parking lot. It was paved long ago, so gravel and dirt are more apparent than asphalt. You'll descend about 30 feet as you follow the path, then the ground levels out and the trail turns sharply right. It continues gently sloping toward a sturdy wooden bench facing Blue Hen Falls. This picturesque point is an ideal conversation spot, and about the only place to sit along the trail.

Blue Hen Falls tumble 15 feet over the edge of a massive hunk of sandstone, landing in Spring Creek—which your feet will soon meet. Behind the bench is

KEY AT-A-GLANCE INFORMATION

Length: 1.2 miles

Configuration: Out-and-back

Difficulty: Moderate

Scenery: Two waterfalls, a meandering creek, deep ravine, deciduous forest, and really big rocks!

Exposure: Completely shaded

Traffic: Moderate

Trail surface: Dirt trail: rooty, rocky, and steeply banked in places

Hiking time: 45 minutes for hiking; allow extra dawdle time at the falls

Season: Open all year; tread carefully when wet or icy

Access: 7 a.m.–10 p.m., but best done during daylight hours

Maps: Cuyahoga Valley National Park maps available at visitors' centers in the park; the closest is at Boston Store, on Boston Mills Road just east of Riverview Road

Facilities: None

Special comments: The parking lot holds eight cars at most; a few additional spots can be had in the unmarked, but cleared, area on the south side of Boston Mills Road

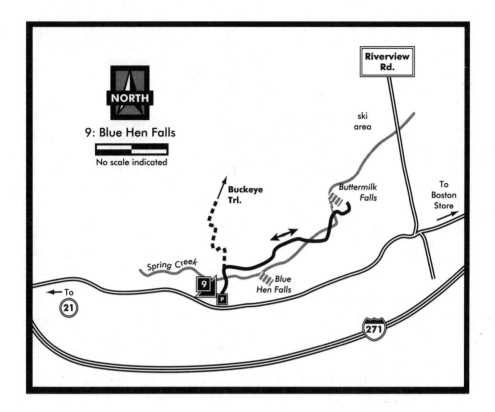

9: Blue Hen Falls

No scale indicated

NORTH

Riverview Rd.

ski area

Buckeye Trl.

Buttermilk Falls

To Boston Store

Spring Creek

9

P

Blue Hen Falls

To 21

271

a long wooden bridge, follow it across Spring Creek and you'll see the blue blazes of the Buckeye Trail, rising to the left. You should continue on the path as it veers right, instead, descending through the deep, thickly forested ravine. During the spring, the pockmarked limestone and shale seem to glow with a green hue; in the fall, they appear darker, and they blush a bit under the reddening leaves. Moss aficionados should be on the lookout here and especially along the bottom of the trail as it approaches Buttermilk Falls. Many of the National Park's moss and fern varieties thrive in this cool, moist hollow.

The path that winds down the 50 feet or so between the two falls is narrow. It twists, bumps, and grinds over the trunks of fallen trees and along the edge of the ravine. You'll have to jump, skip, or splash

your way across the creek at least three times, and you may cross trickles and runoff water several other times, depending on recent rainfall. The widest points you'll cross are 15 to 20 feet across, but don't worry—a slip here will land you in just a few inches of water. At the first wide crossing, look to your right (east) to see where layers of Bedford Shale and Berea Sandstone slammed into each other, forming the geological equivalent of a layer cake in the hillside. In the winter, when trickles of water have frozen while falling down the wall, it's easy to imagine it has been recently frosted, awaiting a giant's first bite.

Since the trail forms a crescent around the top and bottom of the falls, you can hear Buttermilk Falls before you can see it. Follow the trail as it bends right after the second wide creek crossing. The trail then heads down a final, sharp decline and a hairpin turn to the left before reaching the pool at the bottom of the falls. This is the spot to play, in the warmer months at least. The pool at the point closest to the falls is several feet deep, so it is not safe for children to be unsupervised here. Anyway, this is a good spot for adults to play, too. Let your eyes adjust to the shadowy world under a few inches of water, and you are likely to see a small toad or tiny white crayfish playing hide-and-seek among the large, flat shale stones.

On your way back up, stop about 20 feet above the second creek crossing. If you're quiet for a few minutes, you'll surely witness a few feathered fly-bys. This bend in the trail above the creek is a popular corridor for woodland birds.

After passing the bench near the end of the trail, pause again at the crook of the wooden fence. Here, you can look almost straight down onto Blue Hen Falls. After viewing her louder, longer-legged sister at the opposite end of the trail, you'll appreciate Blue Hen's unique and quiet beauty from a different perspective.

NEARBY ACTIVITIES

Blue Hen Falls is just around the corner from Boston Mills Ski Resort, also located in the Cuyahoga Valley National Park on Riverview Road. Reach the ski area by phone at (330) 467-2242. If you want a snack, more hiking, or both, take Boston Mills Road about 0.25 miles east of Riverview Road to the Boston Store. On the south side of the road sits the old company store, dating back to 1836; it has been given new life as a visitors' center in the National Park. In addition to maps and information you'll find there, you can cross the street to a small snack shop where ice cream, beverages, and other trail essentials await, next to the towpath trailhead.

IN BRIEF

Ohio's grandest canyon, carved by Tinker's Creek, was almost spoiled in the mid-1960s. Thanks to concerned citizens, today you can peer into the nearly 200-foot deep gorge and enjoy its cascades and waterfalls along the trail.

DIRECTIONS

Exit I-271 at Broadway/Forbes exit and head west on Broadway about 1.5 miles, then veer left onto Union. After crossing Northfield Road (Route 8) in Bedford, turn left on Egbert Road, and make a quick right onto Gorge Parkway. Head west about 2 miles to the parking area for Bridal Veil Falls Overlook, on the left.

DESCRIPTION

Cross the parkway and enter the trail, following 65 wooden steps down to the overlook. Along the way there are several places to stop and admire the water gently bathing the shale as it trips along to the falls. At the bottom of the steps, the walking and bridle paths cross. Horses cross the shallow water on hoof; the rest of us use the bridge. As you look north from the bridge, notice the layers of Bedford Shale that line the side of the hill.

At the bottom of the 85-foot drop, you'll find a small observation deck with benches. Stop here to enjoy the view.

Once you've had a good look, get off the deck and step onto the bridle trail, continuing west. You'll roll up and down several gentle hills, under the shade of

KEY AT-A-GLANCE INFORMATION

Length: 2 miles

Configuration: Loop

Difficulty: Easy

Scenery: Waterfall, 190-foot gorge, lush forest; great fall color, wide variety of wildflowers in the spring

Exposure: Completely shaded except for overlook itself

Traffic: Moderate to heavy

Trail surface: Dirt/gravel trail on loop's north side, paved on south

Hiking time: 45 minutes

Season: Open year-round

Access: Open from 6 a.m.–11 p.m., parking lots that close at dusk are clearly posted

Maps: Available at all Metroparks nature centers and at www.clemetparks.com

Facilities: Pay phone, water, and flush toilet at ranger's station at corner of Egbert Road and Gorge Parkway; portable rest rooms at Gorge Overlook, water and rest rooms at Hermit's Hollow picnic area, about 1 mile west of the overlook

Special comments: Learn more about Tinker's Creek and the surrounding watershed at Garfield Park Nature Center; call (216) 341-3125.

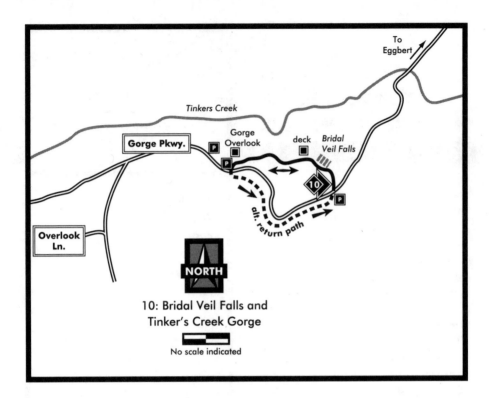

NORTH

**10: Bridal Veil Falls and
Tinker's Creek Gorge**

No scale indicated

thick maple, oak, and hemlock trees. The eastern hemlock is common in this area, often simply lumped in with the "evergreen" family. Hemlocks can be distinguished by their tiny opposing leaves, deep green in color, that lie flat along their branches. Look for narrow white stripes on the leaves' undersides.

The wide dirt and gravel trail you're on performs double duty here. It is both the Metropark bridle trail and a portion of the Buckeye Trail, and it is well marked. A mile west of the falls, you'll rise up to meet the parkway again, soon reaching the Gorge overlook.

The area was declared a National Natural Landmark in 1968. The overlook itself is wheelchair- and stroller-accessible (parking is available directly off Gorge Parkway). The view is the main attraction, of course, but the history is also interesting.

Tinker's Creek, the largest tributary to the Cuyahoga River, begins in Kent, Ohio—about 15 miles southeast. Once it reaches this area, it winds its way nearly 5 miles through Bedford Reservation. In 1965, public officials planned to dam the gorge, intending to flood it to create a large, inland lake they would call Lake Shawnee. A five-year study by naturalist William F. Nimberger, however, highlighted the valley's unique blend of plant and animal species. Public opinion, swayed in large part by Nimberger's study, convinced politicians to abandon their plans to dam the gorge. Today the gorge is a National Natural Landmark.

To return to your car, retrace your steps on the bridle trail or cross the parkway to the south, and take the all-purpose trail back to the parking area at Bridal Veil Falls. The difference in the two paths is negligible—about 0.1 miles.

#11
Canal Fulton, Towpath, and Olde Muskingham Trail

IN BRIEF

Settled in the early 1800s, Canal Fulton has triumphantly maintained and celebrated its rich canal history. Following the towpath trail on the eastern side of the river and the Olde Muskingham Trail on the west, hikers and bikers can enjoy historic landmarks and shopping on both sides of the Tuscarawas River.

DIRECTIONS

From I-77, take Route 21 south to Route 93, heading east. Route 93, also named Cherry Street in town, passes by a canoe livery. Follow signs to the St. Helena boarding area in Community Park, where towpath parking is available.

DESCRIPTION

As you step up onto the towpath in Canal Fulton, you may plod alongside a couple of draft horses pulling the *St. Helena,* a restored canal boat. About 1 mile south of your starting point, you'll lose the horses and find a canal lock that still works. If you're lucky, you might catch a live lock demonstration, thanks to the Canal Fulton Heritage Society. Even if you don't see the demo, stop at Lock 4 and read the interpretive sign.

Continue south, enjoying the view as you stroll along about ten feet above both the canal bed on your left and the river on your right. In many places from this point south, the canal bed is overgrown with thistles and cattails,

KEY AT-A-GLANCE INFORMATION

Length: 11 miles

Configuration: Loop (or one-way with shuttle)

Difficulty: Moderate

Scenery: Historic town of Canal Fulton, the Tuscarawas Riverbed, thick with wildflowers and a working canal lock

Exposure: Shaded by deciduous trees; almost completely exposed when leaves have fallen

Traffic: Busy, especially on warm weekend afternoons

Trail surface: Crushed limestone (towpath) and grass and gravel (Olde Muskingham Trail)

Hiking time: 4.5–5 hours

Season: Open year-round

Access: Open dawn–dusk; no permits required

Maps: See www.starkparks.com or call (330) 477-3552; also see maps nos. 20–22 in *Towpath Companion, A Traveler's Guide to the Ohio & Erie Canal Towpath Trail* (2002).

Facilities: Rest rooms and pay phone at Community Park on Cherry Street in Canal Fulton; portable rest room at Crystal Springs Bridge Park

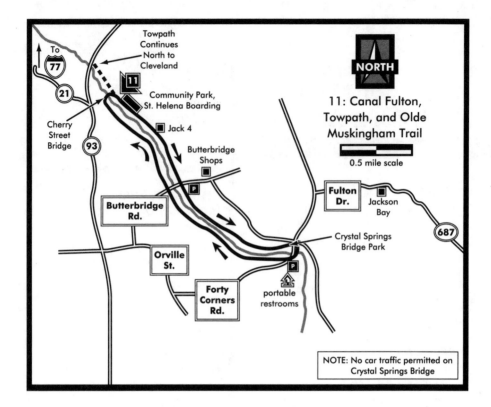

Towpath Continues North to Cleveland

To 77

21

Cherry Street Bridge

93

11

Community Park, St. Helena Boarding

Jack 4

Butterbridge Shops

P

Butterbridge Rd.

Orville St.

Forty Corners Rd.

Fulton Dr.

Jackson Bay

Crystal Springs Bridge Park

687

P

portable restrooms

NOTE: No car traffic permitted on Crystal Springs Bridge

providing a haven for birds and butterflies. Pick a quiet evening for your trip and you're almost certain to see warblers, finches, robins, jays, and cardinals.

One mile south of the trailhead, you'll be tempted to leave the trail for the shops at Butterbridge, just east of the trailhead of the same name. Immediately west of the trail, a private farm with a majestic red barn paints a scene typical of Stark County's beautiful farmland.

About 5 miles south of your start, you'll reach Crystal Springs Bridge. Its old iron grid floor has an almost lacey appearance. The bridge was built in 1914 (the lacey floor came later), and in 1996 it was designated Crystal Springs Park Bridge. This unlikely park now closes the gap between the Olde Muskingham Trail, on the west, and the towpath on the east bank of the river. If you turn left

at the bridge, you'll find the "Towpath CabInn" serving food and drink. Across the bridge to the west, at the intersection of Forty Corners Road and Riverside Avenue, there's a parking lot and an entry point to the Olde Muskingham Trail. Turn right, crossing the bridge to the north, then turn right again to travel north on the rail-trail.

(*Note:* Here, on the southern portion of what is sometimes called the "Little Loop" of the statewide trail, you may notice blue paint on nearby trees, as you are crossing paths with the Buckeye Trail.)

From this point south, the Buckeye Trail follows the river into Zoar.

If you've timed your hike right, you'll be able to watch the sun sink slowly in the sky as you head back to Canal Fulton. Stretches of farmland reach out to the west; the panorama is quite pretty, with or without the sunset. Because the trail surface here is more conducive to hikers than to bikers, you will have far less company on this part of the loop. You won't be lonesome, though, as toads, rabbits, and deer will join you, bumping along this old railroad right-of-way.

After crossing to the north side of Butterbridge Road, the trail winds back by Community Park, bending slightly to the right before depositing you onto Cherry Street. Turn right and cross over the bridge, heading east. Pause to look upstream, and perhaps to wave at a canoe as it drifts under the bridge that has carried traffic through town for nearly 100 years. Your historic trip ends here if you want it to; the parking lot and your car are behind you.

NEARBY ACTIVITIES

Canal Fulton was incorporated in 1814. Today's visitor may feel he's entered a time warp, walking by the "Toys Time Forgot" toyshop and under the historic street lamps that line the brick streets. Wander around above the river, or get a view of history from the river itself. From May through September, the *St. Helena* offers an authentic canal experience; call (330) 854-3808 for a schedule and rates. Those who prefer to paddle down the river can rent canoes from one of two liveries that operate just north of Community Park.

Budding botanists should visit Jackson Bog, 2 miles east of Crystal Springs Bridge. The bog is managed as a State Nature Preserve; more than 20 endangered plants can be viewed from its boardwalk trail.

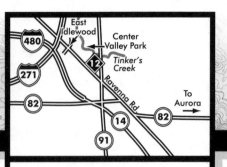

#12
Center Valley Park Trail

IN BRIEF

Leapin' Lizards! These trails offer salamanders, herons, forest, hills, wetlands,
old fashioned pump swings, and shiny,
new playground equipment. A flat, paved
trail—perfect for bikes and blades—cuts
through this heavily wooded corridor.
Seven rustic hiking paths shoot off the
main trail, wind through the woods, and
return to the center. In a word, this valley is versatile.

DIRECTIONS

From I-480 exit "Twinsburg/Route 91"
go north on Route 91 to Ravenna
Road. Turn left onto Ravenna Road and
go about one mile west to Dodge Middle School. Park in the school's lot and
enter the trail by the school's ball fields.

(*Note:* Alternate parking is available at
Idlewood Park, about 1 mile farther up
Ravenna Road. A third, smaller parking
lot sits at the trail's northern tip, off
Glenwood Drive—take Ravenna Road
to Glenwood, and turn right. Trailhead
parking is 0.5 miles from Ravenna
Road, on the right.)

DESCRIPTION

The city of Twinsburg did something
brilliant when it created this corridor of
park that connects residential neighborhoods with city amenities. The paved,
multi-use trail connecting the 1.2-mile
stretch between Glenwood Avenue and
Dodge Middle School was built in 1998.

KEY AT-A-GLANCE INFORMATION

Length: 4 miles

Configuration: Out-and-back
with loops

Difficulty: Flat and easy; Green
Heron Way is moderately strenuous

Scenery: Thick deciduous forest,
pines, wetlands; amphibians, birds

Exposure: Paved path is exposed;
dirt trails are shaded

Traffic: Paved path sees constant
traffic; nature trails see far less

Surface: Center trail is paved; foot
trails are dirt with some wood chips

Hiking time: 1–3 hours, depending on length

Season: Open year-round

Access: Daylight hours

Maps: Posted at trailhead and available at Twinsburg Parks and Recreation Department offices, 10075
Ravenna Road

Facilities: Emergency phones at
Dodge Middle School and Idle-
wood parking lots; rest rooms in
Idlewood parking lot

Special comments: This hike covers a little more than 4 miles, but
you can hike from 1–9 miles
depending on the loops you choose;
bikes are not allowed on nature
trails; pets are allowed, on leash.

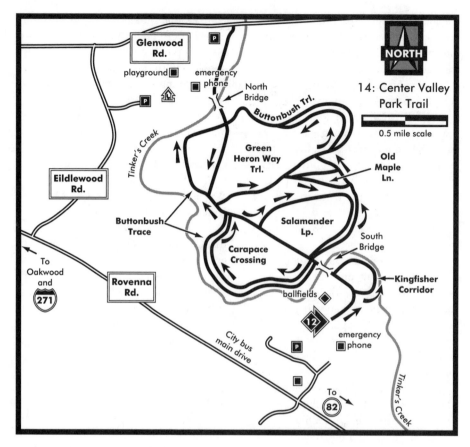

Glenwood
Rd.

playground   emergency
             phone

North
Bridge

Buttonbush Trl.

Green
Heron Way
Trl.

Old
Maple
Ln.

Tinker's Creek

Eildlewood
Rd.

Buttonbush
Trace

Salamander
Lp.

South
Bridge

Carapace
Crossing

To
Oakwood
and
271

Rovenna
Rd.

Kingfisher
Corridor

ballfields

12

City bus
main drive

emergency
phone

To
82

Tinker's Creek

Over the next few years, the city carried out a thoughtful plan, adding playgrounds, benches, and seven nature trails, which loop off of the relatively straight, north-south path. Today, the trails are well traveled and much appreciated by Twinsburg-area residents and workers.

The trail configuration allows you to tailor your hike to the desired length. For a short, satisfying hike, leave the school parking lot on the paved path, follow Kingfisher Corridor, and loop back to the lot in less than a mile. Or for a longer hike (and very little of it on pavement), follow Buttonbush Trace. It incorporates most of Carapace Crossing and Green Heron Way, and features many valley highlights, in just over 2.5

miles. The following hike description covers about 4 miles.

Begin from the southeast end of the Dodge parking lot, where a metal map of the entire park is posted. You may be disappointed to realize that you're facing the Twinsburg wastewater treatment facility. But stop and think for a moment—isn't this a fabulous "development" for a strip of land that other cities might have discounted as mere right-of-way space? With that perspective (and knowing you'll soon leave the plant behind), hit the trail.

The wide, paved trail sees heavy traffic on warm days after school is dismissed, as students and teachers walk, jog, and blade away the day's cares. During the summer months, you're likely to encounter groups of parents and children on their way to or from the pool, the library, or a ball game. The foot trails are generally quiet and shady.

Just beyond the trailhead sign, the path veers left. Soon, a sign on the right points to Kingfisher Corridor. Take this short loop as it twists alongside Tinker's Creek, about four feet above the water level, where kingfishers are often seen. When the dirt path deposits you back on pavement, turn right and cross over South Bridge. Just north of the bridge, turn left onto Carapace Crossing—my favorite of the trails here.

With the woods to your right and Tinker's Creek now on your left, you will need to jump over the creek in a couple of spots as the trail winds. It's perfect to whet the appetite of young hikers and to groom them for longer, more adventurous treks. As the path snakes back and forth, you find yourself nearly 50 feet from the water's edge. Then, at water's edge, carefully cross over a trickle of water on a makeshift "log bridge," or find a spot where you can step across.

About a mile into your hike, you'll be able to see homes on the western side of the creek and the remnants of an old stone bridge.

Amid the mud, Virginia creeper, and mayapples lives a dense population of birds, bugs, and small mammals. The "carapace" for which this trail is named refers to a hard covering, usually describing a turtle's shell. I've not seen turtles on the trail, yet this area is full of life. The calls of various birds, the rustle of chipmunks darting about, and slower-moving snakes and frogs accompany your every footfall. Dragonflies, California-potato beetles, and some of the largest bumblebees I've ever seen live here in the summer.

At about 1.3 miles into your trek, the trail bends to the left. Here duckweed sits on top of a small wet area practically bubbling with spring peepers and their buggy dining companions. After you cross over a wooden boardwalk, take a long step over a drainage culvert and a ditch, you'll see the paved path. Take it to the left.

Ahead, on the right (east) side of the trail, is the entrance to Green Heron Way and its little offshoot, Old Maple Lane. Turn right and wander down Green Heron Way, which is a loop trail that offers short, steep hills, and yes, green herons are often sighted here. (Old Maple Lane is a 0.3-mile loop that abuts Green Heron Way and Buttonbush trails. It is a "side trip" more beautiful than it is long; take it too if you have allowed time. The hike as described here sticks to Green Heron Way.) At the Maple Lane intersection, stay to the left, following Green Heron Way and for a time, Buttonbush. (Buttonbush, the outer loop, shares its path several times with the other trails here.)

In spite of its proximity to some of Twinsburg's residential areas, you could believe you were traveling in a vast forest. Interpretive signs point out the history of the area along Green Heron trail (and on Old Maple, you'll get a good look at our sap-making trees). Returning to pavement again, now on the north side of the park, turn right and head up to the playground on the western side of the paved path. Pump swings there remind me of several playgrounds of my childhood. You don't see many of these anymore. If you have an opportunity to introduce a swingset-age kid to a pump swing, you'll both have a good time. If swings aren't your thing, you may just be glad to know there's a portable rest room over the North

Bridge, on the western side of the playground.

Continuing your hike from the playground, turn right heading south on the center path (or following the western portion of Green Heron Way). About 0.5 miles south, you'll come to the entrance to Salamander Loop on the left (east) side of the path.

You'll encounter a hard-packed, dirt-and-grass trail, but as soon as you enter the woods, you'll see a wet and perfect salamander home to your right. Smart trail design keeps the trail—for the most part—dry. About 0.8 miles into the trail, Buttonbush Trace and Salamander Loop intersect (see p. 45). Turn right, following Salamander, heading south and making an extended S-shaped curve. You'll soon reach the nature overlook, a raised wooden platform where you can enjoy a view of the wetland. Each spring, park staffers lead special "salamander crossing" hikes here. The hikes are designed especially for elementary school–age children, who leave with no doubt as to how this trail got its name. Exit the platform, descending about 30 stairs, and end up south of the wetland area. Emerging from the trees, your feet find pavement again. Turn left and return to Dodge Middle School parking lot.

NEARBY ACTIVITIES

Twinsburg's city square is small but interesting. It has served as the center of town festivals since the early 1800s. An historic church, bandstand, and war memorial grace the square, located at the junction of Route 91, Ravenna Road, and Church Street.

#13
Chagrin River Park

Lake Erie   Lake Blvd. →   20   90
Chagrin River Park   13
East Lake
2
271   91
To
↓ Solon

IN BRIEF

The crooked Chagrin River runs wide through here, and this park takes full advantage of the river that serves as its southern boundary. A canoe launch near the park's entrance doubles as a shallow wading area. On dry land, a playground satisfies active little ones; grown-ups who want to play will enjoy the volleyball court. Seasonal wetlands on the park's north side attract a wide variety of birds, and therefore bird-watchers, to the park.

DIRECTIONS

From I-90, head east on Route 2 and exit at Lost Nation Road; follow it north to Reeves Road. Turn left (west) onto Reeves and left again to enter the park on the south side of the road. Follow the park road west 0.2 miles to the main parking area, by a playground and picnic shelter.

DESCRIPTION

From the south side of the parking lot, enter the wood-chip path, then turn left at the intersection. Follow the trail northeast about 0.2 miles to the canoe launch area. Wooden steps lead down to the river and launch area, which doubles as a wading spot. The Chagrin River is shallow here, and a flat sandstone area in the middle of the river serves as a good gathering spot. Kids like it because they can wade out to their own space and sit in the middle of the river, within

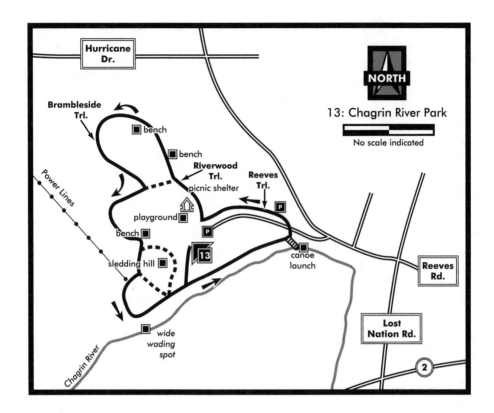

sight (but out of earshot) of dry adults on the river's edge.

From the top of the steps, cross the park road and turn left onto the paved Reeves Trail. Several memorial trees have been planted here, among them cimarron ash and celebration maple. As you approach the main parking lot and playground area, turn right onto the Riverwood Trail. The 0.7-mile trail is flat with a gravel surface. It passes through dense shrubs and woods that are as heavily populated with birds as the playground is with children. As you walk along on a summer afternoon, the songs of birds, the drone of insects, and the squeals of playful children mix together in a surprisingly loud but delightful way.

About 0.5 miles into your hike, the Brambleside Trail juts off to the right. Follow it past tangled trees and shrubs.

Deer beds are evident along here; angel wings bloom in July and August; and goldenrod appears in the early fall to make some of us sneeze. Tall, strong maples and oaks also grow on Brambleside, and their fallen friends lie alongside the trail. The park department leaves them here so woodland critters can make good use of them. What looks like dead wood to us looks like a new restaurant and a condominium development to chipmunks, raccoons, frogs, and other animals that make their homes in, or eat, rotting trees.

Leaving the Brambleside Trail, turn right to rejoin the Riverwood Trail and continue your trek southwest. This part of the Riverwood Trail is the most exposed portion of the gravel trails. In the relatively open area just north of the trail intersection, a few lonely corn stalks grow. No doubt they were planted by a fly-by farmer, perhaps a jay, who dropped a few kernels he stole from the nearby cornfield.

Stay on Riverwood as the trail veers left, where it grows considerably shadier. Inside the horseshoe of the turn, a park bench is positioned so that you'll sit with your back to the trail, facing a thicket of tall bushes and weeds. This is an absolute haven for birds, and therefore, it's inviting to bird fanciers, too. At this point, you've logged about 1.1 miles. The sledding hill in front of you poses a challenge: will you climb over it for an aerobic challenge, or stay on the trail as it wraps around the south side of the hill? Either way, don't miss the narrow, grassy trails heading from the south side of the trail to the river.

Follow the skinny trail through a field of tall grass for less than 0.1 miles to reach a wide and quiet stretch of the Chagrin River. The tawny heads of bull thistle grow in the clearing along the river. At this point, some hikers step down a couple of feet from the sandy banks and wade in. Follow this loop trail back onto Riverwood Trail, and turn right to return to the parking lot.

Chagrin River Park is a Metropark that truly embodies the "metro" in its name. As soon as you pull in, you'll notice the park is on the bus line. In the middle of the park, a habitat management area spans several acres underneath an electric power line corridor. The deer here are so accustomed to their human neighbors, they often stand by the trail instead of bounding away when you walk by. It's eerie, like passing beautiful manikins that are a little too lifelike.

Walking along the Brambleside Trail one hot August day, I passed a doe and her fawn. They stood about six feet away and watched with interest as I stopped, settled my dog, put down my notepad and got out my camera. Only then did they decide to leave, I missed a great photo opportunity, and I learned that the deer here are quite comfortable among the humans who share their space. Perhaps you'll meet a deer on the trail here, too. My advice? Have your camera ready.

NEARBY ACTIVITIES

A volleyball court and large playground by the main parking lot can occupy kids of all ages. If it's more hiking you want, head north on Route 2 to Mentor Lagoons (see p. 122), about a 15-minute drive from here.

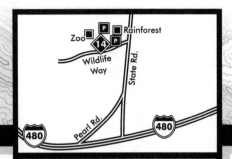

#14
Cleveland
Metroparks Zoo

IN BRIEF

You're thinking, "this isn't a trail, it's an amusement park." Well, yes and no. You can hike 3 or 4 miles at Cleveland's Zoo, and the kids will never complain. And where else within 60 miles of Cleveland can you see polar bears *and* kangaroos?

DIRECTIONS

I-480 to State Road exit, follow State Road north until it dead-ends at Pearl. Turn right, follow Pearl approximately 0.5 miles; then turn left onto Wildlife Way, which leads to the zoo's main entrance.

DESCRIPTION

Once upon a time, zoos added to their collections by going on safaris to capture wild, exotic creatures. In 1955, the Cleveland Zoo added some elephants, hippos, and rhinos to their collection that way. Since then, the zoo has added far more to endangered animal populations than it has taken and continues to grow and change every year.

The zoo dates back to 1882, when Jeptha Wade donated 73 acres in the University Circle area where the Western Union Telegraph Company kept a small herd of deer. Over the years, other local animals such as Canada geese and raccoons were added to the collection. Eventually, plans to establish the Cleveland Museum of Art in Wade Oval

KEY AT-A-GLANCE INFORMATION

Length: 3.5 miles (add The Rain-Forest for a total of 4)

Configuration: Interconnecting loops

Difficulty: Easy, except for one long hill

Scenery: African savannah, desert, beaver dam, expansive greenhouse, outdoor sculptures, rain forest

Exposure: Path is mostly exposed; exhibits provide shade/shelter.

Traffic: Moderate, with crowds for special events

Trail surface: Asphalt

Hiking time: 4 hours to see it all

Season: Closed December 25 and January 1

Access: Hours 10 a.m.–5 p.m.; admission $8 (adults), $4 (children), and free for ages 2 and under

Maps: Free map at the entrance gate

Facilities: Rest rooms, water, and pay phones at Welcome Plaza and scattered throughout the park

Special comments: In the winter, admission is discounted; visit www.clemetzoo.com or call (216) 661-6500.

51

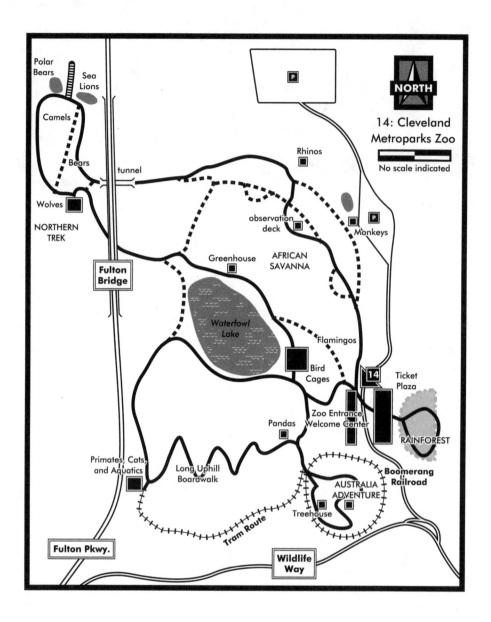

14: Cleveland Metroparks Zoo

No scale indicated

NORTH

Polar Bears

Sea Lions

Camels

Bears

tunnel

Wolves

NORTHERN TREK

Rhinos

observation deck

Monkeys

Greenhouse

AFRICAN SAVANNA

Fulton Bridge

Waterfowl Lake

Flamingos

Bird Cages

14

Ticket Plaza

Zoo Entrance
Welcome Center

Pandas

RAINFOREST

Primates, Cats, and Aquatics

Long Uphill Boardwalk

Treehouse

AUSTRALIA ADVENTURE

Boomerang Railroad

Tram Route

Fulton Pkwy.

Wildlife Way

meant the menagerie must move. In 1909, the animals were relocated to the zoo's current site, then called Brookside Park. The Works Progress Administration completed many projects at the zoo during the Depression era. Since then the zoo has had several caretakers: The Cleveland Museum of Natural History from 1940 to 1957, the Cleveland

Zoological Society from 1957 to 1975, and the Cleveland Metroparks since 1975. Each has added to the zoo's history and attractions; each addition seems more fascinating than the last.

The RainForest opened in 1992. Inside the two-acre habitat you'll find some of the world's strangest animals. In 1997, Wolf Wilderness opened, exposing

The only place in Cleveland where you can spot polar bears

us to a pack of gray wolves, a beaver dam, and a variety of other species both indoors and out. The newest exhibit (at this printing) is the Australian Adventure. You won't believe it until you see it, so lace up your boots, mate, and walk this way . . .

From the Welcome Plaza, head north (right) to the Savannah. As the path curves to the west, you'll encounter gazelles, great African cranes (some of the largest birds in the world), and finally, the Masai giraffes. The Masais are hard to miss: they are the tallest animals on earth, reaching 16 to 18 feet. A male born here in July 2001 was 6 feet tall and weighed 185 pounds at birth! If they aren't near the fence as you round the park's northern edge, don't worry; observation decks on both sides of the exhibit give you plenty of chance to catch them, if only on film. At about 0.5 miles, visit with the black rhinos before heading under the impressive Fulton Avenue Bridge.

Following the signs to the "Northern Trek" section, turn right to visit some of the zoo's older exhibits. The sea lion and polar bear pools were both built of native stone quarried from Euclid Creek Reservation. Climb the steps between the two exhibits to watch both from above.

Continuing through the Northern Trek, you'll walk by the placid Bactrian camels (two humps) before reaching Wolf Wilderness. Step inside the cabin-style building to see a variety of exhibits, including turtles, snakes, and beaver. Watch for the wiry gray wolves from behind the cabin's glass wall. They are hard to spot until they move; be patient and you can get a good look. Leave the cabin for the center of the Northern Trek to visit with several bear species, tigers, and reindeer. Heading east, back under the Fulton Bridge, you'll pass the African Savanna again. The greenhouse, at about 1.5 miles, is a must-stop spot for gardeners. Opposite the greenhouse is the original zoo building. Relocated from Wade Park in the mid-1970s, and completely refurbished in 1992, it has evolved into a Victorian-style ice cream parlor.

Continuing south, you'll pass the former "Birds of the World" exhibit. At the time of this printing, the area was undergoing a major renovation, so watch for something new and exciting here. On your right you'll find a towering birdcage. It has to be towering because it houses condors, some of the world's highest flyers, along with eagles and other large birds. On the southern edge of Waterfowl Lake, turn left, then right again, to visit the koalas in "Gumleaf Hideout." On your right, just past the koalas, looms the only serious hill in the park: a 1,250-foot-long boardwalk climbing 800 feet up from the Australian Outback to the land of primates, big cats, and big fish above. Before you tackle that, head for the 'land down under.'

"Australian Adventure," the zoo's newest section, is serious fun. The "Boomerang" railroad track encircles a walk-through lorikeet aviary, kangaroos and wallabies, and a 55-foot tree house. You'll "climb" inside the man-made baobab tree on a swingy suspension bridge. Bats, snakes, and a creepy animatronic crocodile await your entrance. The exit is a slide, disguised as a long snake. (Note: Much of the Australian Adventure area is wheelchair accessible; the tree house, though, isn't.)

Next, you'll take the 1,250-foot boardwalk up 800 feet to the southwest corner of the park. (You can take the tram instead, but then you'll miss the only serious aerobic workout of the hike.) Steps in the middle of each zigzag along the ramp allow walkers a bit of a shortcut, while strollers and wheelchairs roll up. At the top of the climb, you've logged about 2.5 miles and several dozen species. Pause to enjoy a shady view of the Big Creek ravine before proceeding to the Primate, Cat, and Aquatics exhibits.

Heading north from the top of the park, follow the path as it winds by Waterfowl Lake. Flamingos will signal your returning to the welcome plaza. Now you've got about 3.25 miles on your sneakers and, probably, a freshly shot roll of film.

If you leave the zoo and head east to the RainForest building, you'll add 0.75 miles to your hike, and as a bonus, you'll get a new perspective on rain forest habitats. Consider this: a 10-acre plot of land in Ohio is home to about 34 different species; on 10 acres in Ecuador's rain forest you'll find about 200.

Inside the dome-shaped exhibit, you can watch as hundreds of bats feed, fly, and crawl about a red-lit room. If you're more interested in birds than bats, you'll enjoy the exhibit highlighting the southern-hemisphere species, such as the yellow-billed cuckoo, that make their summer homes in Ohio. Beyond bats and birds, the rain forest is home to thousands of other animals; many are exhibited here.

Thanks to Sue Allen of the Cleveland Metroparks Zoo for reviewing this hike.

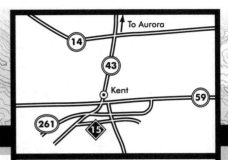

#15
Cooperrider/Kent Bog
State Nature Preserve

To Aurora
14
43
Kent
59
261
15

IN BRIEF

Kent Bog is one of only three places in Ohio where the small cranberry makes a stand. It is also home to what may be the largest stand of tamarack trees in Ohio, the southernmost grouping of the trees in all of the United States. You can see what's left of this 12,000-year-old bog from a boardwalk made of recycled plastic.

DIRECTIONS

From Cleveland, take I-480 (or the turnpike) east to State Route 14 in Streetsboro. Turn right, heading south on Route 43, through Kent. About 0.5 miles south of Route 261, turn right (west) onto Meloy Road. The bog's entrance is about 0.5 miles west of State Route 43 in Kent.

DESCRIPTION

Long, long ago, a retreating glacier left behind a giant ice cube. It was buried with silt, clay, and gravel. Eventually, the ice melted, forming a glacial "kettle" lake. Over the next 10,000 years or so, the lake was covered by boreal plants, and then completely filled in with peat. Today, in what is left of this tiny bog, you'll find a host of rare, bog-loving plants, including sphagnum moss, Virginia chain fern, small cranberry, and tamarack trees. It is the best stand of tamarack in Ohio and probably the southernmost stand of tamarack in the

KEY AT-A-GLANCE INFORMATION

Length: 0.5 miles

Configuration: Loop

Difficulty: Easy

Scenery: Rare bog plants, and the birds and animals that relish them

Exposure: About half shaded

Traffic: Moderate

Trail surface: Flat boardwalk trail, accessible to all

Hiking time: 30 minutes

Season: Open year-round

Access: The bog is open dawn–dusk, but sometimes the gate is locked; when the lot is closed during "open" hours, you may park on the grassy shoulder of Meloy Road.

Maps: A large map is posted on the trailhead signboard; a map and trail guide is usually available there as well.

Facilities: None

Special comments: The entire boardwalk is ADA compliant; pets, bikes, and skates are prohibited here, as the bog is designated as a State Nature Preserve.

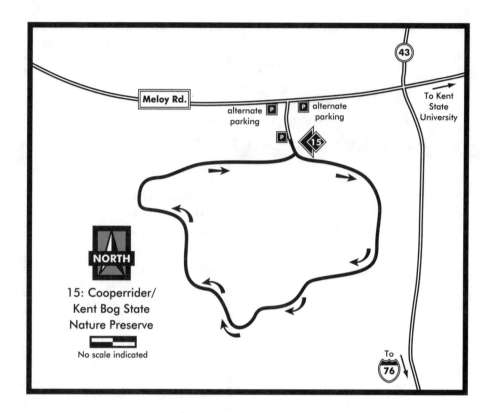

Meloy Rd.

alternate parking

alternate parking

43

To Kent State University

P P P

15

NORTH

15: Cooperrider/
Kent Bog State
Nature Preserve

No scale indicated

To
76

continental US. This is a bog full of history, firsts, and rarities.

In 1985, Cooperrider/Kent Bog State Nature Preserve was the first State Nature Preserve purchased with money donated by Ohioans through the State Income Tax Refund "check off" program. The boardwalk was added in 1993, which also was a first. Paid for in part by a grant from the Division of Litter Prevention and Recycling, this walkway is made of recycled plastic shopping bags, stretch wrap, and bottles. What you recycle at home today, you may find underfoot tomorrow!

A bog is a harsh environment; its climatic conditions are called "limiting factors." Extremes in temperature, wetness, nutrient levels, and acidity significantly limit the plants that can survive in a bog. During summer, root level temperatures

in the peat can be as much as 40 degrees cooler than the surface temperature. Bogs favor plants that can thrive in an acidic, mineral-poor environment, since nutrients from dead plants are tied up in peat, and therefore unavailable to nourish the plants. That's one reason carnivorous plants tend to show up in bogs. Many other unusual species thrive here, as well.

Sphagnum moss is one. A rootless moss, it continually grows from the top while dying at the bottom. Sphagnum moss can hold up to 27 times its own dry weight in water, is more than twice as absorbent as cotton, and has antiseptic properties. Where it grows, it lowers root temperatures and oxygen levels. Its peculiar properties have earned it at least two footnotes in history: Native Americans used sphagnum to diaper their babies, and during the civil and first world wars, doctors used the moss as emergency field dressings.

Small cranberry also grows here—one of only three spots in the entire state it calls home. Most people are surprised to see that cranberries are not so much trees as viney, woody shrubs that creep over the ground. Poison sumac is here, too. Like its mean, nasty cousin poison ivy, poison sumac has white berries. Several other sumac species, which sport red berries, are harmless.

If you visit the bog in the fall—October is your best bet—you'll notice the needles on the tamarack trees have changed from green to yellow, and they may be falling off. The tamarack is a deciduous conifer, so it sheds needles like other trees shed leaves. Tamarack trees love the cold; they grow as far north as trees can grow in Canada. This far south, they are rare. Walk through the bog in the winter, when the tamaracks are nearly bare, and you'll spot "cat berry," a bog holly identified by its bright red berries.

To see all these and many other bog oddities, step onto the boardwalk trail from the south end of the parking lot. Turn left, following the loop clockwise. The walkway circles a sedge meadow and runs northeast through a marsh and wooded stretch of land. As you stroll through, stop along the way to read the many educational plaques that offer perspective on the bog's unusual conditions and inhabitants.

Six park benches placed along the boardwalk provide good places to observe wildlife. Birders will watch for Rufous-sided towhees and berry-loving waxwings. The bog is also home to deer, foxes, and cottontail rabbits. Rare spotted turtles also live here, but it's unlikely you'll see one. The spotted turtle is palm-sized, with brilliant yellow spots on its shell. To protect these slow bog residents, "turtle tunnels" were built into the boardwalk's underside. They allow the turtles to move freely about the bog, out of sight of most visitors as they walk over the relatively new boardwalk.

As you leave the bog, you'll cross a dry moat-like depression that surrounds it. This trough around the bog brings excessive shade and leaf-litter from the adjacent upland trees. That, and the well-oxygenated runoff that enters here, allows other species to creep into the bog. The main peat mass, with its limiting factors that control bog ecology, is reduced and threatened by the invaders. Eventually, the bog will naturally go the way of the glacier, and its long history will be, finally, just history. Visit now, so you can say you were here when . . .

NEARBY ACTIVITIES

Head north from Kent and visit the bog's nearest relative, an alkaline fen. Herrick Fen in Streetsboro is about a 15-minute drive up State Route 43. See hike description on page 88.

This state preserve was named to honor Tom S. Cooperrider, PhD, a nationally recognized botanist who played an instrumental role in discovering, and protecting, this unusual and important area.

#16
Dix Park

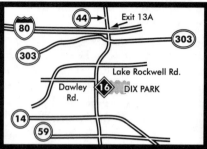

IN BRIEF

This new addition to the growing Portage Park District offers a short woodlands trail set amid lovely farm fields. Depending on the time of year, you may get to watch planting, harvesting, or other farm work. Go in the spring to enjoy the best wildflower display in the woods.

DIRECTIONS

Take I-80 to Route 44 (Exit 13A). Follow 44 south about 5 miles. Dix Park is on the eastern side of 44, just south of Dawley Road. *Alternate directions:* Follow I-480 to Streetsboro/Route 14, and continue east on 14 about 10 miles; turn left onto Route 44. Follow 44 north about 0.7 miles to park entrance.

DESCRIPTION

In the fall of 2000, the Dix family donated the property and development funds to create a new county park in memory of Robert Dix. There was one request, however: the family asked that the neighboring dairy located on a 25-acre portion of the land be allowed to continue operations. The Portage Park District agreed, and the park came into being. While the farm is not part of any formal programming, visitors can still walk by and see a little of what a working farm looks like while enjoying a rich woodland hiking trail.

KEY AT-A-GLANCE INFORMATION

Length: 2.2 miles

Configuration: Loop

Difficulty: Easy

Scenery: A working farm on the premises, plus a variety of trees and spring wildflowers

Exposure: Mostly shaded

Traffic: Moderate

Trail surface: Dirt on woodland trail, old farm lane is gravel

Hiking time: 45 minutes

Season: Open year-round

Access: Dawn–dusk

Maps: Posted at trailhead

Facilities: Picnic tables in parking lot; portable rest rooms may be added in the future

Special comments: This is strictly a hiking trail; no bikes or horses are permitted. The farm fields are not open for public use. On occasion, agricultural activity may temporarily close the farm lane, and subsequently the woods trail. To check on farming activity before you go, call the Portage Park District at (330) 673-9404.

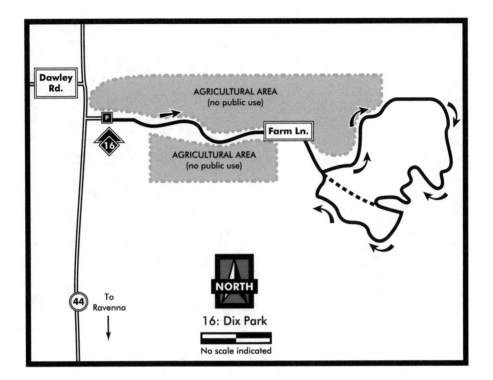

AGRICULTURAL AREA
(no public use)

Farm Ln.

AGRICULTURAL AREA
(no public use)

16

NORTH

16: Dix Park

No scale indicated

44 To
Ravenna

A trail system loops through approximately 60 of the park's 103 acres. An old field near the front of the property is scheduled to host bluebird nesting boxes. Other than a small parking lot, the rest of the property has been left for cultivation.

From the parking lot, follow the farm lane east. This is the most exposed portion of the hike, and good birding opportunities exist along the hedgerow that parallels the gravel lane. The farm is on your left; maple and cherry trees line the fields of corn, soybeans, and hay. This lane is in use by the farm, and hikers will occasionally meet farm equipment here.

About 0.6 miles east of the parking lot, a trail sign invites you to turn left into the woods. Follow the narrow dirt trail as it wanders by yellow birch and a few sassafras trees. You'll tramp across at least two footbridges (more may be added) over the wettest spots in the trail.

What looks like a small creek in the early spring is actually an ephemeral (or seasonal) water flow. Usually dry in the summer months, the temporary drainage provides a perfect setting for buttonbush.

Typical of Portage County, the woods here are rich in glacial history. Small erratics are strewn about as you skirt the higher ground around the drainage depression.

As the trail bends to the right, it rises slightly before returning to the farm lane. Throughout the trail, tree buffs should look for sugar and red maple, black cherry, tulip poplar, white oak, red oaks, bigtooth aspen, and dogwood. Wildflower watchers may spot trilliums, dutchman's breeches, toothwort, anemone, marsh marigold, blue cohosh, violets, trout lily, and bellwort.

Along the trail, see if you can spot a spicebush. Its light brown bark is coated with white speckles, and when you rub

Year-round, this farm lends character to Dix Park

the soft leaves, it smells like a ripe mix of lemons and oranges.

When you reach the lane, turn left and follow it about 250 feet to pick up the southernmost portion of the loop trail. You'll turn right off the lane, following the trail sign back into the woods. In the spring, this area is alive with wildflowers as well as the peculiar skunk cabbage. Its blooms usually appear in May, and while it is not as pretty as wildflowers, it has its own odd charm. In early spring—as early as February in a warm winter—the bulbous heads of new cabbage plants pop up through the soil. Inside the flower of the new plant, it warms itself. The warmth is thought to appeal to pollinating insects that need the heat to move around. The temperature inside the flower may be as much as ten degrees warmer than the outside air.

As the path bumps along through the woods, wildflowers, and self-warming cabbage, you'll notice this portion of the trail is generally higher than the northern loop. From here, you have a good view of the landscape-in-progress and the seasonal drainage that sustains a variety of plants and animals.

The southern loop quickly returns to the lane. Turn left onto the gravel road to return to the parking lot. As you walk past the farm fields again, it's easy to draw comparisons between the water flow and the farm operations. Both are seasonal, and both supply the land—and the park—with a measure of diversity and richness.

(*Note:* As of this book's printing, the trail in Dix Park was not yet named.)

NEARBY ACTIVITIES

To hike more woodland trails, visit nearby Towner's Woods (see p. 193) or go north to Nelson's Ledges (see p. 136) for a very different hiking experience.

Special thanks to PPD staffer Brad Stemen, who created the trail, for a pre-opening tour of Dix Park, and also to PPD Director Christine Craycroft for reviewing this hike description.

#17
Downtown
Cleveland Highlights

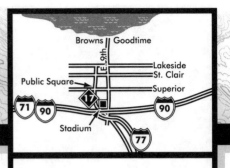

IN BRIEF

Got out of town guests who want to see the big city of Cleveland? Haven't been downtown yourself for a while? This mini-tour stops at highlights, from stately Public Square to the anything-but-square Rock and Roll Hall of Fame and Museum.

DIRECTIONS

Exit I-77 north at E. 9th Street. Follow signs to Public Square, going north on Broadway. Turn left onto Huron to park at Tower City Center parking garage.

DESCRIPTION

How many hikes start at a historic landmark and shopping mall? This one does. Park in Tower City's lower lot, and go inside Tower City Center, up the escalator and wander north, through the fabulous shopping center. The history behind the mall is interesting. The van Sweringen brothers planned the 52-story tower, and they massaged public opinion and political decisions to have it built as they wanted. As the main tower in the Cleveland Union (railroad) Terminal, it was the tallest building outside of New York City from its opening in 1930 until 1967. Today, the tower-turned mall-and-office space, complete with dancing water fountains, has far outlived the railroad line for which it was planned; it remains the signature flourish on Cleveland's skyline.

KEY AT-A-GLANCE INFORMATION

Length: 3 miles

Configuration: Loop

Difficulty: Easy

Scenery: Cleveland's landmark buildings (both old and new), our Great Lake, public art, fat pigeons, and peregrine falcons

Exposure: Mostly exposed

Traffic: Moderately heavy

Trail surface: City sidewalks

Hiking time: 1.5 hours

Season: Year-round

Access: Most shops, museums, and attractions are open 7 days

Maps: Downtown area maps are posted at each RTA stop

Facilities: Public rest rooms at Tower City and Galleria (E. 9th and Lakeside)

Special comments: The Tower City observation deck was closed on September 11, 2001, and had yet to reopen as of this book's printing. Call (216) 771-0033 or inquire at the Tower City Center information desk for the latest. As of March 2002, there were 6 nesting pairs of peregrine falcons in the Cleveland area. If you don't see them cruising around the tower, check in on them at www.falcons.apk.net.

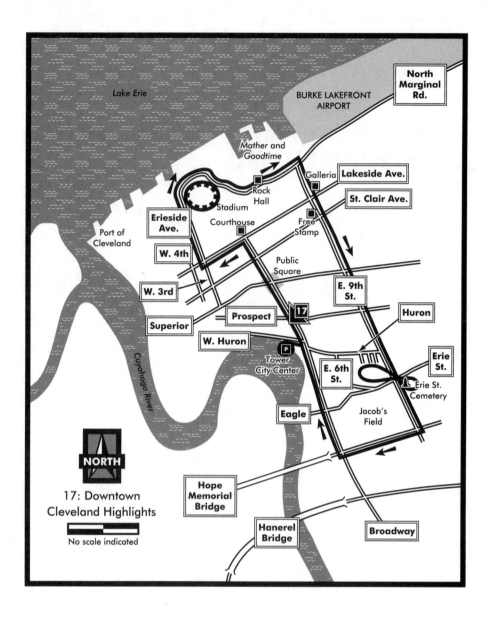

Lake Erie

BURKE LAKEFRONT
AIRPORT

North
Marginal
Rd.

Mather and
Goodtime

Galleria

Rock
Hall

Stadium

Courthouse

Free
Stamp

Lakeside Ave.

St. Clair Ave.

Erieside
Ave.

Port of
Cleveland

W. 4th

Public
Square

W. 3rd

E. 9th
St.

Huron

Superior

Prospect

17

W. Huron

P

Tower
City Center

E. 6th
St.

Erie
St.

Erie St.
Cemetery

Eagle

Jacob's
Field

Cuyahoga River

NORTH

17: Downtown
Cleveland Highlights

No scale indicated

Hope
Memorial
Bridge

Hanerel
Bridge

Broadway

Exit Tower City Center onto Euclid
Avenue and find yourself on Public
Square. The Soldiers and Sailors Monument, built in 1884, sits to your right, on
the eastern side of Ontario. The monument to the 10,000 Cleveland area soldiers who served in the Civil War is
open inside; you can walk right into it if
you like.

Continue north across Public Square
to the Old Stone Church. The church
was established here on the corner of
Ontario and Rockwell in 1834; it has
been rebuilt a couple of times since. The
building you see today dates back to
1855. If your timing is good (no wedding in progress), you can go in—it's
beautiful inside. Follow Ontario north,

"Sports Stacks" are among the more modern sculptures you'll see on this quick tour

across St. Clair, to the Cuyahoga County Courthouse. As you approach, crane your neck to take in six stately sculptures atop the building's façade. These marble figures were created by Herbert Adams in 1911; each honors an individual for his contributions to English law. Simon de Montfort (1200–1265) for example, helped establish the House of Commons. Below, Alexander Hamilton and Thomas Jefferson sit on opposite sides of the main entrance steps.

With a nod to Misters Hamilton and Jefferson, turn left in front of courthouse and follow Lakeside Avenue west about half a block; turn right onto West 3rd. From the top of the hill you'll catch a glimpse of the lake. Follow West 3rd downhill, passing the Port of Cleveland on your left, and wind around the 31-acre site of Cleveland Browns Stadium. This may be a good place to get some landscaping ideas: an estimated 24,700 trees, plants, and flowers grow on the stadium grounds.

Follow West 3rd it east as it bends right, heading south into Erieside—the 171-foot-tall stadium now stands to your right. Turn left onto North Marginal, walking east past the Great Lakes Science Center and the Rock and Roll Hall of Fame and Museum. The Rock Hall, designed by architect I. M. Pei, is a futuristic and shapely icon. As you continue east and approach E. 9th Street, you'll see the 618-foot-long *William G. Mather* steamship to the north, as well as signs for the *Goodtime* tour boat. (Both tours are fantastic, and they, along with a walk-and-crawl-through tour of the nearby *USS COD* submarine, are well worth the time. (See "Nearby Activities" on p. 58.) Continue your walk from here by turning right, going south on E. 9th Street. Cross over busy Route 2, also known as "the Shoreway," and begin to head uphill.

Just south of Lakeside Avenue, you'll find the Galleria. The beautiful mall was something of a loser in terms of retail occupants after the prestigious Tower City Center opened, but the food court inside the Galleria remains popular with downtown workers and visitors.

Farther down East 9th, you'll see the always-good-for-a-conversation-starter "Free Stamp" sculpture at Willard Park, on the north side of St. Clair. Ahead and on your left, at the corner of East 9th and Superior, is St. John's Cathedral. The ornate sandstone church was built from 1848 to 1852.

Continue south (crossing Vincent, Chester, Euclid, and Prospect) to reach Bolivar. Jacob's Field, home of the Cleveland Indians, is on your right. If you would like to see some of the interesting sculptures designed for the new ballpark in 1994, take a brief detour and follow Eagle Street west. Several of the sculptures function as fashionable benches: "Who's on First," "Meet Me Here," and the abstract "Sports Stacks." (Between you and me, I see a baseball bat in there, but you decide for yourself.) Once you've peered inside the gates of Jacob's Field, return to East 9th and turn right, heading south again.

On the eastern side of East 9th (on your left) is old Erie Street Cemetery. How old is it? It was created in 1826, when Erie Street was constructed. As the city's first "official" cemetery; many bodies buried at church cemeteries were relocated here when Erie Street opened. And here lies Chief Thunderwater, the most likely inspiration for the city's baseball tribe. Thunderwater appeared in *Buffalo Bill's Wild West Show* and was known as the "official" Cleveland Indian. Today, Thunderwater shares the grounds with Cleveland's earliest permanent settlers, Lorenzo and Rebekah Carter, and other folks notable in the city's history.

From the cemetery, take East 9th to Carnegie, and head west past the front of Jacob's Field. Here you'll face the oft-photographed entrance to Hope Memorial Bridge, which opened in 1932 as the Lorain-Carnegie Bridge. Impressive stone carvings on each entrance represent the progression of transportation. The figures hold various icons—a covered wagon, stagecoach, car, and several trucks. Water transportation isn't represented by the figures, but the bridge itself reminds us—it was built 93 feet above water level, to allow for shipping clearance.

With your transportation (your feet) now on Broadway, turn right (north) to Huron, and return to the parking garage at Tower City Center.

NEARBY ACTIVITIES

It's okay to act like a tourist here—even if Cleveland is your hometown. Grab your camera and go see the *USS COD*, for starters. Open May–September, the World War-II submarine is only for the agile. Visitors enter and exit through original hatches and climb ladders over equipment inside. For information call (216) 566-8700. Less constraining is the *William G. Mather,* the 1925 flagship of the Cleveland-Cliffs Iron Company. Now operated by Great Lakes Historical Society as a floating maritime museum, you may call (216) 574-6262 for information. You can cruise the Cuyahoga River aboard the *Goodtime,* enjoying fabulous views of Cleveland's industrial "flats" and the area's many different bridges. I've always wanted to say this—For a *Goodtime* call (216) 861-5110. Want another hike, with a different view of the skyline? Edgewater Park is just off the Shoreway, just two exits west of East 9th (see p. 65).

#18
Edgewater–Cleveland
Lakefront State Park

IN BRIEF

Edgewater offers pleasant hiking along the Lake Erie shore, good fishing, and a 900-foot-long public swimming beach. It also offers the best seat in the house for Cleveland's annual July 4th fireworks display.

DIRECTIONS

Edgewater Park sits between downtown Cleveland and the City of Lakewood. From downtown, go west on Route 2 to the Lake Avenue/West Boulevard exit. Go north on West Boulevard until it intersects Cliff Drive then turn right. Parking is straight ahead and on the left. Signs directing drivers to the scenic overlook are visible from Lake Avenue/West Boulevard exit.

DESCRIPTION

From the "scenic overlook" parking lot, follow the paved trail east. At the west end of the parking lot, you'll meet German composer Richard Wagner. Actually, it's just his statue, but he's a towering presence sculpted from limestone. From the base to the top of his hat, Wagner stands 18 feet tall, and he's been looking out over the lake and the skyline since 1911. If only he could talk . . .

But since Wagner's not talking, continue east on the bike path. Several unmarked paths on your left lead down to a sandy, dirt trail about 25 feet closer to the lake, and as many feet below you.

KEY AT-A-GLANCE INFORMATION

Length: 2.5 miles

Configuration: Figure-8

Difficulty: Easy

Scenery: Lake Erie views, beach, bird-watching opportunities from the western end of the trail

Exposure: Mostly exposed

Traffic: Moderately heavy

Trail surface: Mixed: paved Parcourse trail, dirt path

Hiking time: 1 hour

Season: Open year-round

Access: Open from 6 a.m.–11 p.m.

Maps: Available online at www.dnr.state.oh.us/parks/parkmaps/cleveland.gif or www.ameritech.net/users/bfischbach

Facilities: Pay phone and rest room at beach area concession and by fishing pier in lower Edgewater Park; rest rooms also at picnic pavilion in upper Edgewater Park

Special comments: To reserve the shelter at Edgewater, or to find out more about the beach, fishing pier, and marina, call (216) 881-8141.

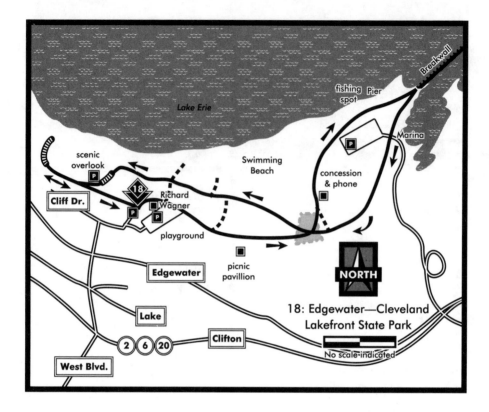

Stay on the paved path; the path below you is your return route.

The paved fitness/bike path offers great lake views to the north as it continues east past a small playground. The path grows shadier by the step as you make your way to the recently renovated picnic pavilion. The melon-colored pavilion, built in 1951, is listed on the National Register of Historic Places. A grant—and a lot of work—returned it to its original state and striking color in the spring of 2001. (The park's boat ramps were renovated at the same time.) Just east of the pavilion, the path begins to slope downhill, on its way to the beach.

Edgewater's swimming beach is 900 feet long, and on warm summer afternoons, you'll hear it long before you see it. It's a popular spot for swimming and just hanging out. In the off-season, you'll hear the coos and cries of hundreds of other visitors: sea gulls. They are some of the only wildlife you'll spot here most days, but they make up for lack of variety with their sheer numbers.

Continue on the path downhill, veering to the left at the "triangle" intersection. This is the middle of the figure-8 of the hike formation; you'll cross this way again on your return. Walk past the beach house and concession stand and head toward the lakeshore. The path curves to the right past the concession building, and from here you'll have a great view of the city skyline and the Cleveland West Pierhead Light. The 30-foot-tall lighthouse was built in 1911, adjacent to the fog signal building built in 1910. It remains an active US Coast Guard facility, marking the entrance from the lake to the Cuyahoga River.

Follow the path along the shore, past the fishing pier, and as far east on the breakwall as you dare. The old, uneven sidewalk is popular with anglers; on good days, they catch perch and walleye here. The footing can be challenging, but if you are willing to take a few "giant steps" over breaks in the path, you can continue to the end. As always, be very careful. The wind blows hard on the breakwall; if you turn your back to it and look south, you'll have a good view of the marina. It's a busy place, with boats coming and going almost constantly during the too-short summer; in the winter it seems eerily abandoned, the only noise coming from the water will be the screeches and whistles of gulls.

As you return west along the concrete breakwall, you'll notice the rocks stuck into the side of the breakwall have strange, weather-beaten faces. Lean over the edge a bit to peer in the water, where there are oodles of freshwater clam and zebra mussel shells.

From the western end of the breakwall, follow the Parcourse FitCircuit path, which heads left (south) along the east edge of the park's other parking lot. The path soon bends right and heads west again, past Washington hawthorn trees full of bright red berries much of the year. The path connects at the "triangle" just east of the beach, and from there, converges with a rocky path. Follow the rocky trail—not the paved path—straight ahead.

Here, you'll walk under the shade of deciduous trees. You'll follow a staircase up and over a large drain culvert and continue along the path, heading west. You'll get an entirely different perspective on the shore from this lower trail, which extends almost all the way to the scenic overlook. Before you return to your car, though, take the steps at the far western end of the park about 30 feet down to the beach, for one last look at Lake Erie and the Cleveland skyline. Many days, you can even see the stack of Perry Nuclear Power Plant from here.

NEARBY ACTIVITIES

You can see it from here: downtown Cleveland beckons! You can walk around, or just stop in the flats for fun.

Special thanks to Carol Ward, naturalist, of Cleveland Lakefront State Park, for reviewing this hike, and especially for tracking down the identity of those "berry" pretty trees.

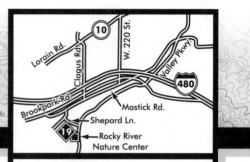

#19
Fort Hill Earthworks

IN BRIEF

While the initial climb might make your legs wobble, this hike provides spectacular views of the Rocky River that will leave you breathless. There's lots for natural history fans, too—a nature center, a "terrible fish," and ancient American Indian ceremonial grounds.

DIRECTIONS

From I–480 west, exit at Clague Road. Turn left off the ramp and follow Clague south until it ends at Mastick Road. Turn right, heading west 4 miles to Rocky River Reservation. Turn left onto Shepard Lane; follow it to Valley Parkway. Turn right on Valley Parkway and park in the nature center lot, located on the right at 24000 Valley Parkway.

DESCRIPTION

The earthworks on the Fort Hill trail are considerably less impressive than the mounds of southern Ohio. But what these ridges lack in size they more than compensate for in location. To reach the earthworks, you'll have to do some climbing. One hundred and thirty steps of climbing, to be precise. The view is worth it. From the top of the stairway, you'll look upon the east branch of the Rocky River, more than 100 feet below, where it bends like a fishhook and snags the breath from your gaping mouth.

However, before experiencing the climb and the view, you might find

KEY AT-A-GLANCE INFORMATION

Length: 1.5 miles

Configuration: Loop

Difficulty: Moderately difficult, with lots of stairs to climb

Scenery: River views, earthworks

Exposure: Mostly shaded

Traffic: Can be busy, especially on warm weekends

Trail surface: Dirt trail, wooden boardwalk and stairs

Hiking time: 45 minutes

Season: Open year-round

Access: Open from 6 a.m.–11 p.m.

Maps: Available inside nature center or at www.clemetparks.com

Facilities: Rest room, pay phone, and water inside nature center

Special comments: This hike will not be enjoyable for those with a fear of heights. Others will find it gorgeous, a trip not to be missed. Note that the steps leading to the Fort Hill Earthworks are closed when icy; if in doubt, call ahead to find about weather conditions. The nature center is open daily from 9:30 a.m.–5 p.m. Phone (440) 734-6660.

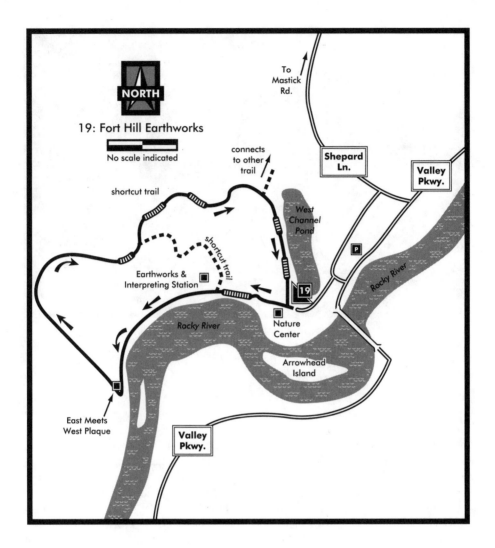

19: Fort Hill Earthworks

No scale indicated

connects to other trail

shortcut trail

shortcut trail

Earthworks & Interpreting Station

West Channel Pond

Shepard Ln.

Valley Pkwy.

To Mastick Rd.

Rocky River

Nature Center

Rocky River

Arrowhead Island

East Meets West Plaque

Valley Pkwy.

yourself gasping for breath in front of the nature center. There, where a welcome mat should be, you'll be greeted by the "terrible fish," or *Dunkleosteus.* The huge hunter swam the oceans that covered Ohio millions of years ago, eating sharks and probably terrorizing other ancient sea critters. The *Dunkleosteus* was discovered in the nearby shale cliffs above the riverbed, where it was both well preserved and difficult to retrieve. The fossil remains were moved to the Cleveland Museum of Natural History,

but an informational display about the beast is located inside the nature center.

Before beginning your hike from the back of the nature center, you can relax for a moment by watching for birds in the feeding area to your left, and around West Channel Pond, on your right. Now take a deep breath and head up the stairs, on your left.

One hundred feet higher, take another deep breath. Once you tear yourself away from the edge, you'll notice a sign about a hundred feet ahead and on your right.

Dunkleosteus makes you glad you're visiting now, rather than 360 million years ago

It explains what researchers understand about the earthworks in front of you.

The earthworks' ridges lie like mussed-up blankets under the shade of pin oaks. More than 1,000 years ago, Native Americans formed these earthworks, probably for ceremonial purposes. The mounds they left here are small, but the mystery is great: who were these people? What, besides the view, was so special about this spot? Inside the nature center, you can learn more about these Native Americans and the earthworks they left behind.

(*Note:* An alternate, shortcut trail here allows you to walk on both sides of the earthworks. The shorter trail, however, decreases your distance only slightly and cheats you out of more breathtaking views.) Continue on the main trail, following the bright yellow markers of the Fort Hill trail, and look forward to more spectacular views of the river far below.

About 0.6 miles into your trek, you'll find an interpretive sign titled, "Where East Meets West." It describes how the river has changed, and continues to change, the landscape. Approximately 360 million years ago, all but the southeast portion of Ohio was under ocean. While the ocean is long gone, the Rocky River continues to cut away at the land. It's obvious as you look at the trees clinging to the cliff sides, the soil that once supported them having eroded and washed into the river below. The soil and other sediment has formed islands in the river, and the trees that grow there—sycamore, cottonwood, and willows—are ones that can survive the silt and changing water levels. The story told on the "East Meets West" sign is a compelling one about the power of nature. It's difficult to read, however, since the spectacular view distracts you from the text. Try to appreciate the magic of both before you continue along the trail.

From here, the dirt path leaves the ridge and curves clockwise, descending slowly into thick woods. Wildflowers and a variety of trees, including hemlocks, are sprinkled along this portion of the trail.

As you "bottom out" near the northern edge of West Channel Pond, you'll find an interpretive station explaining the rusty red color in the groundwater. When Ohio was covered with seawater, minerals like iron pyrite were trapped in the silt. Gradually, the rust sediments formed a new rock we call bog iron. It was mined extensively in the 1800s, and several large pig iron furnaces were constructed between Toledo and Cleveland. One of the largest was in nearby Westlake.

As you head back to the nature center, the trail is mostly boardwalk. You'll complete the clockwise loop by West Channel Pond, walking up a slight incline to return to the rear of the nature center.

Before returning to the parking lot, stop in at the wildflower garden in front of the nature center. Even in the dead of winter, you'll find that you can identify some flowers—wild leek and wild ginger, for example—just by their stalks. A single dogwood stands in the center of the garden. A plaque there explains that there's more to the tree than its pretty spring blooms. In that way, it's rather like the earthworks here in the park—there's much more to both than meets the eye.

NEARBY ACTIVITIES

Don't leave the park without a good look around inside the nature center. There, children can wander through a tree-shaped activity center filled with fun, educational displays. Then explore the rest of the Rocky River Reservation —it offers more than a dozen hiking trails, plus bridle trails, a fitness trail, and the paved all-purpose trail.

Special thanks to Keith Kessler, Park Manager, Rocky River Reservation, Cleveland Metroparks, for reviewing this hike description.

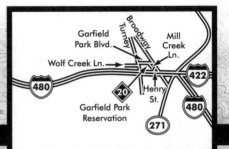

#20
Garfield Park
Reservation

IN BRIEF

Garfield Park Reservation is rich in both history and features. The nature center on the park's eastern side offers a wide variety of educational programs; on the west, a solar-system walk provides hikers with a perspective on space. A paved trail encircling the park offers two heart-pounding hills for joggers and in-line skaters. In the middle of it all, there are a half-dozen nature trails.

DIRECTIONS

Exit I-480 at Broadway Avenue. Go north on Broadway about 4 miles. Turn left onto Wolf Creek Lane, just north of the Henry Street intersection. Turn left again onto Mill Creek Lane to reach the nature center. To start the Solar System Walk, follow Wolf Creek west to Trolley Turn picnic area, approximately 1 mile west of the Broadway Avenue entrance.

DESCRIPTION

Garfield Park opened in 1895 under the name Newburg Park. In 1896, Cleveland officials called it "an ideal place in the country to get away from it all," and are a residents traveled miles to reach the park's tennis, fishing, and boating facilities. It became a part of the Cleveland Metroparks system in 1986. While volleyball and in-line skating probably are more popular than tennis today, the park remains busy. Start at Trolley Turn

KEY AT-A-GLANCE INFORMATION

Length: 2 miles

Configuration: Teardrop-shaped loop

Difficulty: Easy, with two steep sections

Scenery: Solar system walk, old boat pond, historic stonework, old iron spring

Exposure: Mostly shaded

Traffic: Moderate to heavy

Trail surface: All Purpose Trail is paved; nature trails have dirt and crushed limestone surfaces.

Hiking time: 1 hour, if you read all about the solar system

Season: Open year-round

Access: Open from 6 a.m.–11 p.m. except where otherwise posted

Maps: Ask for the Garfield Park Reservation map and trail legend inside the nature center or see www.clemetparks.com.

Facilities: Pay phone, water, and flush toilets are inside the nature center; grills, water, and rest rooms are located at each picnic area.

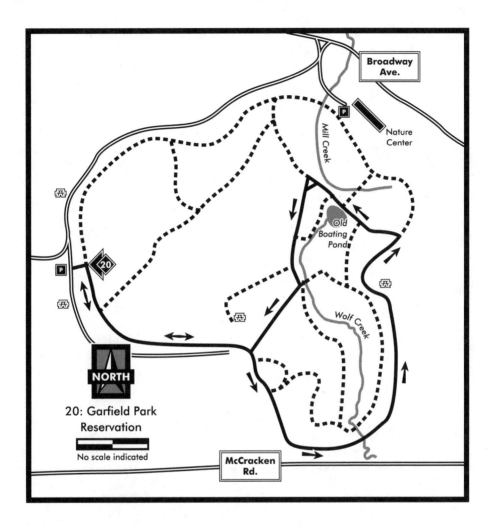

20: Garfield Park Reservation

No scale indicated

Trailhead, immediately south of Garfield Park Boulevard.

The hike begins on the 0.75-mile Solar System Trail. The Solar System Trail, which shares the path with the All Purpose Trail here, was built with the cooperation of the Metroparks, the Cleveland School System, and NASA Lewis (now Glenn) Research Center. It is designed to give us an appreciation of the immensity of our solar system, and signs along the way offer descriptions of the various planets.

The journey (and the hike) starts with a visit to the sun, our closest star. As you

follow the All Purpose Trail counter-clockwise, you'll visit each of the nine planets, from Mercury to Pluto.

A plaque describing each planet is placed at the proper distance along the trail to represent the planet's average distance from the sun on a scale of 1 foot equaling 1 million miles. If you've had trouble grasping the enormity of our solar system in the past, this will either help put it in perspective, or it will completely boggle your mind.

Either way, the Solar System Trail offers an appropriate metaphor for a hike. As one sign points out, the English word "planet" comes from the old Greek word meaning "wanderer." All the planets orbit the sun, or "wander" around it, spinning on their axes all the while. As we wander along, we should take a clue from the planets, and remember to turn around on occasion to get a better view of our universe.

Following the All Purpose Trail, you'll see a forest of maple, beech, and elm on your left. Heading downhill along the southern end of the loop and curving left, you'll notice the lines of Bedford shale in the ravine walls above Wolf Creek. At this point, Wolf Creek begins to tumble over a series of stone ledges, descending nearly 70 feet. On the north side of the park about a mile away, Wolf Creek empties into Mill Creek and eventually into Lake Erie.

On the eastern side of the park, the All Purpose Trail is actually the old park roadway. As such, it gives wide access to strollers, bikers, joggers, and skaters. Happily, hikers can find a narrow and slightly higher footpath just inside the loop of the All Purpose Trail that affords better views of the ravine and creek so far below.

Just north of Red Oak picnic area, take the stone staircase down to your left to pick up Iron Springs Trail. At the bottom of the stairs, you'll find the old boating pond and get a good look at some of the beautiful stone work that remains from the park's early days. Pretty willows dot the edges of the small pond. This is a good place to watch for birds and butterflies, which are attracted to the cattails and other wildflowers that grow here.

Cross the stone bridge to the north and pass the entrance to Cattail Trail.

Turn left onto Iron Springs Trail (signs marked by a bird's profile). As you walk along here in the summer, angelwings tower above you; in the fall, goldenrod bends down over the trail, brushing your arm. You may also see turtlehead in bloom here in the late summer.

A bit further south, you'll notice the stairs to your right that leading up to Meadow Trail. They are part of a master park plan, developed in the 1890s, with the assistance of landscape architect Henry Law Olmsted. (Olmsted also assisted in the design of New York's Central Park.)

Following the Iron Spring Trail south past the stairs, you'll notice wild grape trees on your left. These small trees provide good coverage for wood thrushes and other birds; so keep your eyes out for low-flying companions as you walk through here. You'll climb up a small hill as you come to the old iron spring for which this trail is named. A sign reminds you that the water is unsafe for drinking, as if its rusty color weren't enough to scare your thirst away. Follow the shallow stone steps up to your right, alongside the spring. You'll emerge on the all-purpose trail, near the Old Birch picnic area, and about mid-way through the Solar System walk. Turn right, heading west again, to retrace your steps through space. From here you'll return to earth, and then to your car in the Trolley Turn parking lot.

NEARBY ACTIVITIES

Be sure to visit the nature center on the park's eastern side, where educational programs are held all year long. Call (216) 341-3125 for program information or check www.clemetparks.com.

#21
Gorge Trail

IN BRIEF

With "pudding rocks" and "lucky stones," waterfalls, caves, and an American Indian tale, this trail is irresistible to kids and anyone with a sense of amusement. Don't be fooled by its fun nature, though—Gorge Trail offers enough up-and-down rock rambling to qualify as a serious hike.

DIRECTIONS

Follow State Route 8 south from Cleveland, exit onto Howe Avenue and turn right. Take Howe southwest about 1 mile, making a sharp right turn onto Front Street. Follow Front Street north, past an entrance to Gorge Metro Park, and turn left into the larger parking lot about 500 feet farther up the road.

DESCRIPTION

The Cuyahoga River provides tremendous water power that has been put to good use here for well over a century. In 1882, High Bridge Glens Park opened on this spot, and patrons enjoyed a roller coaster and dance hall. Electric cable cars powered by the dam were added later. After the amusement park closed, the local electric company donated this 144-acre tract to the Metro Parks. Several educational signs along the trail offer history and geology lessons.

From the northwest corner of the parking lot, head west on the wide dirt path. You'll follow the yellow circles on

KEY AT-A-GLANCE INFORMATION

Length: 2 miles

Configuration: Loop

Difficulty: Moderate, with a few steep sections and lots of steps

Scenery: Two small caves, a waterfall, large rock passes, river views, and a 50-foot-high dam

Exposure: Entirely shaded when trees have leaves

Traffic: Moderate to heavy

Trail surface: Dirt and rocks

Hiking time: Allow an hour, so you can investigate the cave and enjoy the rock passes

Season: Open all year, but it's smart to avoid this trail when icy

Access: Park open from 6 a.m.–11 p.m., but Gorge Trail closes at sunset

Maps: Available at trailhead

Facilities: Rest rooms at the trailhead; water at the picnic area

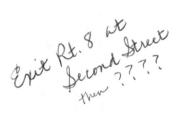

Exit Rt. 8 at Second Street then ?????

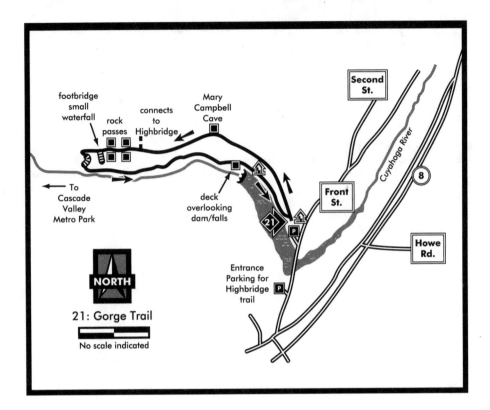

footbridge small waterfall   **rock passes**   **connects to Highbridge**   **Mary Campbell Cave**

Second St.

To Cascade Valley Metro Park

deck overlooking dam/falls

Cuyahoga River

8

Front St.

21

P

Howe Rd.

NORTH

Entrance Parking for Highbridge trail   **P**

21: Gorge Trail

No scale indicated

---

wooden signs that identify Gorge Trail. Pass three picnic shelters and the skating pond, all on your left.

About 0.4 miles into the trail, just beyond a small hill, you'll reach Mary Campbell Cave. The cave is named for a young girl who was captured in Pennsylvania by Delaware Indians. She lived in this cave with the tribe for five years before she was released at the end of the French and Indian War in 1764.

As the path goes downhill from the cave, it is studded with fist-sized and larger rocks. The small ones are called "lucky stones." These milky white pebbles were smoothed by an ancient river, while other, softer minerals eroded into mud. As a result of the way the sand and pebbles settled, layers of lucky stones can be seen in the Sharon Conglomerate. "Pudding stone" refers to larger rocks

that contain lucky stones of various shapes and sizes. The term probably came into use because the stones resemble British-style chunky pudding. Mind your lucky stones, then cross over a footbridge and head uphill to another small cave. The trail becomes rocky here, and water tumbles over a 20-foot drop from above, sometimes spilling across the trail.

Continuing west, you'll notice at least three unmarked trails to the left. They are shortcuts, to be sure, but if you were to follow them you'd miss some great sites, including a gigantic oak tree on the south (left) side of trail. About 0.9 miles west of your starting point, you'll find yourself between two boulders, each nearly 20 feet tall. Climb up a short but steep hill between the rock walls, and then turn left as the trail heads south through another rock pass.

This one is almost a cave—it's not a difficult climb, but it is a narrow passageway. (An alternate route is available to the left for those too wide or too claustrophobic to pass through it.) Twenty-two stone stairs have been laid inside the pass. At the top of the steps, turn around and watch as the hikers behind you emerge from what appears to be a tiny crack between the two rocks. As you continue west, you'll walk through a short "hallway" of dark gray and white-washed shale; lucky stones decorate the walls on both sides.

A Gorge Trail marker indicates a sharp left turn, and from there, you'll slip-slide down a sandy hill. The trail curves right again, heading west for the last time before dropping down a log staircase which is neatly stitched into the side of sandy ravine. As the trail straightens out, you'll soon notice what looks like a root maze underfoot. From the large surface of exposed roots, you can overlook the shallow rapids of the Cuyahoga River. The trail earns its name here, providing beautiful views and sounds of the river gorge.

The trail bends left to cross over a long footbridge, and you may notice some fossil remains in the rock here.

You'll cross another footbridge and hit a few more small hills as you continue east. Once over the hills, a short log stairway takes you down to the dam overlook, where you can relax on a bench and enjoy the view.

Rested? Good. You'll climb up 105 wooden steps from the dam overlook before you veer right and east again. On your way back to the parking lot, you'll pass by a large, wooden, fishing pier. If you have time, hop onto it and enjoy a look at the water, so smooth here just above the dam. You'll pass by the south side of the picnic areas, and a water fountain, before returning to the trailhead.

NEARBY ACTIVITIES

If you're just getting warmed up after this hike, head south on Front Street and turn into the smaller Gorge Metro Park lot to venture onto Highbridge Trail. It's a 3.2-mile hike connecting to the Cascade Valley area of the Metro Parks Serving Summit County (see the Oxbow Trail, p. 140). In cold weather, the skating pond is open and even lit for night skating. Call the seasonal information line at (330) 865-8060 for details.

#22
Green Leaf Park

IN BRIEF

Not so long ago, a gravel pit sat at the corner of Medina Line Road and State Route 162. When a young park district converted the parcel into a 45-acre park, it became the first of many lovely Medina County Parks. Instead of gravel, visitors here now pick up bits of history. Green Leaf Park features an old log cabin, three picnic shelters, a lake to fish in, and a nature trail that winds around a small herb garden.

DIRECTIONS

From I-271, exit onto Route 94 (Ridge Road) and follow it south to State Route 162. Turn left, heading east. When you reach Medina Line Road, turn right, heading south. You'll soon pass the northern entrance to Green Leaf Park. Continue south about 500 feet, turning right into the larger parking lot.

DESCRIPTION

Start your walk at the north end of the main parking lot, in front of Willow shelter. Your first few steps follow a low, pretty sandstone wall as it bends around the eastern side of the shelter. From there, follow the wide grass and gravel path north toward the fishing lake. As you walk, you'll pass a ball field and a grassy hill on your right. The tall thick trees on your left offer afternoon shade.

Two park benches just west of the trail provide pleasant views of the little lake.

KEY AT-A-GLANCE INFORMATION

Length: About 1 mile

Configuration: Loop

Difficulty: Easy

Scenery: Forest, fishing lakes, historic log cabin, and herb garden

Exposure: About half shaded

Traffic: Moderate

Trail surface: Dirt and grass

Hiking time: 30 minutes

Season: Open year-round

Access: Park closes at dark

Maps: Not available

Facilities: Portable toilets near fishing lake

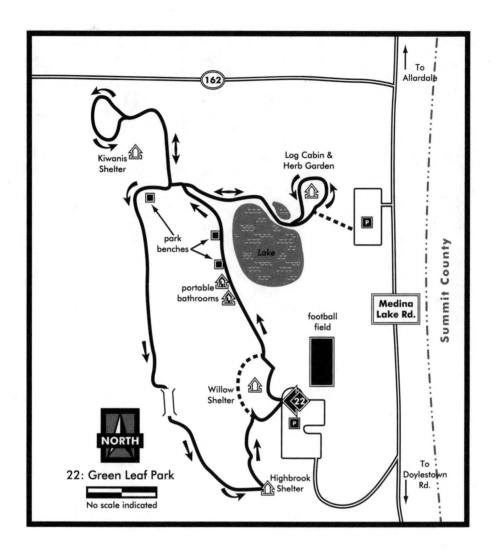

To
Allardale

Kiwanis
Shelter

Log Cabin &
Herb Garden

park
benches

Lake

portable
bathrooms

football
field

Medina
Lake Rd.

Summit County

Willow
Shelter

22

NORTH

22: Green Leaf Park

No scale indicated

Highbrook
Shelter

To
Doylestown
Rd.

From the north end of the lake, turn right onto a sandy path leading through the woods and to the old log cabin. The Hard family constructed this house in 1817, shortly after they arrived in Ohio. Abraham Hard and his wife, Rebecca, had left Vermont a year or so earlier, with five of their ten children. They headed for Tallmadge, where their son Cyrus had settled; eventually, they put roots down in what would become the eastern edge of Medina County. They put down roots not only by building

this home, but also by expanding their family. Moses Knapp Hard was born in 1818, when Rebecca was 50 years old. It seems Mrs. Hard was made of tough stuff, indeed—when she died in 1860, she had lived an amazing 91 years.

Today, the Hard family log house is surrounded by an herb garden, established by the Medina County Herb Society. Once you've circled the perimeter (or gone inside, if it is open), head back through the woods past the lake, and continue west on the grassy path.

The Hard Family log house

Ahead on your right, nestled in the shady northwest corner of the park, is the Kiwanis picnic shelter. Behind it, a couple of short, unmarked paths have been worn over several sandy knolls. Some of the hills are steep and slippery, but they are all short—so there's little chance of getting hurt, even if you slip. Across the path from the shelter, a park bench marks the spot where the path turns south, running under tall shade trees and over a footbridge to the park's two other shelters. The path winds a bit before it takes you to Highbank shelter on the south side of the parking lot. From there, a path to the left leads you back to Willow shelter, just 0.1 miles north of Highbank.

NEARBY ACTIVITIES

All three of Green Leaf's picnic shelters have grills; shelters can be reserved by calling the Medina Park District at (330) 722-9364. Fishing is permitted at the lake. While you're in the area, visit Allardale (see p. 11) on Remsen Road, just a few miles north of Green Leaf Park. You can learn more about the Hard family, and other tough cookies in Medina's past, at the county's historical society. The John Smart House Museum and Research Center is located at 206 North Elmwood Street in Medina. The museum's hours vary with the seasons, so call (330) 722-1341 for the current schedule.

Special thanks to Tom Hilberg of the Medina County Historical Society for his time and fact-checking assistance.

#23
Happy Days,
Ledges, and Pines

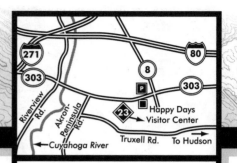

IN BRIEF

This hilly combination of three trails starts and ends at Happy Days Visitors Center in the Cuyahoga Valley National Park. Along the way you'll visit a pioneer cemetery, assorted caves and ledges, and the best spot in the valley to watch a sunset.

DIRECTIONS

Take Route 8 south to Route 303; head west to find Happy Days Visitor Center parking lot, on the North side of Route 303, approximately 1 mile west of State Route 8. Coming from I-77, exit Route 21 and head south to Route 303; at 303 turn right and go east to Happy Days Visitor Center, about 2.5 miles east of Riverview Road.

DESCRIPTION

From the parking lot, you'll cross under Route 303 through a 200-foot-long lighted tunnel, climbing up a few steps to see Happy Days Visitor Center. The trailhead is behind the large, one-story wooden structure, where you'll step onto one of the shortest trails in the park, the 0.5-mile Haskell Run. Haskell Run is dotted with 16 wooden, numbered posts. A self-study nature guide of the trail explains each of the numbers in turn. The guide is available at the trailhead for 50 cents. It's two quarters well spent.

Head east (left) on Haskell and you'll find yourself on the edge of the Mater

KEY AT-A-GLANCE
INFORMATION

Length: 4.3 miles

Configuration: Bumpy loop

Difficulty: Moderate, with difficult sections

Scenery: Large rock outcrops, cave, valley overlook, forest, streams

Exposure: Mostly shaded

Traffic: Moderate to heavy near the cave on Ledges portion, lighter traffic on the Pine Grove portion

Trail surface: Mixed—from large stones to dirt and gravel

Hiking time: 2 hours

Season: Open year-round

Access: 7 a.m.–11 p.m.

Maps: Ledges area map available at Happy Days Visitor Center

Facilities: Water and rest rooms available inside Happy Days visitor center; rest rooms located at Ledges Shelter and by Ledges Overlook

Special comments: For beginning hikers, especially little ones, start with the Haskell Run Trail. Or, shorten this hike by taking the Ledges Loop to return to the Happy Days Visitor Center.

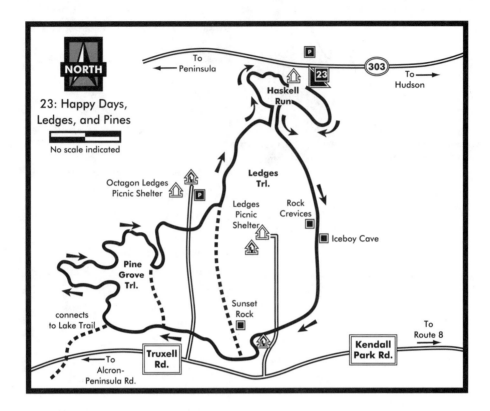

NORTH

23: Happy Days,
Ledges, and Pines

No scale indicated

To Peninsula

Haskell Run

303

To Hudson

23

Ledges Trl.

Octagon Ledges Picnic Shelter

Ledges Picnic Shelter

Rock Crevices

Iceboy Cave

Pine Grove Trl.

Sunset Rock

connects to Lake Trail

To Alcron-Peninsula Rd.

Truxell Rd.

Kendall Park Rd.

To Route 8

Delorosa cemetery, which dates to 1869. Its inhabitants include a Civil War soldier who died in battle, and his parents, a Mr. and Mrs. Coady, who lived to 93 and 83 years old, respectively. (We'll never know the secret to their longevity, but we can guess that they walked a lot.) Many of the cemetery's other souls rest in mystery, as their names have long since faded from their sandstone markers.

Back on the trail, Haskell Run turns to the right and drops about 30 feet, crossing a short wooden footbridge over the meandering creek for which the trail is named. From here, the trail bends sharply to the left, working its way up toward the base of the Ledges Trail. Arriving at the top of 20 or so steps, turn left onto Ledges Trail, and follow the signs to Ice Box Cave.

Ledges Trail offers challenging footing in places. In the 1930s, the Civilian Conservation Corp (CCC) carefully created stairways out of the indigenous stones to provide hikers with a safer path. You will appreciate their work for both its form and its function. The CCC's mission, in part, was stated in a 1910 report of the US Department of the Interior. It declared that "particular attention must be devoted always to harmonizing of these improvements with the landscape." Along this trail (and many other places in the park), you'll see evidence of the CCC's adherence to this goal.

Before you reach Ice Box Cave, you'll be called into one of the skinny, cool crevices along the right side of the path. Giant walls of Sharon conglomerate (300-million year old rock formed of cemented sand and small quartz pebbles) seem to have been dropped like a giant child's blocks, scattered across the Ledges area, creating a playground of sorts

Remembering the Civilian Conservation Corp

Sitting on the flat expanse of rock you're facing west, overlooking the valley. On most days, you can see well past the communities of Bath and Brecksville. Many nights, a crowd gathers here to catch the short sunset performance, and actually applauds as the sun slips out of sight. Move on for now (you won't want to finish the hike without the benefit of daylight), and plan to come back another time to enjoy the nightly show.

The Ledges Trail continues just south of the overlook point, veering west and dropping down 41 wood-reinforced steps into the forest. A sign at the bottom of the steps points right (north) to complete the Ledges Trail loop, but you should continue straight through the cool forest, toward Pine Grove Trail. You'll cross the park road to the Octagon shelter and get a brief view of Truxell Road, about 200 yards to your left. Most days, the woodpeckers and the wind in the trees will distract you from any traffic noises that may come from the road.

Soon the trail turns right, heading north, where you'll notice a few pines amid the tall aspens, beech, and maple trees. About 2 miles into the trail, you'll see a sign noting the connector to Lake Trail, also part of the Virginia Kendall unit of the park.

Midway through the climbing, twisting Pine Grove trail, you'll find yourself overlooking a deep ravine and a small footbridge. Two sharp left turns and a 30-foot drop later, you'll cross that bridge and climb up again, this time ascending 66 wooden stairs (as you huff and puff, remember to thank the Cuyahoga Valley Trail Council volunteers who built them). As soon as you catch your breath, you leave Pine Grove on the connector, heading east to cross over the Octagon Ledges access road again. Follow the signs to the Ledges Trail and

for average-sized humans like us. Park signs prohibiting rock climbing and warning of the dangers of falling off the sometimes-slippery cliffs are posted here. Heed the signs, but have fun.

While the entire Ledges Trail is naturally cooled thanks to the surrounding rocks, you'll notice a distinct drop in temperature as you approach Ice Box Cave. South of the cave you'll cross two tiny streams. Further south, the trail veers right and leads you across the park's driveway to the Ledges picnic area. The trail rises a bit, revealing the south end of a large, open field where people on blankets often vie for space amid kite-fliers and dogs chasing flying discs. Permanent rest room facilities are also here. Follow the path up another 30 yards to a sign directing you left (south) to the Ledges Trail or straight ahead to visit Octagon Ledges overlook. The overlook is a sunset-watcher's paradise.

Happy Days Visitor Center, veering left to complete your clockwise jaunt around this rocky place.

Your final quarter-mile is the second half of Haskell Run. It takes you by numbers 10 through 15 of the self-guided nature trail markers. Your legs will get one more workout as you climb up a gravel trail and then a dozen stone steps to arrive on the western edge of the field adjacent to the visitor center. Several grills and picnic tables here may seem rather inviting at this point, as you have likely worked up an appetite on the trail.

NEARBY ACTIVITIES

Enter the visitor center to request free maps and information brochures about the park. Art related to the National Parks is often displayed here as well. To find out what's going on at Happy Days Visitor Center before you leave home, call (330) 650-4636.

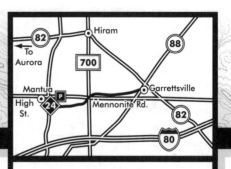

#24
Headwaters Trail

IN BRIEF

This rail trail in Portage County makes for peaceful, easy walking. Running east and west between Mantua and Garrettsville, it abuts the Mantua Bog and Marsh Wetlands State Nature Preserves, making for dandy bird-watching.

DIRECTIONS

From I-77 or I-480, take State Route 82 east into Mantua. Trailhead parking is on the south side of Mennonite Road (known as High Street in Village of Mantua) about 0.25 miles east of Route 44 and immediately east of Buchert Park. *Alternate directions from northeast suburbs:* Take I-271 to Alt. 422 east to Route 306. Turn right and follow 306 south to Route 82; turn left and continue into Mantua.

DESCRIPTION

Step onto the crushed limestone trail, walk up a short slope to meet the old rail bed and head east. The trail more or less follows Eagle Creek, a tributary of the Cuyahoga River, but you won't see much of it.

Starting 0.5 miles east of trailhead you'll reach the northwestern edge of Mantua Bog (actually an alkaline fen). It was designated as a National Natural Landmark in 1976 and as a State Preserve in 1990. Next, you'll stroll alongside Marsh Wetlands, a 152-acre site situated west of Peck Road (County

KEY AT-A-GLANCE INFORMATION

Length: 7.5 miles (one way)

Configuration: Out-and-back is 15 miles

Difficulty: Easy, flat surface with a short stretch on a country road

Scenery: Beech forests, creek ravine, lots of waterfowl; Western Reserve architecture in Mantua and Garrettsville is worth a look, too

Exposure: About half exposed

Traffic: Moderate

Trail surface: Crushed limestone

Hiking time: 3 hours

Season: Open year-round

Access: Open dawn–dusk; no permits required

Maps: Available from the Portage Park District, call (330) 673-9404

Facilities: Rest rooms and water at the eastern end of the trail in Garrettsville Village Park and at Buchert Park at the west end in Mantua

Special comments: Pets must be leashed. Horses and bikes frequent the trail. One day, this section of trail could be incorporated into a trail system, stretching from Washington, DC, to Indiana.

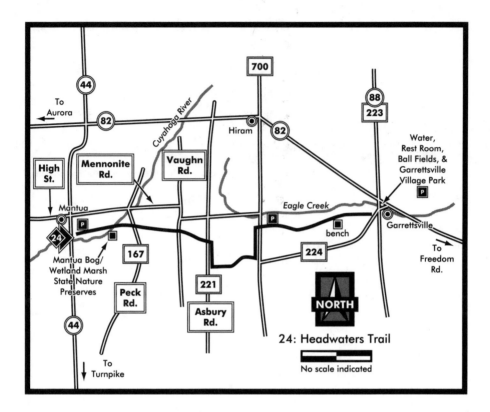

24: Headwaters Trail

NORTH

No scale indicated

Road 167) and south of Mennonite Road (Township Road 256). Both the Wetlands and the bog are protected by the Ohio Department of Natural Resources and are open by permit only. So, while you can't see the beaver in the marsh or the cranberries in the bog, you can enjoy the migrating waterfowl as you stroll by the edge of these protected areas. You might also find a generously sized garter snake, or even a skunk that has wandered away from its protected habitat to gawk at the funny two-legged creatures plodding along the trail.

At 1.4 miles, you'll cross a gravel road. From here you'll enjoy some gradual changes of scenery: shallow but pretty ravines, cornfields, and a mix of both old and new home sites. The trail cuts through some shallow but pretty ravines at 2.7 miles. You'll rise up a slight hill (a

big hill, for a rail trail) for about 0.3 miles. The trail ends at Asbury Road.

As of this writing, the Park District is hoping to gain access to and continue the trail through the privately owned corridor between Asbury Road and Route 700. For now, you'll have to be contented with some road walking. Turn right, leaving the trail going south on Asbury. Be sure to stay on the left, facing traffic, through this next section.

I usually don't enjoy walking on roads, but I enjoyed this stretch for several reasons. Walking by sun-dappled farm fields was quite pleasant and a moderate hill broke up an otherwise level walk. When you reach Hankee Road, turn left and climb up another hill, passing more scenic farms. Hankee is narrow, with uneven soft shoulders, but traffic is light. It bends to the right and rolls downhill, intersecting Route 700 at about 4 miles. Turn left, and rejoin Headwaters Trail about 0.7 miles north of here. While the traffic on Route 700 can be too fast for comfort, the thistle and cattails along the road are lovely, attracting butterflies by the dozens. With such distractions, the road section of the hike passes quickly.

As you join the trail east of Route 700, stop and look into the ravine on the north. Continuing east, you'll notice the landscape changes on both sides of the trail rather quickly. To the north— the ravine slopes down gently in places—it is deep and steep in others. To the south (right), the land rises up toward distant farms in an area that is heavily wooded.

Six miles into your hike, you'll come to a park bench. Here, you'll see the backside of a quiet industrial park; you're just 1 mile west of Garrettsville.

In the late summer, you'll find big milkweed pods at the end of the trail: Andrew Rowley field in Garrettsville Village Park. You've logged 7.5 miles at this point. (*Note:* You'll see a sign just west of here describing the trail as 6 miles long; it is accurate, but does not count the roadway portion of the hike.)

If you've planned to hoof it back, you may stop for a bite nearby. A grocery store sits just east of the park. About 0.5 miles to the west, just a few steps off the trail at White Street, is a convenience store. As you head west in the afternoon, you'll have great sunset views for company.

If you've parked a rendezvous vehicle here, you may want to drive into Garrettsville and have a look around. The Western Reserve was settled largely by pioneers from Connecticut. Mantua, Hiram, and Garrettsville were all settled before Ohio became a state (1803). All three towns conjure up visions of New England—including central village squares with imposing churches, surrounded by large frame-style houses.

When John Garrett, of Christian Hundred, Delaware, purchased 300 acres of land in Nelson, he obtained Silver Creek water power rights and built a gristmill here. In January of 1806— reportedly on the day the mill opened— Garrett died of pneumonia. Under his wife's direction, the mill thrived, and the town grew up around it. The old mill is now vacant. In 1889, the thriving community built an opera house at a cost of $15,000. It was razed in 1964, but the clock from the tower was saved. It still chimes the hours away at the corner of Main and High Streets. Before you leave Garrettsville, be sure to pick up a pack of Lifesavers. Clarence Crane invented the candy here, in 1912.

NEARBY ACTIVITIES

Eagle Creek State Nature Preserve is just east of Garrettsville on Freedom Road (Route 223). The 440-acre area offers nature trails and a sturdy wildlife observation blind at the edge of a large open swamp. There's plenty to see. Eagle Creek is home to many reptiles, birds, mammals, and more than 120 woody plant and fern species, including ostrich ferns that stand nearly five feet tall! The preserve is open dawn to dusk year-round; call (330) 527-5118 for more information. Also nearby: Nelson's Ledges State Park (see p. 136).

Special thanks to Christine Craycroft, Executive Director, Portage Park District, for reviewing this section.

#25
(J. Arthur) Herrick
State Nature Preserve

IN BRIEF

Who knew carnivorous plants could be so cute? Who knew beaver could cause such trouble? As pretty and peaceful as this place is, you may not notice the battles raging all around you. This fen harbors the tiny insect-eating sundew plant, endangered bayberry, and tamarack trees. Tamaracks are Ohio's only native deciduous conifer; visit here in the fall when the trees' needles turn bright yellow before they fall off. Visit here anytime to watch for birds and stay, perhaps, for a sunset.

DIRECTIONS

From Route 14 in Streetsboro, take Route 43 south 0.2 miles to Seasons Road. Turn right. Approximately 2 miles west of Route 43, Seasons Road curves sharply to the left and crosses a railroad track. Turn left into the preserve access driveway on the eastern side of Seasons. Follow the drive past a stream crossing to the small parking lot on the right.

DESCRIPTION

If you know the difference between a fen and a bog, you probably paid very close attention in biology class. If you think bogs, swamps, and marshes are all about the same, and aren't sure you've ever seen a fen, here's the abbreviated version:

For starters, a fen is alkaline and a bog is acidic. Both areas are ecologically important, too scarce these days, and

KEY AT-A-GLANCE INFORMATION

Length: 1.5 miles

Configuration: Out-and-back, with a small turnaround loop

Difficulty: Easy

Scenery: In addition to rare plants, this fen is a popular spot for spotting beaver, muskrat, and heron, and is good for bird-watching in general

Exposure: Mostly shaded

Traffic: Moderate

Trail surface: Wooden boardwalks and dirt trail

Hiking time: 45 minutes

Season: Open all year

Access: Daylight hours

Maps: Trail map may be available at the park.

Facilities: None

Special comments: As a State Nature Preserve, pets, bicycles, and motorized vehicles are prohibited. The first portion of the trail is a wide, hard-packed gravel road that allows handicapped-equipped vans to access the boardwalk. The boardwalk is ADA compliant and includes several turnaround points.

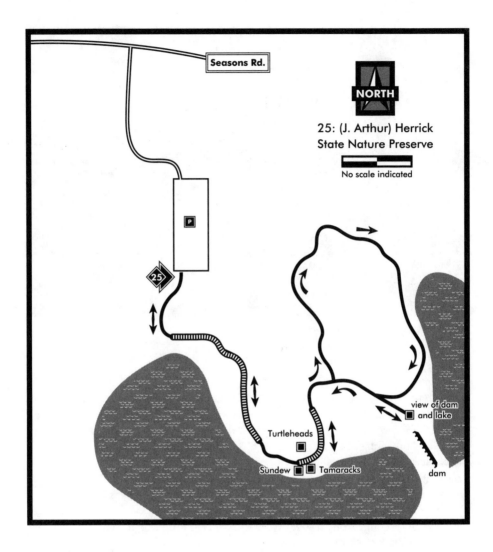

NORTH

25: (J. Arthur) Herrick
State Nature Preserve

No scale indicated

25

Turtleheads

view of dam
and lake

Sundew ◼ ◼ Tamaracks

dam

generally damp. Bogs receive their water from above-ground sources (mostly rain and snow), and they may have a surface outflow. Groundwater seeps and springs, usually coming out of permeable glacial deposits, feed fens. True bogs are isolated from groundwater—sometimes from impermeable soil conditions, but often also from an impermeable layer of compressed, humified peat. Peat is the thing that really sets bogs and fens apart from other wetlands. The peat, combined with the continual wetness, causes and perpetuates extreme soil conditions. You don't have to be a science whiz to realize that different types of plants live in alkaline and acidic soils. But shades of gray exist in nature, and in the relative acidity of bogs and fens. Because bogs and fens both are generally wet with nutrient-poor soil, some plants exist in both. In fact, some of those species cannot exist anywhere else. Thus ends the science lesson—now let's do some research in the field, *er,* fen.

From the parking lot, head south down a wide gravel path. A brilliant red barn sits on a small hill to the east. Tall

Catch a sunset from the wooden boardwalk here

marsh grass and seasonal wildflowers grow on both sides of the path. When the goldenrod explodes under a sunny fall sky, the scene is as colorful and glossy as a still-wet painting. But behind the pretty picture there is turmoil. Battles rage, quietly but constantly, among the fen's inhabitants.

About 0.2 miles from the trailhead, you'll come to a large stone recognizing the work of the Nature Conservancy and the Akron Garden Club in preserving this land. Step onto the boardwalk, where you'll have a chance to stop at three inviting benches. These are good seats to watch the heron and marsh wren that commonly appear here. Believe it or not, these seats are in the middle of the battlefield.

A wall of cattails seems to stand guard along the boardwalk. But are they here to protect, or invade? The answer depends on whom you ask. Cattails provide high-energy food for migratory birds and butterflies; so birds and butterflies, and people who watch them, may root for the cattails. But the answer also depends on the type of cattails. Some are native and non-aggressive, content to enjoy their view of the fen without overtaking it. Other cattail species are invasive and quite aggressive, threatening some of the fen's indigenous plants. The bayberry, for example, is on the state's list of endangered plants. This fen is one of just three spots in Ohio where it grows. Unfortunately, the cattails and bayberries aren't the only species at odds in this preserve. The invasive cattails and reed canarygrass threaten the open fen as a whole, driving out the sedge meadow and shrubby cinquefoil. The glossy buckthorn, a small tree or large shrub (distinguished by its shiny oval leaves and speckled bark) threatens the tamarack population as well as the bayberry. The skirmishes among the plants and animals here started long ago, and along the way, people have stepped in—for better or for worse.

The lakes and dams here date back to the 1940s and 1950s, when the Frame family raised minks and muskrat here. J. Arthur Herrick bought the initial tract of land that would form the preserve in 1969; for some time after that the area was known as Frame Lake Bog. The muskrats (who didn't care what the place was called) stayed, and beaver joined them. The beaver, like the cattails, can be troublemakers. Beaver dams cause the water levels to rise, threatening the tamarack population. The tamaracks in this fen comprise one of the few reproducing populations of this tree in the US.

What can—and what should—be done to tip the balance in favor of the bayberries and the tamaracks? Again, the answers vary depending on whom you ask, and a resolution is not expected in the near future. The good news is that the fen has been preserved, so the battles may continue. The Nature Conservancy sends aid in the form of volunteers. They diligently thin the ranks of invaders in hopes that the natives can continue to fight for themselves. While some of the natives are under duress, the volunteers who visit typically report finding the battlegrounds overwhelmingly beautiful. So march on . . .

As you continue south on the boardwalk, tamarack trees line the trail; you're likely to see or hear a catbird at this point. It's easy to spot the mayapples and skunk cabbage growing along the boardwalk, but notice, too, the fen-loving shrubby cinquefoil, whose bright yellow flowers bloom from spring through midsummer. You'll have to look hard for the less common sundew, a small but mighty carnivorous plant resembling a sunburst. When an insect lands on the plant's hairy, sticky leaves, it triggers an enzyme reaction that makes a leaf grow very quickly—so quickly that it wraps up the insect like a burrito before absorbing the bug's nutrients. Another unusual plant to look for is turtlehead. It has dark, waxy, green stems and white flowers. Each bloom is about one-half-inch long. When viewed from the side, with just a bit of imagination, the bloom indeed forms the outline of a turtle's head. Also look for poison sumac, cousin to the more common sumacs that only occur in fens. Admire, but don't touch it if you are remotely sensitive to poison ivy!

Just 0.4 miles into trail, the boardwalk ends, and you'll step down onto a narrow, rooty dirt trail that winds between the base of a wooded hill and the shrub swamp. Soon, the boardwalk begins again, curves to the left, and then re-deposits you on the dirt trail.

The hard-packed dirt path bends left, leading you up a small hill into a beech-maple wood that offers color-charged, spring wildflower displays. Circling back down the hill you'll find two lakes separated by a narrow dam. The trail loop rejoins the original path at this point; you will retrace your steps back to the boardwalk and home from here. You probably won't have any war stories to tell when you return, but you should bring home some lovely pictures.

NEARBY ACTIVITIES

This nature preserve sits about 5 miles north of Towner's Woods (see p. 193), and about 5 miles south of Tinker's Creek State Park (see p. 190) and State Nature Preserve in Aurora/Streetsboro (see p. 187).

Special thanks to Jennifer Hillmer, Nature Conservancy land steward and Herrick Fen site manager, for reviewing this section, and for continuing to fight the good fight.

#26
Hiram Field Station

306 Hiram College **700** **88**
Wheeler Rd.
422
Aurora
82 **26**
80 **700**
To turnpike
14
43 To Ravenna **88** **700**

IN BRIEF

Wandering through these woods, you can breath easy. One of the largest beech-maple forests in Ohio, Hiram Field Station is also quiet, beautiful, and teeming with diverse plant and animal life. Watch for barred owl and pileated woodpeckers in the trees.

DIRECTIONS

From Cleveland, take I-480 east to route 422. Follow Route 422 east (toward Solon) to Route 700. Turn right on Route 700 and continue south about 5 miles into Hiram. Turn left, heading east on Route 305 about 1.5 miles to Wheeler Road. Turn right and follow Wheeler 1.3 miles to the entrance of the James H. Barrow Field Station.

DESCRIPTION

If urban sprawl is getting to you, this is the place to come. The woods are thick and quiet, and the trail is not well worn. Established in 1967 at Hiram College, the James H. Barrow Field Station is one of the largest forests of its kind in Ohio and the fourth largest in the United States. The 260-acre woods works like an oxygen factory situated between Cleveland and Youngstown's industrial development. Come here and get a lungful of scents, including pine, sassafras, decaying wood, and other really organic smells.

KEY AT-A-GLANCE INFORMATION

Length: 4.5 miles (optional 2.4-mile hike)

Configuration: Loop(s)

Difficulty: Moderate

Scenery: Wide variety of trees, ferns, wildflowers, wildlife, maple-sugaring operation (in season)

Exposure: Mostly shaded

Traffic: Light

Trail surface: Dirt and leaves

Hiking time: 1.5 hours

Season: Open year-round

Access: Dawn–dusk

Maps: Available at www.hiram.edu /global/academics/fieldstation and posted inside Frohring Lab Building

Facilities: Public rest rooms in the museum/interpretative center near entrance to the trail; nearest pay phone is in Garrettsville.

Special comments: As part of Hiram's outreach program, the Field Station offers educational visits for students, preschool through 12th grade. For information about the outreach programs, call (330) 527-2141. (*Note:* The Field Station trail is for foot traffic only. Dogs (on leash) are permitted, but bikes, horses, and motor vehicles are not.)

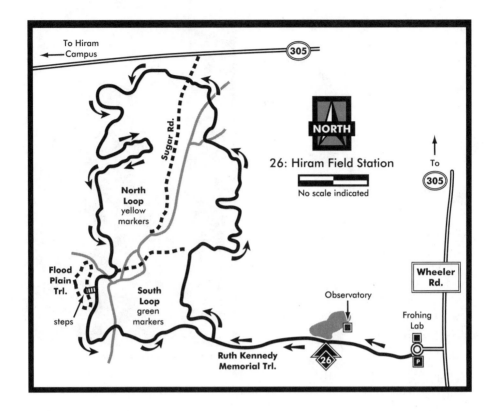

To Hiram Campus

305

NORTH

26: Hiram Field Station

To 305

No scale indicated

Sugar Rd.

North Loop
yellow markers

Flood Plain Trl.

steps

South Loop
green markers

Observatory

Wheeler Rd.

Frohing Lab

P

Ruth Kennedy Memorial Trl.

26

Start your hike in the small gravel parking lot by the green museum building known as Frohring Lab. Inside, you'll learn about biodegradation cycles and some of the animals you're likely to find on the trail, such as the mudpuppy and the painted turtle.

From the museum, take the gravel road west to the Observation Building. There, on the edge of a pond, you can enjoy watching birds from inside or outside. In addition to wild birds, a pair of trumpeter swans lives here year-round.

The official trail sign for the Ruth E. Kennedy Memorial Trail stands by an apple tree, just south of the Observation Building. Follow the signs west past another pond. Walking through young but dense growth, a farm field slants down to your left, revealing a nice view of the gentle hills of Portage County.

Soon the trail begins to roll downhill as well. The path is not well worn. But well marked it is, with yellow and green markers and numbered signs too. (Speaking of signs, you'll note an intersection where the trails' loop will return you; keep going straight, following the trail markers.) The numbered signs along the southern loop correspond to an interpretive guide, available in the museum. Even without the guide, you'll benefit from the tree identification signs listing the trees' common and botanical names. They will help you spot tulip poplar, white pine, sassafras, black cherry, musclewood, and others. When you see the *Acer saccharum* (sugar maple) and *Fagus grandifolia* (beech) signs, you'll see you're entering a forest that is still used for maple sap collection. (The commercial sugar-maple operation fulfills terms of the donation of the land, and does not harm the forest.)

As the trail begins to go up a slight hill, the yellow and green trails split. Here, at about the 1-mile point, you can turn left to follow the shorter green trail (about a 2-mile loop) but this hike follows the longer (4-mile) yellow trail by veering right. Follow the trail as it heads east, then wiggles north, from here.

As you wiggle with the trail, five little platform bridges help you through the muddier parts of trail. You're on your own at a stream crossing—but don't worry, you can cross the shallow, three-foot-wide expanse with the aid of a few large rocks. Like a beacon on the other side of the stream, a yellow tree marker tells you that you're going the right way. Soon after crossing the stream, you'll be able to hear cars passing along Route 305 to the north. That's about the only time that civilization will re-enter your thoughts on this trail.

You'll soon cross the sugaring road. It runs north to route 305, but you continue west. A map posted by the road crossing indicates you've gone about 2 miles. The trail parallels Route 305 for a few more steps before bending left, taking you into dense woods

Pines, pin oaks, and Christmas ferns keep you company as you head, generally, south. But to go south, you must zigzag along each wiggle of the creek bed here on the forest floor.

As you're generally heading south, you have to make repeated sharp turns east to west, east, then south as you wiggle on down the path. After crossing another bridge, the path seems to narrow. The trees that grow along here are young and skinny, so they don't impose on you with their size, but they do give the unmistakable impression that you are outnumbered.

A shallow stream running through Field Station

In this thick forest of thick trees, you'll head up a slight hill and then to go down a fun, sharp incline to cross the steam again. No bridge, no problem—the rocks make for another easy crossing. Across the stream, a map indicates that 1.7 kilometers (about 1 mile) remains ahead of you. The trail goes right, then up a few steps, to reach a bench overlooking the stream.

After descending a steeper set of stairs, the yellow and green trails meet again, sharing a single path heading south by southwest. You're heading downstream, at this point, along the shallow but friendly creek. Its babble provides a bit of conversation here in the middle of the woods.

Soon you'll reach the intersection of the short (0.25-mile) Floodplain Trail. Turn right and follow the loop around and return back to the main trail. Just beyond the Floodplain Trail, you'll find two benches perfectly situated for conversation. Or perfectly situated so you can sit on one and put your feet (or your lunch?) on the other.

Moving on, you'll cross the creek again and bound over a pair of bouncy wooden bridges, going uphill a bit to reach another observation bench. Walking on acorns, you'll pass shagbark hickory trees as the path twists left, then right again before leveling out to find a bitternut tree.

At the top of the hill, grapevines create a natural arch—you'll have to duck to walk under it. Soon after you'll come to the sign marking the point where the yellow and green trails originally split. They join again by a dogwood tree. At this point, you've logged about 4.3 miles. From here, you'll follow the trail, then the road, east past the pond, the observation building, and back to your car.

NEARBY ACTIVITIES

Before leaving Hiram, you may want to tour the college and the town, both of which reflect their Western Reserve heritage. You may also want to visit the Headwaters Trail (see p. 85), about a five-minute drive from the Field Station. To get there, follow Wheeler Road south to Twinsburg-Warren Road (Route 82). Turn right, heading west to Route 700. Turn left and follow Route 700 south about 1 mile to the rail-trail parking lot.

Special thanks to James H. Barrow Field Station Director Samuel D. Marshall, for supplying background information on the station and for reviewing this hike description.

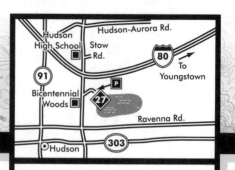

#27
Hudson Springs Park

IN BRIEF

Young hikers have a lot to look forward to when they set out to complete this counter-clockwise loop hike. On the north side of the lake, there's a great playground and a hedge maze just for them. If you time your visit right, you can catch the sunset from a westward-facing bench or from the elevated pier nestled on the north side of the lake.

DIRECTIONS

From Cleveland, take Route 8 south to Route 303. Turn left, heading east into Hudson's historic downtown. Continue east approximately 2 miles to Stow Road; turn left. The park entrance is on the eastern side of Stow Road, just south of the Ohio Turnpike.

DESCRIPTION

Hudson Springs Park spans 260 acres, and much of it is lake. Fishing and small boats are allowed here. Hudson residents can even rent space on the lakeshore to keep their canoes and rowboats handy. Non-residents may bring their own non-motorized boats to enjoy the water.

Although the park is well used, you will rarely see boats on the water, perhaps because there are so many other diversions here. Bikes are allowed on the trail, but you won't see many of them, either. That may be because the long (25 miles and growing) Summit County Bike/Hike trail runs nearby. Why boaters

KEY AT-A-GLANCE INFORMATION

Length: 1.8 miles

Configuration: Loop

Difficulty: Easy

Scenery: Lake views, lush woods, and a small island

Exposure: Three-quarters of the trail is shaded

Traffic: Moderate

Trail surface: Crushed limestone

Hiking time: 50 minutes (not counting sunsets)

Season: Open all year

Access: Open dawn—dusk; no permits required

Maps: Park map not available

Facilities: Rest rooms in the parking lot; two picnic shelters within the park

Special comments: Western Reserve College was established in Hudson in 1826. In 1882, the college moved to Cleveland, and Hudson took the loss hard. By 1906, Hudson had no water service and the business district went bust. Then Hudson native James Ellsworth stepped in. He told local officials that he'd help out, if they'd rescind all liquor licenses in town. Both sides performed, and, by 1912, Hudson was once again a thriving town.

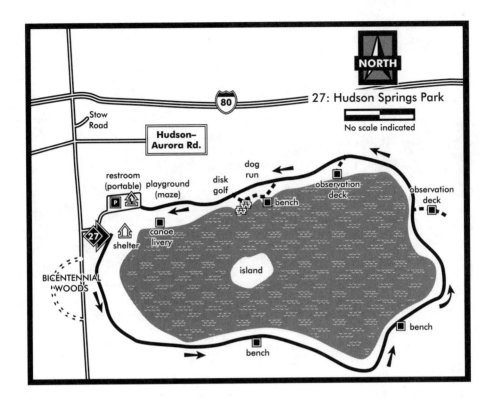

and bikers haven't taken to this park is uncertain, but its appeal hasn't been lost on walkers and others out for a bit of exercise; you will certainly have company as you travel around the lake.

To follow the trail counterclockwise, head south from the parking lot, entering the trail just to the right of the shelter and boat launch area. The dirt and gravel path heads up a slight rise before it curves toward the east. From here, you'll have a good view of the entire lake and its little island.

The trail is wide and relatively flat. On the eastern side of the lake, you will roll up and down over a few hills, ten feet or so at a time, but if you want to do any real climbing, you'll have to wait until you reach the playground on the other side of the lake.

On the south side of the lake, you'll cross over a well-disguised culvert; soon after, you'll notice an unmarked path on your right. It heads east to a housing development. Here, and at a couple of other points along the trail, you'll be able to see some of the homes nearby. It won't detract from your enjoyment of the trail, unless you're overcome with jealousy that the folks who live there can walk here without first driving over.

Rounding the eastern edge of the lake, you'll come to a raised observation deck. It faces west, making it perfect for sunset viewing. For a less direct but equally beautiful view of the sunset, follow the loop northeast to a second, lower, but slightly larger deck.

As you continue (now west) on the trail, you'll come to a dog run area (it is posted as such) and then to a disc golf course. Both are used frequently. Just a few steps from here, on the wet (south) side of the trail, two pieces of land

97

Hikers and bikers alike stop here for the sunset

jut into the lake. The park department wisely planted a couple of park benches and picnic tables here. They are situated so that you can enjoy a peaceful lake view, with your back to the action at the disc golf course and playground. Ah, but peaceful contemplation is only fun for so long. Heading west on the path again, you'll find it hard to resist the playground's charm.

Here, in the northwestern corner of the park, is play equipment—good stuff—for kids of all sizes. (You'd expect that in Hudson, home of Little Tikes Toy Company.) There's a small obstacle course, a tire swing, climbing equipment, and slides—and they're all fun. But none of the equipment compares to the little hedge maze, perfect for pint-size explorers. The maze was dedicated in 1988, "To all children . . . from the Hudson preschool parents." It was a very thoughtful gift, from people who clearly know kids. The playground is adjacent to the parking lot, so when you're done playing, you're free to leave. Bet you'll be back, though.

NEARBY ACTIVITIES
If the hedge maze, trails, disc-golf course, and playgrounds don't tucker you out, cross Ravenna Road west to pick up the 0.5-mile hike/bike trail through Bicentennial Woods. Or, if you prefer a bit of history with your hike, drive into the heart of Hudson.

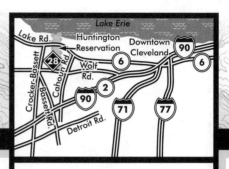

IN BRIEF
Crawl through a hollow log; visit the stars, and hit the beach—all within a mile. What a trip.

DIRECTIONS
Huntington Reservation is located in Bay Village. Exit I-90 at Crocker-Bassett Road. Follow Crocker-Bassett north approximately 2.5 miles to Wolf Road. Turn right onto Wolf. The park entrance is at 28728 Wolf Road, about 1.5 miles east of Crocker-Bassett.

DESCRIPTION
Huntington is one of the oldest reservations of the Cleveland Metroparks. It gets its name from English immigrant John Huntington, who purchased the land in 1881. Huntington built a distinctive tower used to pump water from Lake Erie to irrigate his grape fields. The water tower still stands; today it is an ice cream store, much appreciated by picnickers and beachgoers. A plaque on the side of the ice-cream shop relates the park's history and illustrates some of the improvements made by the Cleveland Metroparks after they purchased the land in 1927.

Start your hike by wandering through the Lake Erie Nature and Science Center (LENSC). It is brimming with life, from turtles and tarantulas to pythons and piranha. Large aquariums full of critters fascinate folks of all ages. Nimble visitors can crawl through a

KEY AT-A-GLANCE INFORMATION
Length: 1.25 miles

Configuration: Out-and-back

Difficulty: Easy

Scenery: A little creek, a Great Lake, and the wild insides of the Lake Erie Nature & Science Center (LENSC)

Exposure: Mostly exposed

Traffic: Path lightly traveled; beach very busy during summer months

Trail surface: Asphalt, dirt, sand

Hiking time: 40 minutes, plus playtime at the beach and inside LENSC

Season: Open all year

Access: Cleveland Metroparks Reservations are open from 6 a.m.–11 p.m. except where otherwise posted; the LENSC is open daily 10 a.m.–5 p.m.

Maps: Inside LENSC and online at www.clevelandmetroparks.com

Facilities: Rest rooms and water inside LENSC and on both sides of Lake Street

Special comments: No pets are allowed on the beach.

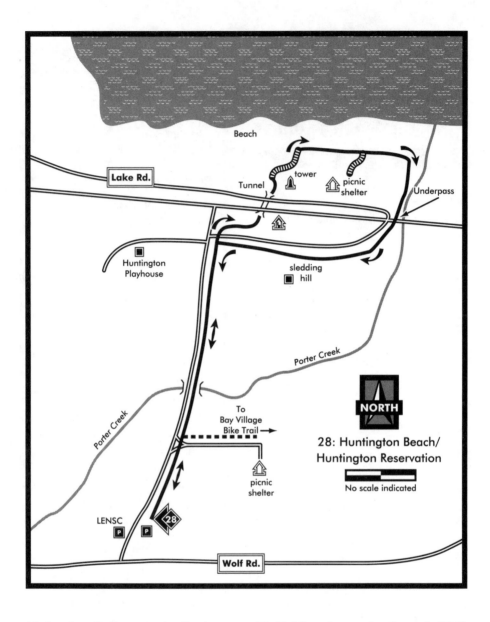

Beach

Lake Rd.

Tunnel · tower · picnic shelter · Underpass

Huntington Playhouse

sledding hill

Porter Creek

NORTH

To Bay Village Bike Trail →

Porter Creek

picnic shelter

LENSC

28

28: Huntington Beach/ Huntington Reservation

No scale indicated

Wolf Rd.

15-foot-long hollow tree that lies just inside the center's front door. LENSC also houses the Schuele Planetarium, which offers regular presentations on weekends. Outside, the center's lovely "backyard" is great for bird-watching and for relaxing.

Once you've soaked up the sights inside and around the nature center, head north on the all-purpose path to the lake.

You'll follow the paved trail past the Wolf Picnic Area (about 0.1 miles), down a slight incline and across a small bridge over Porter Creek. You'll share the way with light car traffic, so stay on the trail as you make your way back up the hill.

Just over the bridge, there's a lovely view of Porter Creek as it heads east before making its final turn to drop into Lake Erie. You'll lose sight of the creek as you climb up a small hill. There, on your left (western side of the trail) you'll see the Huntington Playhouse; on your right is a sledding hill.

You can see the lake from here, but don't cross busy Lake Road to get there. Instead, turn right and follow signs to the pedestrian tunnel underpass (Rest rooms and pay phones are located near the tunnel's entrance).

Emerging on the north side of the park, you'll find a shady playground area, a large picnic shelter and the distinctive tower. Behind the tower (ice cream shop), follow the steep stairs—about 50 of them—down to the shore. During the too-short summer season, the beach is often crowded. In the off-season, however, you can enjoy the beach in quiet. On a windy, late fall day, you may even find solitude along the breakwalls—on those days, the lake seems more green than blue, and the gulls are the only ones playing in the waves.

Walk east along the shore about 0.2 miles, where you'll find another set of stairs that lead up to the picnic shelter. If you continue walking east on the beach, however, you'll soon find a path that curves to the right and stays low. This narrow path along Porter Creek takes you south through the underpass—not the tunnel—under Lake Road.

Follow the dirt path along the side of the road as it curves west, toward the sledding hill and back to the all-purpose trail. From here, turn left to retrace your steps back to the LENSC.

NEARBY ACTIVITIES
You can catch a star-studded show at the Schuele Planetarium here each weekend. Call (440) 871-2900 for a schedule or for information about other programs at the LENSC. Huntington Beach is open during the swimming season from 11 a.m.–9 p.m.

#29
Indian Hollow
Reservation

IN BRIEF

Hikers can observe the effects of glaciers as well as spy herons and myriad birds enjoying this shady stretch of the Black River's East Branch. A gravel loop provides a different experience away from the river near land that was once quarried to make blocks for bridges and millstones for mills.

DIRECTIONS

Take I-80 west, exiting at Route 10. Continue west about 6 miles to Grafton Road. Turn left (south) on Route 57 (Grafton Road) into Grafton. Shortly after crossing a set of railroad tracks, turn right (west) onto Parsons Rd. The park entrance is about 0.75 miles ahead on the right. Follow the park road about 0.5 miles in from Parsons Road to Picnic Shelter no. 1 and the trailhead.

DESCRIPTION

About 30 miles southwest of Cleveland, Indian Hollow Reservation lies under the flight path of Cleveland Hopkins' jets. Watching them fly over, you can't help but feel sorry for the people in the sky, for whom the Black River is just a tiny line wending north to Lake Erie. For you, here on the ground, the river is the beautiful, dominant feature of this hike.

Begin at the trailhead map posted by the picnic shelter and rest rooms. From here, a connector trail to your left leads you down a short hill, and across a

KEY AT-A-GLANCE INFORMATION

Length: 2.5 miles

Configuration: Loop and out-and-back spurs

Difficulty: Easy

Scenery: Black River, exposed sandstone walls, beech-maple forest, variety of wildflowers

Exposure: Mostly shaded

Traffic: Moderate

Trail surface: Loop trail is crushed gravel; spurs are hard-packed dirt.

Hiking time: 45 minutes–1 hour

Season: Open all year

Access: Reservation is open dawn –dusk.

Maps: Available online: www.loraincountymetroparks.com

Facilities: Two picnic shelters, grills, water, rest rooms, and a small playground

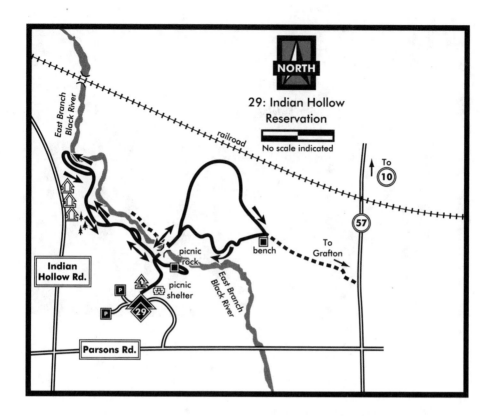

bridge over the East Branch of Black River to a 1-mile loop trail. But before you reach the bridge, you'll want to explore the banks of this beautiful river.

On your left, an unmarked but well-traveled dirt path draws you toward the river's edge and into the woods. Follow the narrow dirt and rock trail north-northeast and enjoy the varying greens and grays of lichen and moss on the rocks along the river. In at least two spots on this trail, the river appears easy to cross, and a path similar to this one calls enticingly from the other side of the river. Don't answer the call—the rocks are slippery, and the river runs several feet deep here. Continue on the dirt path on this side of the river, keeping an eye out for heron and other fishing birds.

At about 0.5 miles, you'll notice deep lines in the sandstone wall across the river. These lines were cut by a glacier called the Wisconsin Ice Sheet, creating a wall that looks much like a layer cake. It is especially striking as you approach an old railroad bridge. Before you reach the bridge, however, you'll find a no-trespassing sign. Heed it, retracing your steps to the base of the bridge. On your return, you'll notice a thick and fragrant stand of pines separating the trail from the private homes on your right.

When you get back to the connector trail, turn left and cross the bridge. As you do, you might appreciate the sand-stone again for a different reason. Because the river bottom is sandstone, the water runs over it clear and bright. Crossing the bridge on a sunny day, the river fairly sparkles up at your shoes.

Across the bridge, the loop trail rises up a slight hill and splits. Veer left, following

The East Branch of the Black River runs clear and bright

the gravel trail clockwise. The path is level and wide, with enough twists and turns to hold the interest of hikers and beginning mountain bikers. The trail lies under the shade of sugar maple and American beech trees. If you look closely, you may spot a tall cucumber tree. Indian Hollow is thought to be the only place in Lorain County where this particular member of the magnolia family grows.

Midway through the loop, a connector trail heads straight into the town of Grafton. In fact, you'll have to make a sharp right turn at a park bench to avoid going into town. After the turn, you're heading due west. This section is especially lovely in the late afternoon, when the sun bounces off the river and bleeds through the trees.

After completing the loop and returning across the bridge, head off the path again, this time to the left (south). Follow this unmarked, well-worn dirt trail to a large, flat rock. Perched just a few

feet above the sparkling river, it seems custom-made for a picnic. Even if you're not packing a snack, stop, sit, and listen to the river rush by.

When you've heard enough, retrace your steps back to the paved connector trail; turn left, and follow it back to the parking lot.

NEARBY ACTIVITIES

Mountain bikes are allowed on the gravel trail. Bikers might choose to roll on into Grafton on the connector to pick up a snack or just check out the town. Or explore a great chapter in American history, in nearby Oberlin. In 1858, Oberlin earned the nickname "the town that started the Civil War." In addition to the town's rich history, the Oberlin College campus boasts beautiful gardens and landscaping, and a fine legacy of its own. You'll find Oberlin by taking Parsons Road west about 8 miles.

#30
Labyrinths, Colleges, and Coffee Shops

IN BRIEF

Walk through the grounds of a Jesuit university to reach the narrow, twisting path of a labyrinth, a 4,000-year-old tradition that could alter you perspective on hiking and life. Then walk through one of Cleveland's Western Reserve neighborhoods, catch a cup of coffee, and reflect on your journey.

DIRECTIONS

To reach John Carroll University, take the I-271/Cedar-Brainard exit and head west on Cedar to South Belvoir—or, if coming via I-480, exit at Warrensville Center Road and follow it north to Fairmount Circle. Turn right on Fairmount Boulevard, then left to reach the parking lot off South Belvoir. Ask the parking attendant for a map of campus.

DESCRIPTION

At first glance, a labyrinth looks like a maze. But more careful inspection finds no dead ends and no wrong turns. By simply following the labyrinth path, you will find the center, and then find your way out again. Like knitting, the motion is measured and repetitive. When walking a labyrinth, your only focus is on "centering."

Labyrinths date back to at least 2,500 B.C.—the circular designs appear on the walls of ancient caves and on early pottery. Labyrinths have been used

KEY AT-A-GLANCE INFORMATION

Length: 2.5 miles

Configuration: Two labyrinths and a loop

Difficulty: Easy

Scenery: Formal landscape, sculpture, and architecture on John Carroll campus and pretty neighboring streets

Exposure: Exposed

Traffic: Moderate

Trail surface: Labyrinths are brick and concrete; campus/city loop on sidewalk.

Hiking time: 55 minutes, more if you repeat the labyrinth

Facilities: Emergency phones on John Carroll campus, pay phone on Fairmont Circle

Season: Open year-round

Access: Daylight hours

Maps: Ask for campus map at South Belvoir parking lot.

Special comments: This is two hikes in one: a stroll through John Carroll University and a walk through the neighboring Western Reserve neighborhoods

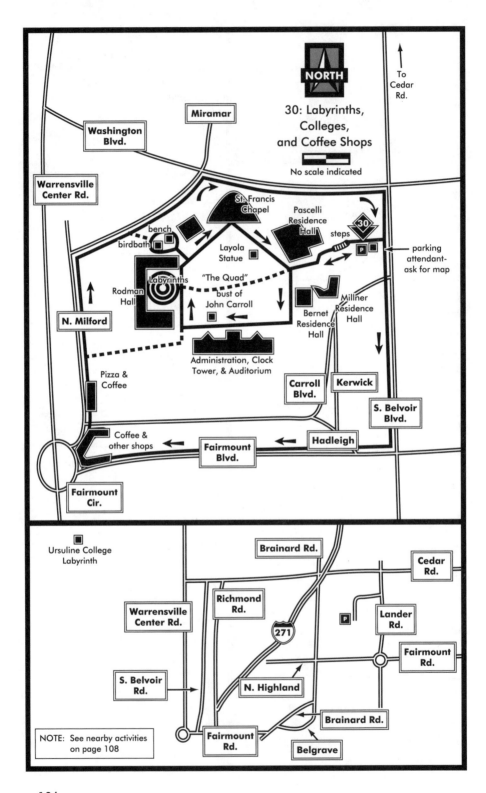

NORTH

↑
To Cedar Rd.

30: Labyrinths, Colleges, and Coffee Shops

No scale indicated

Miramar

Washington Blvd.

Warrensville Center Rd.

St. Francis Chapel

Pascelli Residence Hall

steps

30

P

parking attendant- ask for map

bench

birdbath

Layola Statue

Labyrinths

Rodman Hall

"The Quad"

bust of John Carroll

Millner Residence Hall

N. Milford

Bernet Residence Hall

Administration, Clock Tower, & Auditorium

Carroll Blvd.

Kerwick

Pizza & Coffee

S. Belvoir Blvd.

Coffee & other shops

Fairmount Blvd.

Hadleigh

Fairmount Cir.

Ursuline College Labyrinth

Brainard Rd.

Cedar Rd.

Warrensville Center Rd.

Richmond Rd.

271

Lander Rd.

P

Fairmount Rd.

S. Belvoir Rd.

N. Highland

Brainard Rd.

NOTE: See nearby activities on page 108

Fairmount Rd.

Belgrave

This sculpture of John Carroll was created in Cleveland by William McVey

for prayer and meditation throughout religious history, representing the spiritual process of going in, receiving, and going out into the world. Today, some hospitals incorporate labyrinths into physical therapy, especially for stroke and cancer survivors. You may approach the labyrinth as a pilgrim pursuing a goal, as a tourist searching for a new destination, or simply as a hiker on a new path.

These were my thoughts the first time I walked through—around—a labyrinth:

I smiled with excitement as soon as I stepped into the labyrinth: I was going on a journey! Then a plastic bag blew by. I wanted to snag it and throw it away, but I couldn't. I'd already entered the path; I was committed to finish it. Midway through, the lane I followed abutted the center. I smiled again, thinking I was "so close, and yet so far." I could have just stepped over the line—but then, I would have missed the trip. I reached the center about five minutes after I had

begun. I left by the same path (a labyrinth is not a loop)—even so, it felt like a different trip. At a barely-slow-enough-to-be-reflective pace, I exited about 10 minutes after I'd begun. Round trip: 0.4 miles.

Now that you've got the idea, try incorporating a labyrinth into your hike here on the John Carroll University campus.

John Carroll University was founded in 1886 as St. Ignatius College, a Jesuit school, on the western side of Cleveland. The college changed its name in 1923, honoring John Carroll, the first archbishop of the Catholic Church in the US. In 1935, the school moved to University Heights. Today, it is a busy campus, and you'll have some company on "the quad" almost any time of day.

To enter the quad and find the labyrinth, follow the sidewalk northwest from the parking lot. Pascelli Residence Hall will be on your right. The center lawn is beautifully landscaped. Turn left, still on the sidewalk. As you walk past Bernet Residence Hall, you'll have a nice view of the clock tower atop the Administration building and Kulus Auditorium. Turn right, walking by the red-brick building. On your right you'll soon see the larger-than-life bust of John Carroll. Ahead, you can see the red and slate-gray brick of the labyrinth. It is set in front of Rodman Hall, the school's business and human resources offices.

Go up the steps to Rodman, and step into the labyrinth. One of the peculiarities of labyrinth walking is that you must take small steps around tight corners. It helps to walk with your head down, focused on putting one foot in front of the other. In fact, looking ahead to estimate your distance from the center may make you dizzy. Whether the meditative quality of the exercise eludes you or inspires you; be assured that any hiker who appreciates a twisting trail will enjoy walking a labyrinth at least once.

Once you've been to the center and back, continue your trek left (north) on the sidewalk. Between Rodman and Dolan Hall, a bird feeder and several benches provide a place for you to watch the campus "wildlife" (birds *and* students). Follow the sidewalk's northeast slant to see St. Francis Chapel and a sculpture of St. Ignatius Loyola (who founded the Society of Jesus in 1540). The walkway leads you by Pascelli Hall. Turn left, heading back to the parking lot. So far, you've walked about 0.8 miles; you can end your hike here if you wish.

If the labyrinth left you focused on a longer walk, however, go see the neighborhood. And if the labyrinth left you focused on a cup of coffee or a snack, you're in luck—and on your way. Head south (right) on Belvoir Boulevard, following the sidewalk several blocks to Fairmount Boulevard. Fairmount is a true boulevard, with a tree-lined center aisle. Continue west, past pretty bungalows and prim lawns, to Warrensville Center Road and Fairmount Circle. The Heights area reflects its Western Reserve heritage in the names of buildings and streets, but street patterns are more reminiscent of modern-day Boston and other East Coast cities. Rotaries lined with hip shops and eateries generally confound drivers and delight pedestrians. Fairmount Circle is a fine example. Take your pick of the coffee, crumpets, and crusty pizza pies here.

Turn right again, following North Park and then turn left onto Milford Road, hiking north to Miramar. Several sidewalks along here allow you to cut across the campus green and/or return to the labyrinth. If you prefer to continue on city sidewalks, turn right again onto Washington Boulevard, and follow it back to Belvoir. Turn right, and right again, to return to the parking lot.

NEARBY ACTIVITIES

If you find you like labyrinth walking, good news: there's another nearby at the Ursuline College Campus. To get there from the I-271 Cedar/Brainard exit, take Cedar east to Lander Road. Turn right on Lander and go south about 0.2 miles. Ursuline College is on the west (right) side of Lander road. Follow the signs to the labyrinth and prayer garden, about 0.4 miles southwest of the entrance. The Nature Center at Shaker Lakes is also nearby; see p. 132 for directions and a description.

#31
Lakeshore Reservation

IN BRIEF

Hike in the company of various shore birds, and enjoy the work of Charles Irish, a Lake County arborist whose use of rhododendrons and other non-native plants are still visible today. Take in views of Lake Erie and visit a sculpture garden at this unique park.

DIRECTIONS

Take US 20 east to Antioch Road in Perry. Follow Antioch Road north about 1.5 miles to Lockwood Road, and turn right. Lakeshore Reservation entrance is about 0.2 miles east of Lockwood, on the north side of the road. Enter the park and turn right, until you reach the easternmost parking lot and the trailhead.

DESCRIPTION

Prior to becoming a park in 1968, Lakeshore Reservation was owned by a group of individuals who built summer cottages along Lake Erie. Arborist Charles Irish owned the largest of these properties. His work—placing ornamental trees among the native species and planting a large group of rhododendrons along the east boundary of the park—is still apparent. The property may have appealed to the park system because Irish had laid this "groundwork." However, the park was ultimately acquired because of its naturally stable beach condition and mature stand of trees— the largest such property along Lake Erie in the County.

KEY AT-A-GLANCE INFORMATION

Length: 1.5 miles

Configuration: Two loops

Difficulty: Easy

Scenery: Lake Erie's shore, variety of native and ornamental trees and shrubs, sculpture garden

Exposure: Mostly exposed

Traffic: Moderate

Trail surface: Asphalt, sand, dirt

Hiking time: 45 minutes

Season: Open all year

Access: Daylight to one-half hour past sunset

Maps: Available at the park trailhead and www.lakemetroparks.com

Facilities: Rest rooms, water, two picnic shelters with grills, small playground

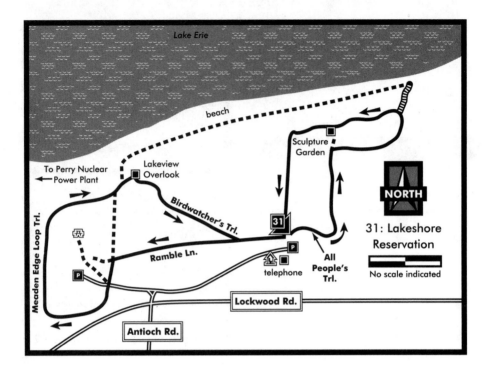

Adding to the park's natural beauty is an interesting sculpture garden. It was dedicated in 1978 and includes work by the nationally known Lake County sculptor Carl Floyd. Sculpture pieces here include a sundial and a cable bridge.

Begin your hike from the easternmost of the two parking areas. Take the All People's Trail as it heads northeast 0.2 miles to reach the Strock Sculpture Garden. As soon as you can see the sculptures, you'll want to go in and have a closer look. Continue hiking; you'll return here soon. Follow the path as it continues northeast a bit, looping north to reach a set of steep and shady steps that lead to Lake Erie's shore. You may follow the steps down to the sand, and walk west the length of the park—but for now, follow the trail back to the center of the sculpture garden and take in the unusual pieces. Wander through the

sculptures (worth the wait, aren't they?), heading west on the paved trail, which turns left, heading south back to the parking lot.

When you arrive at the intersection with Ramble Lane, you will have covered about 0.5 miles. Turn right to follow paved Ramble Lane. Along this section you will have a good picture of the property as it once was—a string of private residences, blissfully situated overlooking the lake. One private home remains here; it is clearly marked and landscaped to blend into the park and afford its residents as much privacy as possible. Please respect the boundaries here. Walk past the intersection with the Birdwatcher's Trail, continuing to head west.

Walk past a picnic area and rest room, then reach the intersection with Meadow Edge Loop Trail near the park's entrance. Turn left, following the still-paved trail as it ventures south, then loops to the right to pass by hemlocks and pretty ornamentals that clearly appeal to birds in the area. The trail straightens out, then once more curves to the right, moving into denser woods, before reaching another set of steps to the shore. The paving ends just past the steps, and the Birdwatcher's Trail begins. At this point, you will have hiked about 1 mile.

The Birdwatcher's trail is graceful, narrow, and grassy. Soon after you step onto it, you're invited to step off again, onto a wooden platform deck overlooking the lake. As the woods, water, and shore converge here, so do the jays, ducks, and gulls. A bench on the overlook invites you to watch and listen to them argue over food and territory.

From the Lakeview Overlook, step back onto the trail and turn left, heading east again. Follow the narrow, hard-packed dirt trail through young woods around the home in the middle of the park, where it merges with Ramble Lane and returns you to the parking lot.

If you didn't succumb to the temptation to walk along the beach before, consider it now. On your way to the beach, notice the tall, reed-like grasses that help hold down the sand here. When you reach the beach and look west, you can't help but notice the Perry Nuclear Power Plant. Of the 103 nuclear power plants in the US, two sit on the Lake Erie shore—Perry, here, and

Sculptures add interest along the trail

Davis-Besse, in Port Clinton. The giant stack you see here is an awesome, if strange, sight along the shore.

NEARBY ACTIVITIES

Perry, perhaps even more than other parts of Lake County, is dotted with nurseries and greenhouses. If you're looking for a specific tree or plant, or advice on growing almost anything, you're likely to find what you're looking for within a mile or two of Lakeshore Reservation.

#32
Lake View Cemetery and Little Italy

IN BRIEF

A cemetery is an unlikely tourist attraction, but Lake View's history and incredible beauty draw thousands each year. Lake View was designed after the garden cemeteries of Victorian England and France. Adding to its European appeal, it lies next to Little Italy, one of Cleveland's tastiest neighborhoods.

DIRECTIONS

From the eastern suburbs of Cleveland, follow Route 322 (Mayfield Road) past Kenilworth Road, and turn right into cemetery at Mayfield gate. From downtown, take East 55th exit off I-90. Follow East 55th south to Euclid Avenue; turn left and head east to gates at 12316 Euclid Avenue on the right. Once in the cemetery, drive to the Garfield Monument and park in front. This is where the hike begins.

DESCRIPTION

Hiking through a cemetery strikes some people as, well—as rather strange. But Lake View Cemetery encourages visitors —tourists, even. Lake View offers tours throughout the year featuring its architecture, geology, history, and horticulture. The grounds are stunning, and if you can shake off that funny feeling that you shouldn't "have fun" in a cemetery, you're in for a wonderful hike.

Established in 1869, Lake View is a Cleveland landmark. President James A.

KEY AT-A-GLANCE INFORMATION

Length: 3 miles

Configuration: Loop through cemetery, out-and-back to Little Italy

Difficulty: Easy

Scenery: Splendid horticulture and architecture, great views of downtown Cleveland and Lake Erie

Exposure: Half exposed

Traffic: Moderate

Trail surface: Dirt, grass, and stone steps through cemetery; city sidewalks in Little Italy

Hiking time: 1–3 hours, depending on interest and stamina

Season: Open all year

Access: Cemetery gates open from 7:30 a.m.–5:30 p.m. every day

Maps: Available at Euclid Avenue office and at the Mausoleum

Facilities: Rest rooms in the Cemetery office, Community Mausoleum, and the Garfield Monument

Special comments: A self-guided driving tour of the cemetery (on tape or CD) is available. Do not walk in areas where there will be a burial, and be respectful of families who are burying or mourning a loved one.

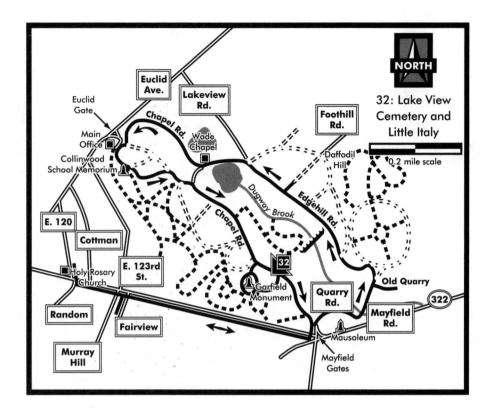

NORTH

32: Lake View Cemetery and Little Italy

0.2 mile scale

Euclid Ave.

Euclid Gate

Lakeview Rd.

Foothill Rd.

Chapel Rd.

Main Office

Wade Chapel

Collinwood School Memorium

Daffodil Hill

Dugway Brook

Edgehill Rd.

E. 120

Cottman

Chapel Rd.

Holy Rosary Church

E. 123rd St.

32

Random

Fairview

Garfield Monument

Quarry Rd.

Old Quarry

Mayfield Rd.

322

Murray Hill

Mausoleum

Mayfield Gates

Garfield and industrialist John D. Rockefeller are both buried here. A tour booklet available in the cemetery administration office identifies the gravesites of all of Lake View's "famous residents." This description highlights only a few of the famous folks buried here and offers a basic introduction to some of Lake View's treasures. When you visit, you will discover many more.

Begin at the Garfield Monument, built in 1890, where you'll enjoy views of Cleveland and the lake. On the north side of the impressive monument is a terra cotta plate showing Garfield in action, teaching geology and other sciences. A professor, Garfield also taught ancient languages at Hiram College. The monument is open from April–October; inside, there are 12 stained-glass windows and four window-like panels, representing the 13 original states, Ohio, and War and Peace. Garfield's statue stands in the middle of the monument; his crypt and his wife's are in the lower level.

From the Garfield Monument, head south on Garfield Road to the Mayfield Gates. Turn left onto Quarry Road. Along the way, you'll pass beautiful Japanese threadleaf maples on your left, and the Mayfield gate and new mausoleum on your right. After crossing little Dugway Brook, look for and follow an old dirt road to the right to have a look at the quarry. In operation from the 1870s through the 1940s, the quarry's contents were never wasted. Dust from the quarry was used as the base for many of the headstones placed here; the rocks taken from this quarry were used in the massive cemetery wall that stretches west from the Mayfield Gates to E. 123rd Street and were incorporated in many of the cemetery's buildings.

Return to Quarry Road and turn right. You'll soon reach a traffic island splitting the road. Follow the road left and walk toward section 30, where the Van Sweringen brothers are buried. The Van Sweringens built Cleveland's rapid transit system and Terminal Tower. You can cross Circle Road to visit their gravesite (no. 117), or continue bearing left to pick up Edgehill Road, passing section 35 on your right and the ravine on your left. You'll soon reach the dam, standing 60 feet high and 500 feet across. It can impound 80 million gallons of water. When it was built in 1978, it was the largest concrete-poured dam east of the Mississippi. That it only has to hold back mild-mannered Dugway Brook seems odd, but suffice to say the waters here are well under control.

Proceed northeast along Edgehill to Summit Road. Just after Summit, turn right into section 3 to find the monument of Jeptha Wade (no. 4), founder of Western Union Telegraph Company, and first president of the Lake View Cemetery Association. Just east of his monument is Daffodil Hill. Each spring, more than 100,000 daffodil blooms burst with color.

Return to Edgehill and head northwest until the road intersects Lake Road. Turn left and follow Lake Road as it passes between two scenic lakes. Just past the lakes, on the south side of Lake Road, is a memorial to Eliot Ness. After bringing down Al Capone in Chicago, Ness served as Cleveland's Safety Director from 1935–1942. He modernized the police department, developed an emergency medical system, and improved Cleveland's traffic fatality record from worst in the nation to twice winning the National Safety Council's award for greatest reduction of traffic deaths. When Ness died in 1957, he was cremated, and his ashes remained with his family for 40 years. In 1997, he was honored with a memorial service and this memorial stone. The grassy area by the lakes is graced with several pieces of sculpture, creating a good spot to sit and enjoy a drink and your surroundings.

When you're rested, continue on Lake Road, then turn right at the intersection to follow Chapel Road as it goes north. On your right is Wade Chapel. Stop to admire the windows, designed by Louis Comfort Tiffany. When the chapel is open, you can go in to appreciate the interior. Also on your right, in section 5-C, are the remains of Carl Burton Stokes, the first black mayor of a major US city and the first black Ohio State legislator.

Continue heading north on Chapel Road to the Euclid Gate. Cross Garfield Road, then follow Maple Road past the Lakeview Office. You'll reach Hatch Road, which bears to the right, but keep on Maple as it bears left and circles around section 26. Look for a road/path that leads right, and cut across section 25 to Garfield Road. In this section, you'll find the Collinwood School Fire memorial. When an elementary school in Collinwood caught fire in 1908, 174 students and 2 teachers died inside. The tragedy caused numerous school inspections nationwide, as well as stricter building codes. At Garfield Road, turn right (south). At the next intersection, turn left, then an immediate right to pick up Chapel Road. Follow Chapel south to section 10, where John D. Rockefeller, founder of Standard Oil Company, is laid to rest. Other notable people in this section include Harvey William Cushing, MD (no. 57), who pioneered brain surgery techniques, and John Hay (no. 73),

President Lincoln's personal secretary during the Civil War and Secretary of State to President McKinley. A granite angel, representing the archangel Michael, guards Hay's grave.

Heading back toward the Garfield Monument and to the Mayfield gates, you'll appreciate the intricate gardening work and incredible planning for which Lake View is known. In the late 1800s, many Italian stonecutters and gardeners migrated to Cleveland for employment at the cemetery. When you leave the cemetery through the Mayfield gate, turn right and walk west to the neighborhood they built.

Walking downhill on the north side of Mayfield Road, you'll appreciate the Cemetery's craftsmen who worked on the impressive wall of Berea sandstone that runs west toward Little Italy. You'll know you've arrived when you see signs for "ristorantes" like Primo Vino, Dino's, and Angelo's. Little Italy offers a wealth of Italian food and culture. Sample some of Presti's donuts or pizza, and then cross the street for a lemon ice at Corbo's Dolceria. To walk off a few of those calories, head up steep Murray Hill Road. Part of Murray Hill and Mayfield Roads are closed to car traffic during the Feast of the Assumption each August. The Feast—a weeklong, Italian-Catholic festival—is celebrated with masses at the church, and with games, music, and dancing. Like an Italian Mardi Gras, the party happens as much on the street as inside the neighborhood's shops and eateries.

Before you say "ciao" to Little Italy, stop at Holy Rosary Church, 12021 Mayfield Road. Built in 1895, the grand, red-brick building is the heart of the neighborhood and of the Feast. As you head back up the hill, east to the cemetery, you're likely to have a belly full of Italian food, and a new appreciation for Cleveland's history.

NEARBY ACTIVITIES

Lake View offers an almost constant schedule of tours and special events. Get a current listing online at www.lakeviewcemetery.com or call (216) 421-2665.

For more information about happenings in Cleveland's Little Italy, call the Mayfield District Council Little Italy Museum and Archives at (216) 231-8915 or the Murray Hill Area Arts Association, (216) 721-4100.

Special thanks to Mary Krohmer, Director of Community Relations at Lake View Cemetery Association, for reviewing this section.

#33
Longwood Park

IN BRIEF

Hidden behind ball fields, playgrounds, and picnic tables, Longwood Park's four "colorful" trails curl through the tall, thick woods in Macedonia's largest park. The soft paths are ideal for hikers and trail runners alike, and the nearby playground makes it a great destination for kids.

DIRECTIONS

From Cleveland, take I-271 south to Route 82 and turn left (east). The entrance to Longwood Park is about 1 mile east of the freeway exit, on the south side of Route 82.

DESCRIPTION

Much of Longwood Park's 292 acres is dedicated to sports—soccer, baseball, volleyball, and basketball. All have a place here. In fact, from the park's entrance, sport fields are about all you can see. A bit further down the entrance road, you'll find playgrounds and picnic tables, shelters, and grills, and finally, a stocked, 3-acre fishing pond. A tall, pretty fountain sits in the middle of the water, and many young fishermen practice patience, as well as casting, on the wooden pier. But those willing to take a 3-mile hike will discover some beautiful woods that the city of Macedonia has set aside. Because the individual trails are rather short and the park is full of

KEY AT-A-GLANCE INFORMATION

Length: 3 miles

Configuration: Four loops (can be combined or hiked separately)

Difficulty: Easy

Scenery: May see frogs, deer, and hawks in the oak-maple forest; wildflowers; small fishing lake with decorative fountain

Exposure: Mostly shaded

Traffic: Moderate

Trail surface: Dirt and mulch trail

Season: Open all year

Access: 7 a.m.–dusk

Maps: Available at the Macedonia Family Recreation Center, 1494 E. Aurora Road

Facilities: Rest rooms and water fountain by playground in Apple Grove picnic area

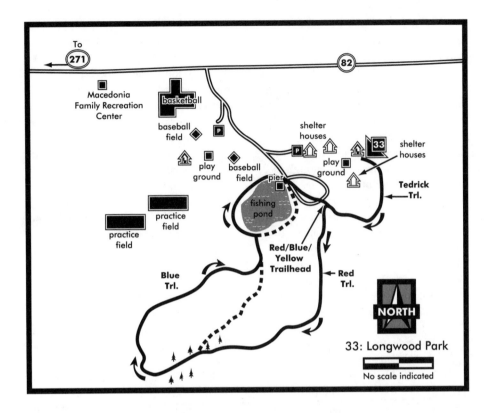

33: Longwood Park

No scale indicated

play equipment, Longwood is a great destination for families with kids. It's also nice for trail runners because the trails are soft, flat, and relatively free of obstructions.

Park in the Apple Grove picnic area lot, east of the lake. Start your hike north of the parking lot, on the trail that's not on the park map (the Tedrick Trail). It begins just east of shelterhouse no. 1; the trail is signed and marked with yellow circles.

Soon after you step onto the wide, dirt trail heading east, you'll find lots of double-trunked (bifurcated) trees here as on the other trails at Longwood. Ferns and picnic benches dot the way as the Tedrick Trail wanders under maple and oak trees, many 60 feet and taller. The 0.6-mile trail bends right, and the

semi-circle brings you back into the daylight and to the southeastern side of the Apple Grove parking lot. You can enter the other trails near here.

The three trails (on the map) are marked Yellow, Blue, and Red. The Red Trail starts here and heads south into the woods. Alone, it completes a 1-mile loop. It also merges with the slightly longer Blue Trail; we'll combine them here to do a longer, wider loop. The Yellow Trail makes a half-circle around the lake—you'll cover it last following this description. All three of these trails are well marked, with signs posted on trees and on posts at trail intersections.

Follow the wide dirt path south underneath tall maples and swamp white oak. In some spots, gravel has been placed to combat the mud. The trail offers plenty of benches, and you'll probably note deer tracks, if not a deer, along the way. About half a mile into this trail, you'll begin to venture west, winding through a stand of fragrant pines. Their needles are welcome on the trail, as they soak up some of the muck in this wet area.

A couple of drain culverts have been placed along the trail, but by and large, the land is unspoiled—wet enough to be home to a variety of mosses and encourage gill fungus to spring from the base of large trees. Swampy grasslands nearby host duckweed and about a billion frogs—give or take a million or so.

Another bench sits at the intersection of the Red and Blue trails. *If you follow the Red Trail north, you'll cross over a park access road, by cattails and weeping willows. The dirt trail gives way to grass soon after merging with the Blue Trail, south of the lake.*

Follow the Blue Trail as it heads generally west through the rest of the pine planting. You'll notice many of the pines are wrapped with poison ivy, others with similar-looking Virginia creeper (if you're not sure which is which, don't touch either one). The pines along here stand 30 to 40 feet tall. The path makes an S-curve to turn you in a northbound direction for the remainder of your trek.

Soon, the Red and Blue trails merge. Grass and moss vie for the opportunity to carpet the trail. (For now, the grass is winning.) Red and Blue continue to travel the same path for a short while, arriving together at the south end of the lake. Turn left onto the Yellow Trail. Along the south end of the lake, you may enjoy the orange blooms of jewelweed, also called touch-me-not. Its horn- or bell-shaped flowers bloom from summer through early fall. You may also look for the orange blooms of jack-in-the-pulpit here.

As you loop around the water's edge, you'll come to the fishing pier on the southeastern side of the lake. The area around the lake is exposed, making this about the only exposed portion of this hike. From the lake, return to the Apple Grove picnic area parking lot (east) to complete your hike.

Now that you've seen Longwood Park's less developed side, you might find its history especially interesting. Longwood sits on the former estate of Colonel William Frew Long, who donated the land for a city park. Ironically, Long aggressively sought industrial development for the city. During his terms as the city's mayor (from 1962–1975) Long said, "Industry is the sole creator of real wealth in any community."

Obviously, Macedonia has much business and industry today. And obviously, the community is also richer for Mayor Long's donation of this wooded property. The sport fields and picnic facilities are popular draws, while the woods and the trails remain relatively undeveloped, quiet, and lovely. Perhaps even Long would agree that "wealth" has various forms, not all of which are derived from industry.

NEARBY ACTIVITIES

Fishing is permitted at the lake (with a license) and cross-country skiing is allowed on the trails.

Macedonia lies just north of the 33,000 preserved acres of Cuyahoga Valley National Park (see hike descriptions of Blue Hen Falls, p. 36; Salt Run, p. 161; and Beaver Marsh, p. 27).

#34
Mason's Landing

Lake Rd.
20
2
91
84
90
Grand River
Vrooman
90
271
34

IN BRIEF

This short hike meanders along the banks of the State Wild and Scenic Grand River. The trail, wisely, lets the river be its guide.

DIRECTIONS

Take I-90 east from Cleveland and exit at Vrooman Road. Follow Vrooman north about 1.5 miles. Mason's Landing Park is located at 5000 Vrooman Road, just south of Route 84, on the western side of the road.

DESCRIPTION

From the parking lot, head west up a slight hill on a sandy dirt trail. The path snakes along the north bank of the river and offers shade and good bird-watching opportunities. Be sure to notice along the trail, and high above your head, the large bird boxes available to sleepy owls. The trail rises and falls and wiggles and bumps over several hills, each five to seven feet tall. Turn south to pass within a few feet of the riverbank, then turn north, running 20 feet or more into the woods. As a result of the trail's wending and winding, your perspective of the river changes almost constantly.

If you veer off the main trail, you can follow a fisherman's trail that runs much closer to the water. On a sunny day, you can expect to find a snake or two soaking up the ray's warmth along the sandy riverbank.

KEY AT-A-GLANCE INFORMATION

Length: 1 mile

Configuration: Out-and-back

Difficulty: Easy

Scenery: The river itself, and good bird-watching along the trail

Exposure: About half shaded

Traffic: Light

Trail surface: Dirt and sand

Hiking time: 35 minutes

Season: Open all year

Access: Daylight to one-half hour past sunset

Maps: Posted at the park and at www.lakemetroparks.com

Facilities: Rest rooms, small picnic area with grills, playground, and canoe launch

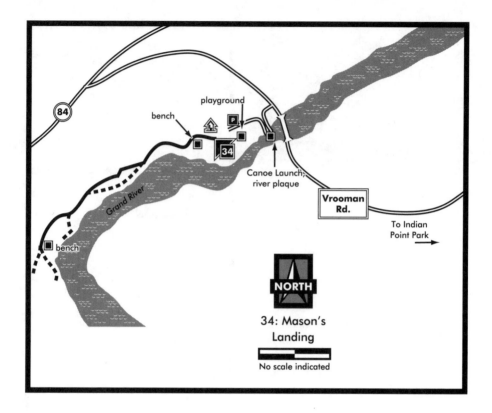

34: Mason's Landing

NORTH

No scale indicated

About 0.5 miles west of the starting point, a park bench waits for you. The "Rivers Edge Trail" ends just a few feet beyond the bench. From the bench, you can watch the river as it heads south, or look east to the bridge. In between, you're likely to see someone wading in, pole in hand, angling for one of the river's many residents. Fishing is allowed, and it is good here in the Grand River.

As you walk beside and contemplate the relatively calm waters of the Grand River, you might wonder what's "wild" about it—there certainly are no rapids here. In this case, "wild" refers to the Grand's inaccessibility (except by trail) and lack of development. Back in 1968, Ohio developed the Wild and Scenic River program, designed to protect the natural beauty of rivers like the Grand.

Since then, portions of ten other rivers have been designated scenic.

The Grand is one of two double designees (Little Beaver Creek is Ohio's other State Wild and Scenic River), due in part to it being home to more than 60 species of fish and at least 25 unique plant species. Bestowing the title in 1974, the state proclaimed, "The Grand River, with its rugged topography and limited human impacts, represents one of the finest examples of a natural stream to be found in Ohio."

As you make your way back along the bumpy path, tread lightly and enjoy deeply. When you return to the parking lot, walk down to the canoe launch on the northwestern side of the bridge. A plaque there relates the history of the Grand River and describes its

A peaceful stretch of the 102-mile-long Grand River

wandering, 102-mile path, which begins in Geauga County. It also explains that this river is more than its wild and scenic designations—the river and its watershed drain about 456,000 acres of northeast Ohio before emptying into Lake Erie.

NEARBY ACTIVITIES

If you have a canoe, bring it here—you can put in and paddle up the Grand River into Ashtabula County. If you prefer to stay on land, head south on Vrooman Road about 0.5 miles, where you'll find an entrance to Indian Point Park on the eastern side of Vrooman. Indian Point is also a Grand River Reservation, and it is listed on the National Register of Historic Places. The park features two earthworks built by some of Ohio's earliest people (between A.D. 900–A.D. 1650), and a totem pole carved by campers in the early 1900s.

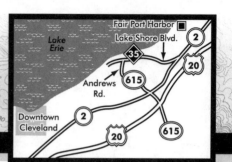

#35
Mentor Lagoons
Nature Preserve

IN BRIEF

This great preserve protects the largest unbroken bluff forest in northeast Ohio and one of the finest coastal dune communities in the state. Rare plants and more than 150 species of birds can be found here—along with some solitude.

DIRECTIONS

From Cleveland, follow Route 2 east to Route 615 exit; head north. Route 615 ends at Lake Shore Boulevard. Turn right onto Lake Shore and then left onto Harbor Drive. Trailhead parking is to the east of the docks and marina office. *Alternate directions:* I-90 east to Route 44. Go north to exit Route 283/Lake Shore Boulevard and turn left. Follow Lake Shore about 3 miles west to Harbor Drive.

DESCRIPTION

Purchased by the City of Mentor in 1998, the 450-acre Mentor Lagoons Nature Preserve protects one of the few riverine marshes still surviving along Lake Erie's shore. Even more land is preserved in the adjacent, 644-acre Mentor Marsh State Nature Preserve. While industry is critical to our livelihood, it is still important to protect what unspoiled land remains, even in bits and pieces like this. We are fortunate to have such beautiful land set aside for exploring.

Heading north from the trailhead parking lot, you'll step onto Marsh Rim

KEY AT-A-GLANCE INFORMATION

Length: 3-plus miles

Configuration: Three interconnecting loops

Difficulty: Easy

Scenery: Lake Erie shore, riverine marshes, woodlands, wildflowers

Exposure: Mostly exposed

Traffic: Moderate

Trail surface: All-purpose trail is hard-packed limestone; nature trails range from hard dirt to soft sand

Hiking time: 1.5 hours for all trails

Season: Open year-round

Access: Closes at dusk

Maps: At trailhead and online at www.cityofmentor.com/parks/lagoons.shtml

Facilities: Pay phone and portable rest rooms by marina office

Special comments: Swimming is prohibited here. Pets are permitted, on leash, on all trails except Marsh Rim and Lakefront Loop. Bikes are permitted on Woods Trail and Marina Overlook. Electric carts are available for those who have trouble walking; to arrange use of one, call (440) 205-3625 prior to your visit. Coast Guard Search & Rescue and other emergency numbers are posted at Marina.

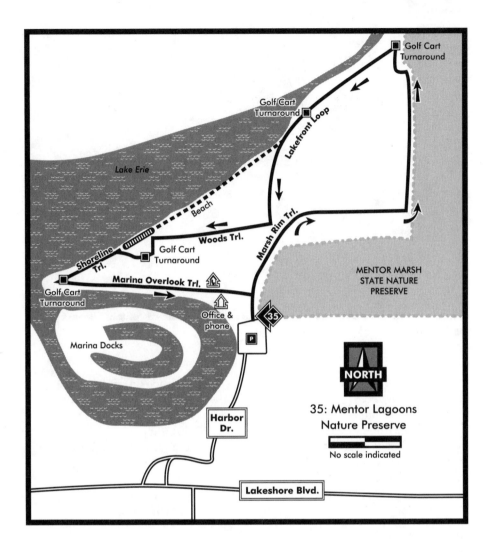

35: Mentor Lagoons Nature Preserve

No scale indicated

Trail. Follow the shady trail north about 0.5 miles. From there it heads east, skirting the border between this park and its neighbor, Mentor Marsh State Nature Preserve. In the summer, you'll hear the roar of outboard motors even here, in the deep of the woods. Tangles of grapevines offer atmosphere for you, and shelter for many small animals, along the trail. Animals and bikes are not permitted on this or the Lakefront Loop trail.

After traipsing about 1 mile through the woods, you'll emerge to find a bench perched high above the lake. You'll also find your feet on the limestone of Lakefront Loop. If you turn right, the trail continues northeast to a gated and a residential area immediately west of Mentor Marsh. Instead, head west/southwest for about a mile along this completely exposed section of Lakefront Loop, walking high enough above the water to enjoy a great view of wildflowers growing amid tall marsh grasses. This is a great place for bird-watching, and since you're not far from Lost Nation Airport,

Mentor Lagoons offers forest and lakeshore views

don't be surprised if a big bird (a small plane) buzzes by, too.

About 2 miles into your hike, you'll reach a cart turnaround. Here, by a rocky outcropping, a narrow unmarked path leads down to a very narrow beach, which is not much wider than a hiking boot. If you're willing to take the narrow path, walk down to the shore and follow along the beach for the next 0.5 miles. (Otherwise, you can continue along the Lakefront Loop, which eventually turns into the Woods Trail and intersects the Shoreline Loop.)

The shore of Lake Erie is interesting. You'll probably spot a working rig or two on the lake; when you look east you can see the east pier light near the Port of Cleveland. On the coarse sand, driftwood as smooth as a baby's skin rests among stones worn smooth and ringed with various pastel colors. Rather than the "sh-sssshh" of an ocean wave, these waves lap loudly, often with a bang and a

crash. Rough-looking, rocky outcroppings and ceaseless wind make the area seem especially wild; at times you can imagine that it is too big to be tamed. Unfortunately, you cannot forget you're surrounded by the "civilization" of a large industrial center, thanks to the eclectic collection of manufactured items also found here on the beach. The odd piece of debris mingles on the beach next to the driftwood and sea oats. Gulls perch on antique machine parts; castaway tires embedded in the sand hold back erosion. It's something of a compromise, this use and abuse of our unique landscape.

As you continue south and west along the shore, about 2.5 miles from your starting point, you'll see two sets of wooden stairs leading up to the Woods Trail on your left. True to its name, the trail is entirely shaded. If you're looking for a cooler, greener trail, head in. It will take you east, and back to the inland portion of Lakeshore Loop, in just about 0.6 miles. If you prefer to continue on the water's edge, you'll soon land on Shoreline Loop, which deposits you onto Marina Overlook Trail.

Marina Overlook is a mix of sand and dirt with a bit of gravel here and there. It takes you east, along the docks, under the shade of tall maples and oaks. The trail leads you up a short hill, and then flattens out into an S-curve, before returning past the marina office and back to the parking lot.

NEARBY ACTIVITIES

Consider taking a tour of Mentor Lagoons aboard a 26-foot BB64 Navy launch. The 45-minute ride is offered on weekends—under $5 for most riders. Call (440) 205-DOCK for schedule and more information.

While you're here, plan a visit to the Lagoon's next-door-neighbor, Mentor Marsh State Nature Preserve. Or you may want to visit Veterans Park, one of the smaller Lake Metroparks, located on Harbor Drive, south of Mentor Lagoons.

IN BRIEF

An easy riverside outing for hikers, especially good for beginning bikers, and wide enough to accommodate both, this trail takes you east from the falls to Kent and southwest to a pretty park in Cuyahoga Falls.

DIRECTIONS

From the eastern suburbs, take I-271 to State Route 8; from the west, take I-80 east to SR 8. Follow SR 8 south to Graham Road. Follow Graham east to Route 91; turn right. Park at Brust Park lot, 130 N. Main Street, immediately north of the Cuyahoga River.

DESCRIPTION

Start your hike at the gazebo north of the falls, where a plaque relates a brief history of the Ohio-Pennsylvania Canal and of the town of Munroe Falls. Head east from here along the paved path on the north side of the Cuyahoga River. Tall, mixed deciduous trees line the path, which generally follows a former railroad right-of-way. Because of that, the few hills along the way are gentle, making this a perfect place for beginning bike riders to get in a couple of practice miles while hikers plod alongside. Part of the Bike and Hike Trail of the MetroParks serving Summit County, this trail runs east to Old River Road in Kent. (*Note:* There are a few parking spaces at the Old River Road entrance—good news

KEY AT-A-GLANCE INFORMATION

Length: 4 or 8 miles

Configuration: Two out-and-backs

Difficulty: A long but easygoing trail

Scenery: Woodlands, marsh, falls, Cuyahoga River, and a fun, family water park

Exposure: Mostly exposed

Traffic: Moderate to heavy

Trail surface: Mostly paved; short stretches of limestone

Hiking time: 3 hours

Season: Open year-round

Access: Sunrise–sunset

Maps: See street atlas of Summit and Portage County

Facilities: Rest room, pay phone, water, and picnic shelters at Brust Park and at Waterworks Park; picnic shelter at Galt Park, assorted play equipment and ball fields along the way

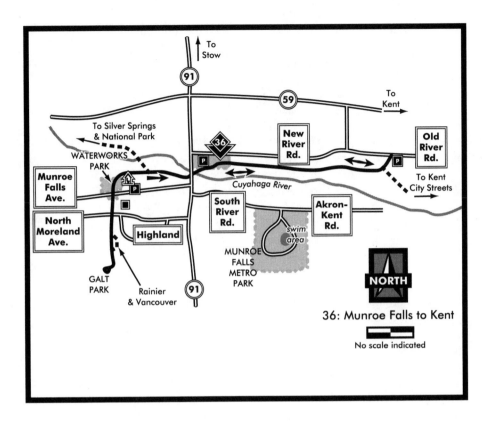

To Stow

91

59

To Kent

To Silver Springs & National Park

WATERWORKS PARK

36

New River Rd.

Old River Rd.

Munroe Falls Ave.

Cuyahoga River

To Kent City Streets

North Moreland Ave.

Highland

South River Rd.

swim area

Akron-Kent Rd.

GALT PARK

Rainier & Vancouver

91

MUNROE FALLS METRO PARK

NORTH

36: Munroe Falls to Kent

No scale indicated

for young cyclists who may need a lift at the turn-around point.)

Green and white signs mark the trail; anglers wade in the river below. Within a few feet of entering the trail you begin descending and, within the first mile, come upon one of several cart crossings cutting through the Pambi Farms golf course. This green space, carved along the Cuyahoga River, borders not only the golf course, but also residential property and even the backside of the Marsh Road water treatment facility.

Instead of bemoaning these "glitches" on the overall scenery, we should be glad that the trail exists, *especially* amid the development. And even when the view on one side of the trail is less than scenic, the other side makes up for it with mature shade trees, an almost con-stant view of the river, and fields of

skunk cabbage and other seasonal wild-flowers.

At the bottom of the trail's steepest incline (about 20 feet), you'll cross a small wooden footbridge; soon after, you'll come to the residential portion of the path. Here you'll reap the benefits of the neighborhood's landscaping, which caters to winged visitors. High above the yards, woodpeckers tap away on either side of the trail. As the path rises above the river again, you'll come to Sulky Lane. On the south side of the trail is a beautiful private residence and tree farm. About 0.5 miles east, you'll arrive at the trailhead on Old River Road in Kent. From here, the Stow-Kent Hike-Bike trail is well marked, with green and white signs leading riders throughout the city of Kent. Foot travelers, however, will want to turn around here.

Retrace your steps, returning to the Monroe Falls trailhead, and cross under Route 91 to continue west on the hike-bike trail. (*Note:* After heavy rains the underpass floods; it is usually signed during such conditions. When this occurs, simply cross Route 91 at the crosswalk at the Brust Park entrance.) Soon the trail splits. The trail to the right continues into Hudson and connects into the Cuyahoga Valley National Park. Turn left, heading south following signs for the Kelsey Bikeway and Galt Park. You'll cross a short bridge over a scenic spot in the river; this is a popular stretch for canoeing.

As you continue south, you'll pass assorted play equipment, ball fields, and picnic areas on your way through Waterworks Park. The park's main attraction is the Family Aquatics Center. An array of water slides, rides, and geysers loom out of the pool, situated just north of Munroe Falls Avenue. Cross the road and continue south on the trail, where you'll find several benches and well-maintained flowerbeds and ornamental trees between the trail and the little creek. About 0.3 miles south of here the trail again splits. The left path heads off behind a school, past ball fields, and into residential streets. Stay on the path to the right, instead, going south to Rainier Street. Rainier runs into Oneida, which ends at Galt Park, about 0.1 miles south. The small and shady park is owned by the City of Cuyahoga Falls.

If you've parked a rendezvous vehicle here, your hike is complete; if not, turn back to retrace your steps to Brust Park.

NEARBY ACTIVITIES

If you like to swim, visit Waterworks Park in Cuyahoga Falls (for hours and admission prices, call (330) 971-8299) or hit the beach at Monroe Falls Metro-Park, off South River Road. Monroe Falls MetroPark also offers volleyball and tennis courts, a sledding hill, and a 2.2-mile nature trail; (330) 867-5511 or www.neo.rr.com/metroparks.

#37
My Mountain Trail and More

IN BRIEF

These two, short, complementary hikes in Cleveland Metropark's Brecksville Reservation give visitors a good leg-stretching and several picture-perfect views. Prairie fields, a vernal pond, and a thinned forest on My Mountain give the budding naturalist plenty to think about.

DIRECTIONS

From I-77, take State Route 21 south to Route 82. Turn left, heading east on Route 82, and then turn right into the park entrance, onto Chippewa Creek Drive. Follow the parkway south to the Harriet Keeler memorial/overlook parking area, about 0.2 miles south of the park entrance.

DESCRIPTION

Start the first of two short hikes at the Harriet L. Keeler Memorial parking area on the south side of Chippewa Creek Drive. Follow the paved path a few yards west to the Keeler memorial. Keeler graduated from Oberlin College in 1870 and then moved to Cleveland. She was a suffragette, a Cleveland Public School teacher, and eventually became the system's Superintendent. Keeler was also a prolific nature writer.

From the memorial, you'll head south on a path of short grass, through a peaceful tall-grass prairie. The path gradually turns eastward, passing an intersection with the Valley Stream Trail.

KEY AT-A-GLANCE INFORMATION

Length: 2.25 miles

Configuration: Three loops plus spur

Difficulty: My Mountain is moderately difficult; the two Metropark loops are easy.

Scenery: Prairie with wildflowers, vernal pool, great views of Cuyahoga River

Exposure: Prairie is exposed; other trails are shaded.

Traffic: Short trails are well traveled; My Mountain Trail offers solitude.

Trail surface: Prairie loop is asphalt and grass; other two are loose dirt and gravel.

Hiking time: 1 hour

Season: Open all year

Access: Cleveland Metroparks Reservations are open 6 a.m.–11 p.m. except where otherwise posted.

Maps: Available inside nature center

Facilities: Rest rooms and water by the nature center, portable rest rooms at My Mountain trailhead

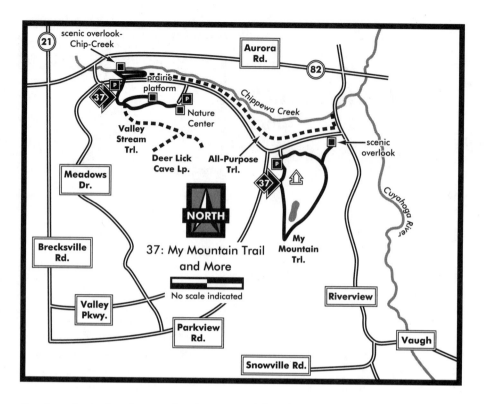

37: My Mountain Trail and More

No scale indicated

Continue forward, and soon after the mown grass trail meets asphalt, you'll find the nature center. (*Note:* Deer Lick Cave Loop leaves from the nature center; if you wish to extend your hike at this time, go inside for a map.) Walk around the nature center clockwise, past a small amphitheatre. As you leave the building, you'll notice the trees along this paved trail are labeled for easy identification. With a bit of studying, you can learn to tell your dawn redwoods from your black cherries. Further west, the trail leads to a raised prairie observation deck.

This prairie is managed so it won't become a forest. It is dominated by tall grasses and brightened by wildflowers most of the year. Foxglove and beardstongue bloom May through midsummer; pretty Shreve's iris blooms in June and July. Tall sunflowers stretch above the grasses from July through early fall, and goldenrod gilds the prairie from August through October.

Continue west on the paved trail (this is the north half of Valley Stream Trail) and you'll see the trees are not only labeled by name, but noted for their achievements as well. (*Note:* Pioneers made chewing gum from the sap of Sweet Gum trees.)

You'll have walked about 0.7 miles when you return to the Keeler Memorial. Now, follow the white trail markers and cross to the north side of Chippewa Creek Drive and down to Chippewa Creek overlook. The path turns right, then left again, sloping downhill. The path here is generally shady; during the fall, your feet noisily crunch over the oak leaves. You'll hear the creek before you see it; once it comes into view, you will follow its path. Eventually, you'll part ways—the creek ducks under Route 82 and out of sight.

Take a sharp left, heading back up the hill on a carpet of leaves and gravel. Follow the trail southwest, back to the all-purpose trail, then across Chippewa Creek Drive to your car. Next stop: My Mountain Trail.

(*Note:* The all-purpose trail runs along the eastern side of Chippewa Creek Drive to Valley Parkway and Plateau picnic area, a distance of 1.2 miles. You may drive or walk; the hiking distance as noted in the "In Brief" section does not include the connecting distance.)

From the Keeler Memorial parking area, follow Chippewa Creek Drive southeast, past the nature center entrance and Valley Parkway, to the Plateau picnic area. My Mountain Trail hugs the hill here, and it makes people who like hills very happy. From the picnic area parking lot, begin walking toward the shelter. About 100 yards in front of shelter, look up to spot orange trail markers nailed to the trees. The signs mark the beginning of My Mountain Trail.

Chippewa Creek Drive falls away to your right as you head up the steep path. You'll be glad you wore your boots here—the going is slippery and uneven due to roots and gravel. The narrow path follows the ridge of the hill (it's not really a mountain) until the roadway lies 40 feet below. Then the trail bends left, looking over the picnic shelter below.

This oak-hickory forest was thinned in 1996 to encourage wildflower growth. Things are pretty quiet up here, and you can imagine it is truly your mountain if you wish. The only sound you'll hear may be the squish of your boots as you near the vernal pool. Here, evidence of thinning is obvious, an aid to hikers to get a good look at the usually wet area. Formed like puddles in contained basin depressions, vernal pools have no permanent above-ground

outlets. They typically follow the water table—rising with winter and spring runoff, drying in summer, filling and freezing in fall and winter. Because they do dry out, they cannot support fish. But vernal pools do support other species, such as frogs, salamanders, and fairy shrimp, which lay eggs in the pools. Depending on the species, the eggs either hatch before the pool dries out, or they incubate throughout the wet-dry-freeze cycle, hatching the next year. While we may see only a puddle, it is an important one.

On the western side of the pool, about 0.3 miles into the trail, you'll make a sharp left and see the blue blazes of the Buckeye Trail. Soon, the trails split, and My Mountain Trail goes to the left, or west. Almost a mile into your jaunt, the trail offers you a spur—take it, if you're not afraid of heights. From the top end of this steep and narrow path, you'll have a bird's-eye view of Riverview Road and the Route 82 bridge.

Retrace your steps down, taking a sharp right to rejoin the loop and continue counter-clockwise. This last leg of the trail offers great wildflower displays in the spring. Your legs, perhaps tired of climbing, will welcome the downhill portion of the loop at about 1.4 miles. A short set of wooden steps leads to the bottom of the picnic area driveway. Turn left to return to the parking area.

If you're not ready to go, you may turn right and cross the parkway to follow the all-purpose trail over a pretty bridge and the Cuyahoga River.

NEARBY ACTIVITIES

Brecksville Reservation offers several other trails with nice hills—Deer Lick Cave Loop, for example, is about 4 miles long. Stop at the nature center, or call (330) 526-1012 for more information.

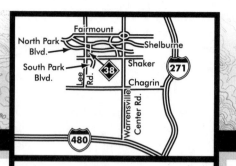

#38
Nature Center at Shaker Lakes

IN BRIEF

Located amid Shaker and Cleveland Heights, this preserved wildness was nearly wiped out in the 1960s by a proposed freeway. Now dirt trails and boardwalks lead visitors past the Nature Center, its wildflower garden, and around Ohio's oldest artificial lake.

DIRECTIONS

The best way to get here is on the Rapid. Take the Shaker Green Line to the South Park stop; walk north about 0.25 miles. The nature center is on the left, at the bottom of the hill, at 2600 South Park Boulevard. *From the south or east by car:* Exit I-271 at Chagrin Boulevard and head west. Turn right on Richmond, going north to Shaker; turn left. Turn right onto South Park Boulevard. *From the west:* Exit I-480 at Warrensville Center Road; go north to Shaker Boulevard (Warrensville turns to Richmond before you reach Shaker). Turn left; cross Lee Road; then turn right onto South Park. Either way, after going down a small hill, the road forks. Veer left; a sign and the driveway to the nature center will be on your left.

DESCRIPTION

In the late 1800s, Cleveland city dwellers escaped to the relative "country" of the city's eastern side Heights area. In the 1960s, it seemed like a good place to run a freeway connecting the city and the

KEY AT-A-GLANCE INFORMATION

Length: 2.5 miles with option to do shorter or longer loops

Configuration: Two loops, with a "sun ray" in the middle

Difficulty: Easy

Scenery: Birds, wetland/marsh/ lake views, wildflower garden

Exposure: Mixed sun and shade

Traffic: Rarely crowded

Trail surface: Wooden boardwalk, dirt trails, some asphalt

Hiking time: 1 hour, plus time for inside sight-seeing

Season: Open year-round

Access: Trails open dawn–dusk; nature center open Monday– Saturday, 10 a.m.–5 p.m., Sunday 1–5 p.m.

Maps: Inside nature center

Facilities: Rest rooms and water inside nature center, water also outside center

Special comments: Seasonal and self-guided tour booklets are available inside the nature center building. The trails here are for foot traffic only—no bikes, blades, or pets are permitted. Special events are offered year round, for all ages— visit www.shakerlakes.org or call (216) 321-5935.

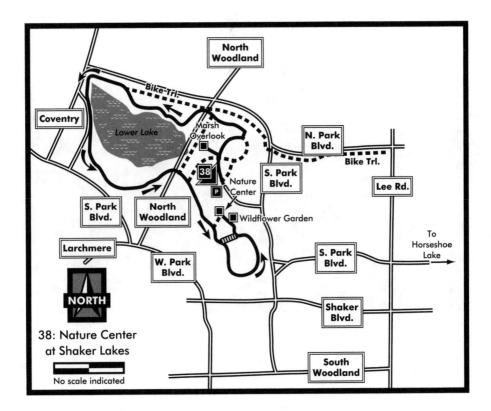

NORTH

38: Nature Center
at Shaker Lakes

No scale indicated

eastern suburbs. That is, it seemed like a good idea to people other than the Heights residents. They were so opposed, in fact, they hustled to establish a nature center, and effectively prevented the freeway's placement. Good thing, too—a few years later, the National Park Service named the center a National Environmental Education Landmark and a National Environmental Study Area. In short, coming here will probably make you smarter—and you'll have a good time, too.

Start exploring on the short "All People's Trail," a boardwalk that will show you marsh and stream habitats and a small waterfall. You'll also get an interesting perspective on the park—from several spots on the All People's Trail, you're surrounded by natural beauty and at the same time, you can hear the cars go by

on North Woodland Drive. That is the defining characteristic of this property: its preserved wildness is firmly entrenched in the densely populated, long-civilized cities of Shaker and Cleveland Heights.

From the north end of the parking lot, follow the All People's Trail north to a marsh overlook. Turn around and follow the trail clockwise. Looping around, you'll see a gate with a sign, "Trail to Lower Lake." Obviously, that's your exit. Go through the gate and follow the wooden steps down to the dirt path and follow it as it curves to the left, up a short hill, to cross North Woodland.

From the north side of Woodland, you can see most of Lower Lake. The bike trail splits off to the right; follow the stone steps down to a skinny dirt path along the lake. (If you aren't so

The view from the north end of Lower Lake

sure-footed, take the "high road," which in this case is the asphalt bike trail. It also offers lake views, but from a wider, flatter trail several yards to the north.) About 0.2 miles north of Woodland, the bike path and walking trail merge into each other for a time, then round the northwest edge of the lake.

At the northernmost end of the lake, you'll have your choice of crossings: over a pretty wrought-iron bridge, or via the smaller, older bridge just north of it. The older bridge, made mostly of wide, flat fieldstone, affords an interesting perspective on the lake as seen from under the wrought-iron bridge. Lower Lake is the oldest man-made lake in Ohio. It was formed from Doan Brook between 1826 and 1837. A few years later, Horseshoe Lake was formed, on the other end of the brook, to power the Shakers' mills. *Note:* After returning to the nature center, you may decide to walk down to Horseshoe Lake—see "nearby activities" section on p. 135.

As the path circles left and heads generally south, you'll parallel Coventry for a while before crossing Woodland again. On the south side of Woodland, and the eastern side of the nature center, the path is wider, part wood and part gravel; as you head south, the grand homes of South Park Boulevard are on your right.

Soon you'll be able to see Stearn's Trail, a series of boardwalks running alongside and over Doan Brook. Under the shade of beech and oak trees, at one point on the trail near the nature center building, you'll pick your feet up to step over a tree root and realize it joins two trees—one on either side of the trail. It begs some rather philosophical questions: Is this a root or a branch? Is this one tree or two? You may pick one of several park benches nearby from which to contemplate the answer . . . if there is one.

Where Stearn's Trail isn't boardwalk, it's hard-packed gravel. Looping and linking trails will take you back—when you're ready—to the nature center. Immediately south of the building, you'll find a small wildflower garden and some alarming news: some of these pretty flowers are actually dangerous!

Purple loosestrife (which can actually be rather pinkish in color), Japanese knotweed, and spotted knapweed have more than unusual names in common. All three are rather pretty pests. They are invasive plants that crowd out native flowers and vegetation, harming animal habitats, and increasing soil erosion in the process. See? You're getting smarter already. When you've learned all you can outside, go inside the nature center so the education, and your fun, may continue.

NEARBY ACTIVITIES:

Add 3 miles or more to your hike here by heading east from the nature center along either North Park or South Park Boulevard until you reach Horseshoe Lake. This is a popular trek for dog walkers. The bike path also runs along North Park Boulevard.

Many thanks to Stephanie Thomas, naturalist at the Nature Center at Shaker Lakes, for reviewing this hike description.

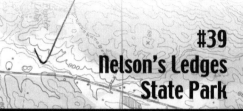

#39
Nelson's Ledges
State Park

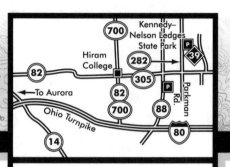

IN BRIEF

Nelson's Ledges offers what may be the wildest 2-mile walk in the eastern United States. Don't let the short distance fool you; you could easily spend several hours here. Dramatic ledges and tight crevasses team up with a waterfall and several small caves, creating dramatic beauty. Bring a flashlight to peer into some of the narrower passages in this small, surprising state park.

DIRECTIONS

From Cleveland, take I-480 east to Route 422. Follow Route 422 east (toward Solon) to Route 700. Turn right on route 700 and continue south for about 5 miles into Hiram. Turn left onto Route 305 and go east about 3 miles to State Route 282 (Garrettsville Road). Turn left. The park entrance is about 1 mile north of Route 305. Parking is on the eastern side of the road; the trails are on the western side of Route 282.

DESCRIPTION

With names like "Devil's Hole" and "Fat Man's Peril," these trails sound a little scary. Dire warnings posted on park bulletin boards don't offer any warm fuzzies, either. The park service strongly (and effectively) discourages horseplay here by posting recent accident information at the trailhead. In less than two years, life-flight rescue was called to the park three times, and there was one

KEY AT-A-GLANCE INFORMATION

Length: 2 miles

Configuration: Three connecting loops

Difficulty: Difficult

Scenery: 60-foot cliffs, creek, caves, crevasses, and a tall, skinny waterfall

Exposure: Mostly shaded

Traffic: Moderately heavy, year-round

Trail surface: Rock surfaces, dirt, peat

Hiking time: 2 hours

Season: Do not attempt when icy conditions exist.

Access: Park closes at sunset; cars in the lot 30 minutes after sunset are subject to towing.

Maps: Online at www.dnr. state.oh. us/parks/parkmaps/ nelonkennedy.gif

Facilities: Rest rooms at parking lot, picnic tables on both sides of Route 282

Special comments: Pets are allowed on leashes; however, I don't recommend bringing them here. Nor is this a good spot for young children. If your kids are longing for a rocky hike, start with the Gorge Trail (see p. 75) and work your way up to this one.

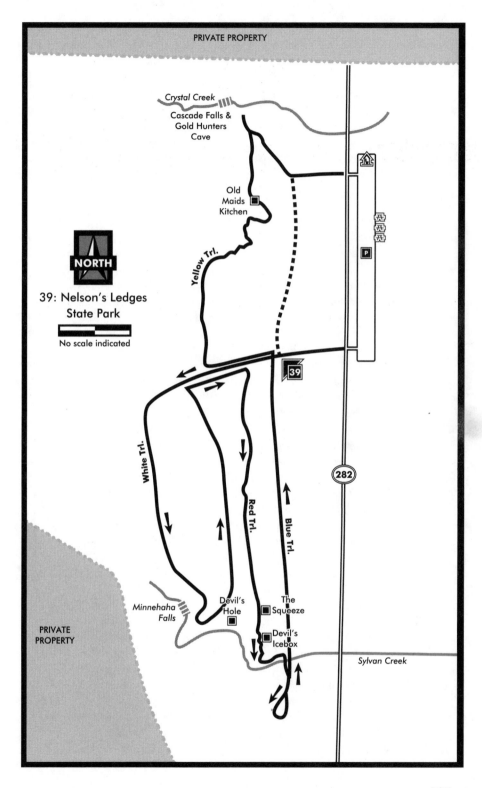

PRIVATE PROPERTY

Crystal Creek

Cascade Falls &
Gold Hunters
Cave

Old
Maids
Kitchen

NORTH

39: Nelson's Ledges
State Park

No scale indicated

Yellow Trl.

39

White Trl.

Red Trl.

Blue Trl.

282

Minnehaha
Falls

Devil's
Hole

The
Squeeze

Devil's
Icebox

PRIVATE
PROPERTY

Sylvan Creek

fatality due to falls. In short, the rock formations that give this park its amazing beauty also make it dangerous. If you heed the posted warnings and proceed with respect and caution, you will certainly enjoy the cliffs, caves and crooked trails here on this little plot of land in Portage County.

Four trails run through the park; their combined length is about 2 miles. While the park's direction is "Hike Only on the Marked Trails," you may be hard-pressed to do so. The trails dart in and out of huge rock formations, and it's easy to lose the trail. Study the map and take care in your exploration—a fall from the tall rock formations here will result in life-threatening injuries or death. With these warnings duly noted, start with the "easy" White Trail.

Head west a few strides from the trailhead sign, passing the Blue, Red, then Yellow Trail, before turning left (south) onto the White Trail. Even though the White Trail is rated the easiest to walk, part of it follows along the top ridge of 65-foot cliffs—highlighting the need to use caution on all of the trails, regardless of their ratings.

The White Trail gives you a good overview of the south end of the park and a glimpse of what to expect on the trails below. About 0.4 miles south, the path loops to the left (east) where you'll see the trickle of Minnehaha Falls tumbling into Sylvan Creek below. A chain-link fence here marks the southern boundary of the park. Follow the trail as it loops back to its beginnings, and turn right, going downhill a few steps to find the Red Trail.

You'll enter the red trail through a "tunnel" of 20- to 25-foot tall boulders. The Red Trail is rated "difficult." No kidding. It leads through a 20-foot-long corridor that will not accommodate

much larger than a size 44 belt. If you make it through there, two more tricky maneuvers await: "The Squeeze" and "Devil's Icebox."

Once through Devil's Icebox (where you and an assortment of moss and ferns emerge by Sylvan Creek) you'll find a short set of steps leading down to the Blue Trail. At the bottom of the steps, turn right, heading south among some relatively small rocks (still taller than you) and loop around to head north, back to the trailhead. While the Blue Trail is rated "moderate," it has much in common with the Red Trail: both give you a squeeze, challenge your knees, and cause you to wonder at the trees, with their roots hanging onto the rocks for dear life. The blue line on the park map is a straight line, but don't be fooled. The actual trail wiggles through the woods and rolls over lots of small rocky bumps —all the way, however, it is well marked.

When the Blue Trail returns you to the trailhead sign, turn left and head uphill again. This time you'll pass the Red Trail. Beyond it, turn right to follow the Yellow Trail (also rated "moderate"). Yellow metal signs point you north; you'll also find yellow markers painted on rocks and trees. Even with these clues, you'll find it's easy to lose the trail.

Like the White Trail, yellow leads you along the top edge of the cliffs. From there it takes you downhill fast, first on a dirt path, then down makeshift stone steps. It bottoms out, cools off, and lurches to the right. (*Note:* If you miss this turn and follow what looks like an obvious trail straight ahead, you'll find yourself bent up like Santa through a chimney flue, wiggling upward, then finally walking upright—to the top of Cascade Falls. This unofficial side trip is all of 0.2 miles long. While it seems no more dangerous than the top of the

White Trail on the opposite end of the park, you're still off-trail. If you accidentally find yourself at this unofficial point, the good news is that you can see the legitimate trail below. Embarrassed but enriched by the view, you may return the way you came.)

The Yellow Trail heads into a closet of sorts, created by two massive boulders. Moving north from there, you'll jog left then right again, to pad along a sturdy wooden bridge into Old Maid's Kitchen. The "kitchen" is about as big as a New York City loft apartment. When you exit the dark and drafty "kitchen," it's nice to see the sky again! You can also see the parking lot across the road—but don't leave yet. Follow the trail abruptly west, turning left and heading along a wooden boardwalk to the bottom of Cascade Falls. The small stream that tumbles over a 40-foot drop eventually makes its way to the St. Lawrence River. (This park sits on a watershed divide. This stream, and water north of here, runs into the St. Lawrence River; Sylvan Creek, on the park's south side, runs to the Mississippi.)

On the bottom of the falls, you can peer into Gold Hunter's Cave. Although the cave is not open to explorers, you can see inside from the wooden platform at the bottom of the falls. Retrace your steps back to the trailhead, or just cross Route 282 to the east to return to the the parking lot.

NEARBY ACTIVITIES
You probably passed through Hiram to get here. Why not visit the the Field Station on your way back? See p. 92 for a description.

#40
Oxbow Trail

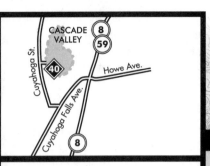

IN BRIEF

Oxbow Trail winds through the Cuya-hoga River Valley, north of Akron. From the burbling rapids of the Cuyahoga River to a cardiac-climb to a fabulous vista, this hike offers variety over a short haul. Though a steep sledding hill and several ball fields are nearby, hikers can get away from the "action" in the center of the park to enjoy this remote wooded trail and the great views of the surrounding valley that it offers.

DIRECTIONS

The Cascade Valley Metro Parks Chuck-ery/Oxbow Area is located off Cuyahoga Street, between Uhler Avenue and Sackett Avenue, in North Akron. From Cleveland, take State Route 8 south. Exit at Howe Avenue, going west approximately 0.1 miles to Cuyahoga Falls Avenue. Turn left. Follow Cuyahoga Falls Avenue about 2.5 miles to Cuyahoga Street; turn right. Follow Cuyahoga Street north about 1 mile; the park sign will be on your right.

DESCRIPTION

If Oxbow Trail were a book—well, it would be a novella—you'd describe it to your friends by saying, "It started a bit slow, but before I was halfway through, I hoped it wouldn't end." In fact, it ends—too soon—by the sledding hill and parking lot where you came in. In spite of its shortness, it's a trail worth picking up.

KEY AT-A-GLANCE INFORMATION

Length: 1.2 miles; "high water detour," about 1 mile

Configuration: Loop

Difficulty: Easy, but all the climbing comes at once; not for weak knees or flatland lovers

Scenery: Average scenery, and nice sound effects, thanks to the rumbling rapids of the Cuyahoga River

Exposure: Shady throughout, except for the steps, which are exposed

Traffic: Moderate most days, busier on snowy weekend afternoons

Trail surface: Dirt trail is carpeted with several seasons' leaves; the first leg of the trail can be very muddy, as it follows along the river; the wooden footbridge can be slippery when wet.

Hiking time: 30 minutes

Season: Open year-round from 7 a.m.–11 p.m.

Access: No fees; dogs allowed on leash

Maps: Available from Metro Parks serving Summit County www.neo.rr.com/metroparks

Facilities: Rest rooms and drinking fountains; a snack concession is open during league ball games.

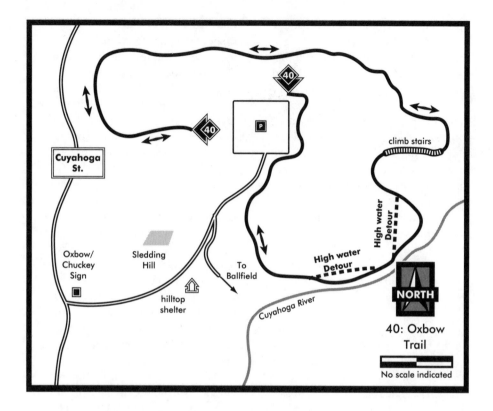

40: Oxbow Trail

No scale indicated

Over a relatively short haul, Oxbow boasts several picnic tables, and they're placed to provide comfortable space between diners. It's entirely possible to enjoy a picnic supper here, with the lilting of the Cuyahoga to entertain you, and never catch wind of the dinner conversation at another table.

Because the trail is somewhat damp, and well shaded, it's advisable to apply some bug repellent when visiting Oxbow during mosquito or fly season. You're likely to hear, if not see, woodpeckers at work on some of the 60-foot tall (and taller) trees along the way. Mostly deciduous varieties—tall oaks and black cherries—shade the trail.

The trailhead marker sends you off toward the east. From there you'll meander through several marshy turns (in dry weather) or large puddles (in wetter

times). In the spring and summer months, you'll be met by white trillium (Ohio's official state wildflower) and a variety of violets that like the wet ground along the river.

About 0.2 miles into the trail, the path turns sharply left, heading north, and meets up with the Cuyahoga River. Soon, you'll hear several rapids providing a musical accompaniment to the sound of your feet on the dirt and leaves. Approach very quietly and you may see great blue or green-backed herons fishing for dinner here.

About 0.3 miles into the trail, you'll pass a picnic table and come to the first "high water detour," where arrows posted by the Metro Parks direct you to the left, away from the river. The trail remains flat and almost entirely shaded until you come to a railroad-tie staircase, climbing

up a set of 80 steps. This is a rise of nearly 100 feet, and you're about mid-way
through this short hike, so pause at the
top of the steps, take a deep breath, and
turn around. The view is worth it.

You'll take several smaller stairways
down the hill and encounter a small
footbridge that may be slippery when
snowy or wet. You'll also find a few
more picnic tables here, set off the trail a
bit—the perfect spot for those who need
nourishment after the climb.

As you descend, the sledding hill
comes into view. Thanks to the lay of
the land, you'll be able to keep an eye on
the sledding hill—and your car in the
parking lot—during most of the final
third of the loop.

When there's no snow and no ball
game, you won't have much company
on the trail. Almost the entire park is
viewable from the Hilltop Shelter, which
is available for free on a first-come, first-
served basis. The shelter, which holds
about 40 people, also can be reserved for
a fee by calling (330) 687-5511.

The trail is patrolled by Summit
County Metro Parks Rangers, who are
dispatched from the Summit County
Sheriff's Office. To report problems at the
park or on the trail, call (330) 657-2131.

NEARBY ACTIVITIES

Oxbow is a popular winter spot thanks
to its traditional sledding hill and in-
ground toboggan runs that the park
service floods for icy fun. The hill is
lighted for night use. Cross-country skiing is permitted on the trail. The park
service maintains a 24-hour seasonal
information telephone line at (330)
865-8060.

Oxbow's greatest value may be in the
diversion it provides for folks who visit
Cascade Valley for a ball game, who also
want to get in a short hike or conversation away from the action on the field.
Spring, summer, and fall, the park's ball
fields—three softball and two soccer—
host league play. The City of Akron's
Recreational Bureau coordinates game
schedules; when the fields are not in
league play they are open for use by park
visitors.

Oxbow Trail is less than 5 miles
(about a 10-minute drive) from the
hustle and bustle of the Chapel Hill
Mall and shopping area. Closer still,
you'll find other hikes waiting at Gorge
Metro Park about 1 mile south of here
(see p. 75), and at Babb Run Bird and
Wildlife Sanctuary, about 2 miles to the
north (see p. 19).

#41
Peninsula and
Quarry Trail

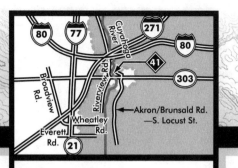

IN BRIEF

Peninsula displays the well-preserved vestiges of a canal-era town and a railroad town, while serving as a portal into the Cuyahoga Valley National Park. Some folks say Peninsula has a lock on history. Actually, it has two—and hikers will see them both on this hike.

DIRECTIONS

From Cleveland, take I-77 south to Route 21. Continue south to Route 303 and turn left, heading east about 5 miles. To reach parking at Lock 29 Trailhead, turn left onto North Locust Street after crossing the river, then left again on Mill Street and into lot. (A sign directs you to "Lock 29 Trailhead Parking.")

DESCRIPTION

Change streamed through Peninsula in the form of a canal in the 1840s and rolled through again in the 1880s when the railroad came to town. And the changes kept coming, with the dedication of the Cuyahoga Valley National Recreation Area (now National Park) in 1975. When the federal government comes to town to claim more than 30,000 acres, "change" is putting it mildly.

While other towns might buckle under the strain of being a gateway to a National park, Peninsula thrives. The town is well suited to serve as a portal back in time; in some ways, Peninsula even serves as an extension of the park. Lock 29 along the Ohio and Erie Towpath Trail

KEY AT-A-GLANCE INFORMATION

Length: 2.5 miles

Configuration: Loop and a cross

Difficulty: Moderate (city portion is easy; Quarry Trail is somewhat challenging)

Scenery: Two canal locks, sandstone quarry, historic architecture, and wildlife along the river

Exposure: Trail is shady; sidewalks are exposed

Traffic: Typically heavy in town and light on Quarry Trail

Trail surface: Mixed: asphalt, sand, dirt

Hiking time: 1 hour

Season: Open year-round

Access: Towpath and Quarry Trail open daylight–10 p.m.

Maps: Peninsula architectural tour guide available at Peninsula Library & Historical Society, 6105 Riverview Road

Facilities: Rest rooms, water, and pop machine at Lock 29 parking lot

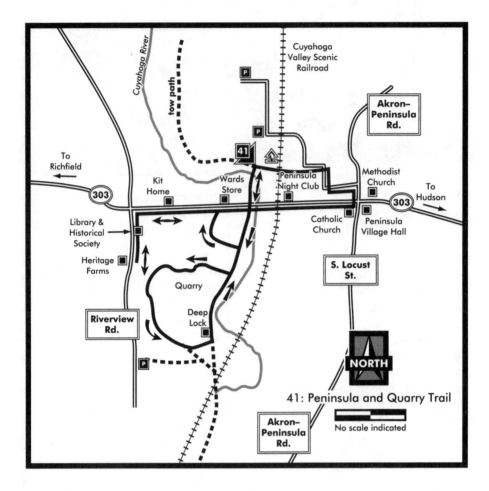

literally deposits through–hikers and bikers into the heart of Peninsula. The local bike shop is an icon to regular towpath riders and a welcome beacon to folks with flats. Peninsula's restaurants are so popular with train riders that the Cuyahoga Valley Scenic Railroad (CVSRR) features a layover lunch stop here.

Start your tour at the trailhead sign and map at Lock 29. Take the steps up to the bridge that literally and figuratively connects the relatively new towpath trail and National Park to the historic town of Peninsula. An interpretive sign on the bridge highlights the building of the Ohio & Erie Canal. When construction began in 1825, workers had to devise it

so that boats could negotiate the 395-foot elevation difference between Akron and Cleveland. Locks 29 and 28 were key to "leveling" the ride, and the canal was key to Ohio's economy.

Go below the bridge and walk into the now earth-filled lock. The mason's marks on some of the blocks are still visible, indicating the quarry and the work group from which the stone came.

Once over the bridge, continue south on the towpath and under Route 303, where the paved path gives way to crushed limestone. The river runs on your left; beyond it, the railroad tracks carry passengers on the Cuyahoga Valley Scenic line north into the park, and

The oldest store in town is one of many historic buildings along Main Street

south into Akron. About 0.5 miles into the trail, a sign points to Deep Lock Quarry; follow this sign as it sends you off the towpath and west. Cross a narrow, wooden footbridge, then head up a steep hill; the bench at the top will be a welcome sight after the climb. Follow the dirt path under tall pines and right over the rocky but now level ground. You'll reach the quarry shortly.

Sandstone dug here helped build many local homes and businesses, as well as several locks along the canal. Today, trees cover the quarry's floor, but the sheer stone walls leave no doubt where you are.

The adventurous may climb into the quarry, but all should take care near the edges as gravel and sand make for slippery footing here. The trail skirts the eastern side of the quarry and heads south. As you go downhill, you'll see Summit County Metroparks trail markers (in yellow), pointing west to the Quarry Trail parking lot, off of Riverview Road. Instead of following

them, stay on the trail heading south and east to return to the towpath.

Turn left on the towpath to find Lock 28, also known as Deep Lock. As its name suggests, it is the deepest lock on the canal. While a typical lock would move a boat up or down 8 or 9 feet, Deep Lock could raise and lower boats 17 feet. For its hard work, Deep Lock was awarded an historical civil engineers landmark plaque, displayed inside the lock.

Continue north on the towpath back to Peninsula. The calls of geese and other birds blend with the bubbling of the river, now on your right. Although you're heading to the city portion of your hike, don't despair—there's still much to see. The Peninsula Business District itself is listed on the National Register of Historic Places, as are many individual buildings in town. At towpath trail marker no. 24, turn left and follow the asphalt path marked "to Peninsula/ Buckeye Trail." At the top of the hill you'll find yourself on the south side of

Route 303. Look across the street at 1663 Main. Built in 1820, it was the oldest store in Peninsula. Like many homes here, it is a good example of the Western Reserve Greek Revival–style.

Turn left, heading west toward Riverview Road. As you go, notice 1749 Main Street. Perhaps the biggest "bargain" on the block, this "Vallonia" model Sears and Roebuck kit home sold for $2,076 in 1926. Its steep roof and white columns have been maintained so carefully you might say it looks brand-new, or "fresh out of the box." It's estimated that about 100,000 kit homes were built in the US between 1908 and 1940. Most models came entirely as pre-cut and numbered pieces of lumber. The homes were inexpensive but not inferior, and were efficient to build, too. The Sears catalog boasted that a kit home could be built in about 60% of the time required to build a traditional home.

Continue west and uphill about a block, following signs to the library. Before you reach the corner of Riverview Road, you'll see the Boston Township Hall and its distinctive bell tower at 1775 Main. Built as a school in 1887, today it houses Boston Township offices, community meeting rooms, and the Cuyahoga Valley Historical Museum. Turn left onto Riverview, and the Peninsula Library and Historical Society will be on your left. Stop in for an architectural tour guide, or to learn more about the area. Across the street, south and west of the library, is Heritage Farms. Operated by the same family since 1848, Heritage Farms holds seasonal events and has a lovely herb garden. Walk through the garden (or pick out your Christmas tree!) before turning around to return to Route 303.

As you walk east, retracing your steps, consider the girth of the maples that line the yards along Route 303. Most of them were planted at or about the time of construction—making these "granddaddy" trees several times over. Walking across the bridge and the railroad tracks, you'll pass a variety of antique shops, cafés, and galleries. The sign for the Old Peninsula Night Club hanging at 1615 Main has been around for many years; the building was a nightclub and a dance hall in the 1930s and 40s. Today, the restaurant is the Winking Lizard, but the owners still display the cool antique sign along with their own in the window.

About a block east of the Lizard, turn right and walk one block south on Akron-Peninsula Road to Our Lady of Sorrows Catholic Church. Originally built in 1882, the church was enlarged in 1935 in a rather clever way. The building was literally cut in half, the west end was moved back, and the middle "filled in" to enlarge the sanctuary. Now turn around and go north on Akron-Peninsula Road. The street name changes to Locust, and you'll pass the Peninsula Village Hall, constructed with sandstone from the local quarry in 1851. Cost to the taxpayers? About $600. It's still used to house village services—talk about getting your money's worth!

Speaking of money, that concludes your "nickel tour" of Peninsula. You can cross Main Street, head north on Locust to Mill Street, and follow it west to return to the parking lot at Lock 29. Or continue to explore . . . there's plenty here to pique your interest.

NEARBY ACTIVITIES

Peninsula's seasonal art walks are fun and friendly. Find out more at www.explore peninsula.com. To explore the National Park from here, you can leave town on foot or on bike, either north or south, on the towpath. Prefer to take the train? Get schedules and ticket information at (800) 468-4070 or www.cvsrr.org.

#42
Plateau Trail

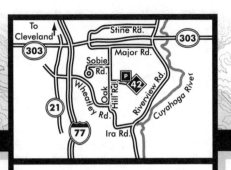

IN BRIEF

While exploring this section of Cuyahoga Valley National Park, you'll encounter a series of S-curves that wiggle through the woods, following a ravine. There's a lovely change of scenery at almost every turn on this loop trail. Be ready—some of these scenes sneak up on you as you round a turn and appear suddenly, breathtakingly beautiful.

DIRECTIONS

From I-77, exit at Wheatley Road and head east to Oak Hill Road. Turn left, going north about 2 miles. The entrance to Oak Hill Picnic area is on your right. (Eastsiders will probably take State Route 8 south to Route 303, then head west to Riverview Road and follow Riverview south approximately 1 mile to Major Road. Turn right, following Major Road west 1.5 miles; then turn left onto Oak Hill Road. The entrance to Oak Hill Picnic Area (and the trails) is on the eastern side of Oak Hill Road. Turn left and follow the driveway 0.2 miles east to the parking lot.

DESCRIPTION

Enter the trailhead at the eastern end of the Oak Hill parking lot. A trail map is posted there on a park bulletin board. Both the shorter Oak Hill Trail and the outer loop of Plateau Trail begins to the left, or north, of the sign. A few grassy steps and a short wooden bridge later

KEY AT-A-GLANCE INFORMATION

Length: 5 miles

Configuration: Loop

Difficulty: Moderate

Scenery: Pine and deciduous forests, two (or three) ponds, lush hemlock ravine

Exposure: Mostly shaded

Traffic: Light

Trail surface: Dirt, with short stretches of grass and gravel

Hiking time: 2 hours

Season: Open year-round

Access: 7 a.m.–10 p.m.

Maps: Ask for the Oak Hill Area map, available at most visitors' centers in the National Park.

Facilities: Portable rest rooms at trailhead

Special comments: Two restricted trails, one on either side of Meadowedge Pond, are clearly signed. They lead to the Cuyahoga Valley Environmental Education Center (CVEEC) and are authorized for CVEEC use only.

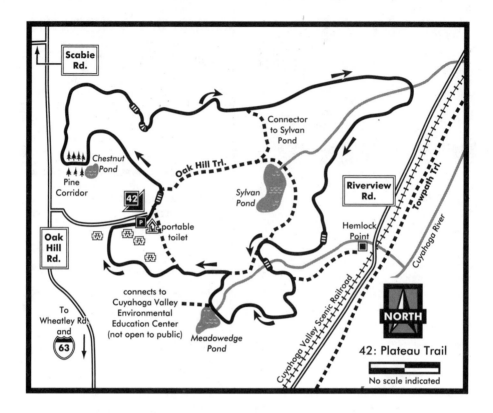

No scale indicated

the trails diverge. Oak Hill Trail turns to the right and loops around the highest point of the plateau in just 1.5 miles. But to do the shorter loop is to miss most of the hills, and much of the fun, of the longer and varied trail.

So stay on Plateau Trail, heading north, as the trail bends left and climbs gradually beneath the cover of hemlock trees. For a few paces, the old trees give way to meadow bushes and growth. This is one of the few stretches of trail where you'll be able to see the sky, as much of the way is completely shaded by hemlocks and deciduous trees. Half a mile into the trail you'll cross another bridge and come to Chestnut Pond. As you turn to look at the pond to your left, peering through thick trees and low brushy growth to see it, you may not realize what is lurking behind you. Here

by the pond, the trail turns sharply to the right. As you spin around, you'll find a long, long, long corridor of tall pines. As you stroll through the hallway of pines, try to keep your feet on the ground while you gaze up at their tops, 60 feet or so above you.

At the western end of the pine corridor, the path veers right again. Gravel and grass work together to keep this stretch of trail nice and dry. Heading north, you'll begin to see evidence of the hard work put into this trail, which was completed in 1997. More than a dozen small culverts have been created alongside and underneath the trail. Designed and laid with care, they are both unobtrusive and necessary. As you round the loop and head east, the ravine is only a few feet from the trail. It's worth a few careful sidesteps to peer

This pine corridor smells as good as it looks

that you're heading uphill for most of the next 0.75 miles. As the trail bends to the right, you'll pass over a feeder stream to Sylvan Creek (unnoticeable during dry periods) and head south, easing downhill. Soon you'll cross another footbridge, this one high enough to warrant leaning over the railing for another look at the ravine.

Just past the 3-mile mark, you'll climb a bit more and veer left to Hemlock Ravine, where a sign directs you to a short side trip. The 0.2-mile, out-and-back trail to Hemlock Point is to your left. Unless you need to conserve your energy, you should take the opportunity to enjoy the overlook. Back on the main trail, you'll follow a series of S-shaped curves. In fact, the trail turns you this way and that, barely righting itself (and you) between the crooks as it slopes up slightly, then takes you down a few feet, to the right. Here you'll see that the twisting served a purpose: directly in front of you is the beautiful Meadowedge Pond—and you didn't even see it coming.

To arrive at Meadowedge Pond in the late spring or summer is perhaps the hiker's equivalent of a carnival visitor leaving the midway's relatively constant panorama for a spectacular, if brief, sideshow. The pond vista is an oasis of color and song. Orioles, goldfinches, and yellow warblers spin colorful, dizzying circles around the pond. Frogs bound in with a splash as you walk by, then scold you for interrupting their day. Lilly pads cover about a third of the pond's surface, and cattails stand like a stockade fence around much of the pond's perimeter, as if protecting it from too-eager visitors.

Linger here as long as you like. The colors and sounds offer an amazing contrast to the forested trail behind you. When you're ready for yet another

over the edge (beware, though—hearty poison ivy hides among the Virginia creeper and young oaks). The ravine is only about 10 feet deep here, but keep an eye on it; it grows wider and deeper as you progress on the trail.

At 1.5 miles, you'll pass a sign indicating a connector trail to Sylvan Pond. If you follow it, you'll also find the short (1.5 mile) inner loop, Oak Hill Trail. But for now, stay on the Plateau Trail . . . you have a lot to look forward to.

Less than 2 miles into the trail, tree buffs will find a special section of the path, loaded with multi-trunked trees. Is there a proper name for this occurrence? If there is, it's elusive, but children—who tend to name things more expediently than botanists—call them "two-headed" and "three-headed" trees. Call 'em what you will, watching for them along this section may take your mind off the fact change of scenery, follow the wide grassy trail to the right, heading north into the shade of pines and hemlocks. The trail unfurls again in a series of S-shaped curves to reach a sign indicating the Oak Hill trail, straight ahead. You can follow it from here, back to the parking lot, or continue on Plateau Trail, by turning left. For the sake of finishing what you've started, then, stay on Plateau Trail.

The ravine is on your right at this point, and the trail is at its flattest. Still, it's not straight. You'll continue snaking along the last three-quarters of a mile in the now-familiar S-shaped pattern. Near the end of the trail, you'll ease down a gentle slope, in the company of young hemlock trees, to emerge in an open grassy area, surrounded by picnic tables and—in the spring and summer, at least—a lovely show of wildflowers, including oxeye daisies, coltsfoot, and clovers. It's somehow fitting that Plateau Trail manages to get in this final change of scenery as the curtain goes down on your hike. The parking lot is a few paces to your right; you'll walk parallel to the driveway as you head east, back to your car.

NEARBY ACTIVITIES

The Oak Hill area is just a few miles from Happy Days Visitors Center, where you can pick up maps of the park and browse a variety of books on the park's history, geology, and wildlife. Find Happy Days on State Route 303, about 2 miles east of Riverview Road. The center's schedule varies; call (330) 650-4636 for hours.

#43
Quail Hollow State Park

IN BRIEF

From an herb garden with a sundial to rough and tumble mountain bike trails, Quail Hollow State Park will satisfy a wide range of interests—even if you want to stay indoors. A unique, glass-enclosed nature viewing area in the lodge allows you to watch birds and small critters up close.

DIRECTIONS

From Cleveland, follow I-77 south through Akron, past I-76 and US 224, exiting south onto Arlington Road. Turn left on State Route 619, following it east into Hartville past State Route 43 to Congress Lake Road. Turn left and then right into the park entrance at 13480 Congress Lake Avenue. Follow the long park driveway approximately 1 mile, following signs to the Manor House on the park's eastern side.

DESCRIPTION

From the manor house parking lot, head south through stone gates to the herb garden. Established in 1986 by the Quail Hollow Herbal Society, the garden includes a rose arbor and features a traditional sundial. The beds are divided in wagon-wheel style, with plantings of irises, lambs ear, and oriental poppies that bloom from late May through early June. Several benches in the herb garden provide rest in the shade of tall trees and offer a view of the Manor House.

KEY AT-A-GLANCE INFORMATION

Length: 2.5-plus miles (total of 12 miles of hiking trails in the park)

Configuration: Loop

Difficulty: Easy

Scenery: Marsh and prairie, pine and deciduous forest, herb and rose garden, a beaver colony

Exposure: Woodland trail is shaded; herb garden and marsh are exposed

Traffic: Moderate

Trail surface: Dirt and grass

Hiking time: 1 hour

Season: Open year-round

Access: Park closes at 11 p.m.

Maps: Available inside visitors center and at www.ohiostateparks.org

Facilities: Rest rooms, water, phone, and pop vending machine by manor house/visitors center parking lot; picnic tables and grills scattered throughout park

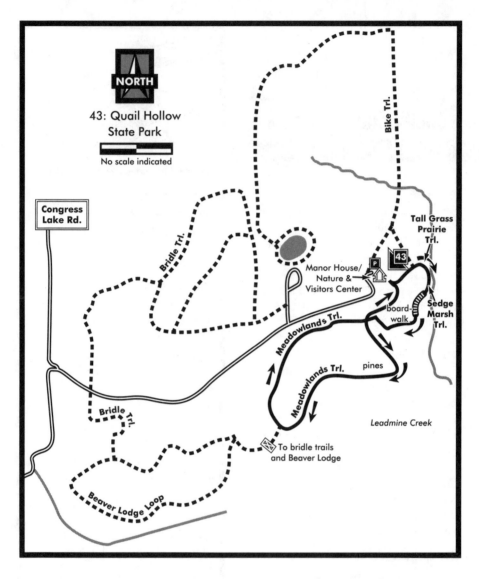

43: Quail Hollow State Park

NORTH

No scale indicated

Congress Lake Rd.

Bridle Trl.

Bike Trl.

Tall Grass Prairie Trl.

43

Manor House/ Nature & Visitors Center

board-walk

Sedge Marsh Trl.

Meadowlands Trl.

Meadowlands Trl.

pines

Leadmine Creek

Bridle Trl.

To bridle trails and Beaver Lodge

Beaver Lodge Loop

From the herb garden, turn left (east) and step onto the short Tall Grass Prairie Trail. As you might expect, it follows a mown grass trail amid taller prairie grasses. Soon you'll turn right, stepping onto Sedge Marsh, a half-mile trail that bends south and then west. Along the trail you'll find sweet flag and cattails and perhaps see some of the many frogs (spring peepers, chorus frogs, and American toads are common here) or birds that frequent this marsh. In the summer, watch and listen for yellow warblers.

A small quiet creek runs along the eastern side of Sedge Marsh trail. On wet spring days, Sedge Marsh can be impassable unless you're wearing high, dry boots. That's okay, because the natives can still get around—the marsh teems with animal life, although much of it is microscopic. Squishy marshes, not surprisingly, are important foundations in food webs. As you move south on a long stretch of boardwalk, the meadow approaches, where larger links in the food chain live.

At the southern end of the marsh, you'll connect with the 1.5-mile Meadowlands Trail loop and turn left to follow the trail clockwise. About 0.25 miles from the marsh, the wide grassy trail turns into a sea of pine needles. You'll rise and fall over several 10- and 20-foot hills as the trail turns along a pine stand. Now you're heading west, and deciduous trees 30 and 40 feet tall line the trail. Among them are crabapples, beautiful in bloom in the late spring.

It's important to note that the thick grass here camouflages some deep holes in the trail; weak-ankled types will need to watch their steps through here. However, if you stop, look into the woods, you may see a red fox, whitetail deer, or a wild turkey on this trail. If you miss them, don't despair. Look carefully and you'll surely see some smaller life forms. Signs along the Sedge and Meadowlands trails encourage you to get down on your hands and knees to look for caterpillars and other small insects and un-usual plants. (The signs don't tell you how to explain yourself to other hikers when they stumble upon you, crawling about.)

As the path bends and rolls along, you'll pass a sign pointing the way to bike trails and to the Beaver Lodge Loop. Stay on the Meadowlands Trail and, as you turn right, you'll come to a clearing where you'll have a view of the entire meadow. It's one of those wide-open spaces where—just for an instant—you'll wish this were your backyard. The view is fantastic.

Looping eastward, the Meadowlands Trail leads you back to the Manor

House; it sits north and to the left of the end of the trail. From here you can go up a dozen wide, stone steps into the Manor House. The house started life as a humble farmhouse, back in 1838. Harry Bartlett Stewart, chief executive officer of the Akron, Canton, and Youngstown Railroad, began acquiring adjacent land in the early 1900s, and he passed it down to his son, Harry Jr. The Stewart family lived here and enlarged the home several times, until 1975, when they offered the property to the state for one-half its appraised value. Today, the 40-room Manor House is used as a natural history study center, hosting a variety of nature-oriented education programs and workshops throughout the year.

Part of the home's lower level serves as a visitors' center and is open weekends from 1–5 p.m. A glass-enclosed room looks out onto a stone landscape featuring a small fountain and bird feeders. Inside, visitors enjoy watching chipmunks, squirrels, bright cardinals, and jays year-round, from the warmth of an old farmhouse.

NEARBY ACTIVITIES

Tours of the Manor House are offered throughout the year—call (330) 877-6652 for dates—and educational programs are offered regularly, both inside the visitors' center and on the trail. Quail Hollow's 698 acres include mountain bike and bridle trails, ice-skating, and cross-country skiing (equipment rentals are even available from the park). Once you've worked up an appetite here, you won't have to go far to satisfy it. Several restaurants in Hartville, near the junction of State Routes 43 and 619, serve hearty meals in the Mennonite tradition.

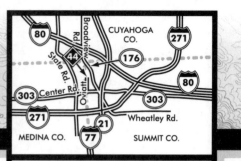

#44
Rising Valley Park

IN BRIEF

This 227-acre park located on the southern end of the Cuyahoga Valley was nearly turned into a federal prison. Fortunately, contemporary visitors can enjoy this beautiful area beside the headwaters of the East Branch of the Rocky River. Here you might spy a variety of mosses, wildflowers, and "pieces of Canada."

DIRECTIONS

Rising Valley Park is on Oviatt Road, just north of Route 303 between State and Broadview Roads. From Cleveland, take I-77 south to Route 21. Take 21 south to 303, turn right (west) to Oviatt. Follow Oviatt north about 2 miles. The parking lot is located at the north end of the park on the left and just before Newton Road.

DESCRIPTION

Parks come about in a variety of ways. Rising Valley was sort of a "gift" from the federal government. The land was originally part of the Cleveland Army Tank Plant proving grounds. The federal government had plans to turn the place into a prison when area residents started to protest. No one wants a prison built in their neighborhood, but this seemed especially poor planning—the adjoining property is a Girl Scout Camp! In 1977, the US government deeded the 227 acres to Hinckley and Richfield Townships for the purpose of creating a public

KEY AT-A-GLANCE INFORMATION

Length: 1.5 miles

Configuration: Loop

Difficulty: Easy

Scenery: Broad expanse of valley, trickles of the East Branch of the Rocky River, and thick young woodlands

Exposure: Mostly exposed

Traffic: Light

Trail surface: Grass and dirt

Hiking time: 45 minutes

Season: Open all year

Access: Dawn–dusk

Maps: Available online at www.hinckleytwp.org

Facilities: Rest rooms at each picnic area, well-water pump by southern picnic shelter, two picnic shelters with grills, small playground, ball fields, soccer field, sled hill

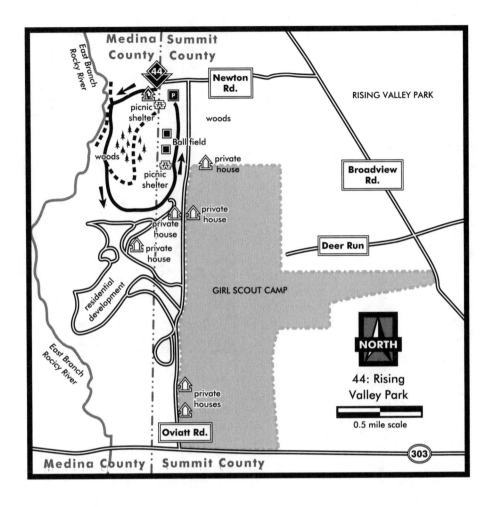

Medina | **Summit**
County | **County**

44

Newton
Rd.

RISING VALLEY PARK

East Branch Rocky River

picnic
shelter

P

woods

Ball field

Broadview
Rd.

woods

private
house

picnic
shelter

private
house

private
house

private
house

residential development

GIRL SCOUT CAMP

Deer Run

East Branch Rocicy River

NORTH

44: Rising
Valley Park

0.5 mile scale

private
houses

Oviatt Rd.

303

Medina County | **Summit County**

park and recreation area. Today, the two townships manage it through a joint park board.

As a condition of the transfer of land, a master plan had to be developed and implemented. The resulting Rising Valley Park Board committed itself to preserving this land and the adjacent East Branch of the Rocky River corridor for future generations. Their goal also includes protecting the flora and fauna indigenous to the area as well as providing access to and interpretation of the wetlands.

There are no trail signs here, but there is a rather obvious path leading west from the parking lot and shelter at the

north end of the park. The wide grassy path is actually a sledding hill, and its steep downhill slope offers fantastic views of the valley. At the end of the hill—ride—the path veers south. Before you turn left to follow it, take a few minutes to really soak up the valley view.

As the path veers left, woods appear on your right. Several unmarked, usually squishy trails meander west into the woods as far as the river. The wet woodlands here, and the river below, are monitored by the park board and the Ohio Department of Natural Resources (ODNR). You may spot jack-in-the-pulpit, skunk cabbage, or trillium along

155

the way. Wild turkeys, pileated woodpeckers, great horned owls, and red foxes
call this area home. The path is easy to
follow for 0.25 miles or so, reaching a few
trickles of the river. Once you are done
exploring, return to the drier, grassy path.

Heading south again, the trail soon
forks. Bear left, going east and up a long,
low-grade hill. (The other path, going
straight and south, soon lands in the residential development). In the middle of
the hill, an unmarked and little-used
path cuts into the woods to your left.
Take this short out-and-back to the relatively small stand of trees.

If you want a shorter hike, continue
walking north; eventually you'll emerge
by a ball field or picnic area. Otherwise,
return to the more-beaten path, where
you'll notice the woods on either side of
the trail are littered with erratics. (The
term "erratics" is used to describe rocks
that weren't made around here, but were
"imported" by glacier ice sheets. They
are also sometimes referred to as "pieces
of Canada.")

Continue south through thick woods,
then turn left as you come into a more
exposed section of the trail. In the thick
of the woods, and even along the more
exposed trail, you'll find a variety of
mosses. In the spring, daffodils pop up
amid maple, oak, and beech trees. The
"exposed" section runs behind a private
home, and then heads north along the
berm of Oviatt Road. Take care to stay
on the trail here as you skirt private
property.

On your way back to the parking lot,
you'll pass the ball fields, picnic areas,
volleyball court, and small playground.
All these amenities may give you pause
to think . . . no matter how rowdy the
ball games, no matter how many picnickers fill the shelters, don't you
suppose it's an improvement on tank

Heading west from the sledding hill

traffic, and far nicer than a prison's
grounds?

NEARBY ACTIVITIES

Lengthen this hike with a 4.7-mile portion of the Buckeye Trail (Medina section) to Whipp's Ledges at Hinckley
Reservation (see p. 207). Take Route
303 west 1 mile, then turn left on State
Road. Follow State Road approximately
4 miles to the Whipp's Ledges parking
lot at Hinckley Reservation.

*I would like to thank the Rising Valley
Park board for reviewing this hike description
and for sharing the history of the park with
me. Also in the interest of giving credit where
credit is due, members of the board pointed
out that they have a generous neighbor in the
Ohio Operating Engineers, who run a train-
ing facility just north of Rising Valley Park.
The engineers have donated much time, labor,
and materials to the Park over the years.*

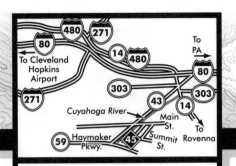

#45
Riveredge Trail and City of Kent

IN BRIEF

This stroll along the Cuyahoga River and through the city of Kent highlights the town's history since the 1800s. It will lead you by Ohio's oldest masonry dam, through a pioneer cemetery, and by some of Kent's historic buildings, many of which are still in use. You'll also stop by a large city park, filled with tall shade trees and fun playground areas.

DIRECTIONS

Take I-480/State Route 14 into Streetsboro. Turn right onto Route 43, heading south into Kent. Turn left onto Main Street, then right onto Water Street. Follow Water Street about 1 mile south to Summit Street and turn right. Tannery Park is about 0.25 miles east on your left.

DESCRIPTION

Legend has it that Captain Samuel Brady leapt across the Cuyahoga River to escape from Indians in 1780. The river is narrow as it runs through Kent; still, it must have been a mighty leap. We'll never know just how far he jumped or how much credence to give the story. Nevertheless, Riveredge Trail in Kent is the setting for this and many other interesting tales in American history.

Start your hike at John Brown Tannery Park, taking the stairs down and to the right, where a small wooden platform overlooks the river. An occasional goldfish hides from the sun under this

KEY AT-A-GLANCE INFORMATION

Length: 2.75 miles

Configuration: Figure-8 loop

Difficulty: Easy

Scenery: Great variety—from river fowl and ravine views to a rail station from the 1870s

Exposure: Mostly shaded, with a few short exposed stretches

Traffic: Moderate

Trail surface: From dirt and wooden boardwalks along the river to sidewalks along city streets

Hiking time: 50 minutes

Season: Open year-round.

Access: Open dawn–dusk; no permits required

Maps: A brochure with map is available inside the Kent Parks and Recreation Department office in Fred Fuller Park.

Facilities: Rest rooms at east end of Fred Fuller Park and at the Kraemer ball fields; a drinking fountain is also located in the parking lot by the ball field.

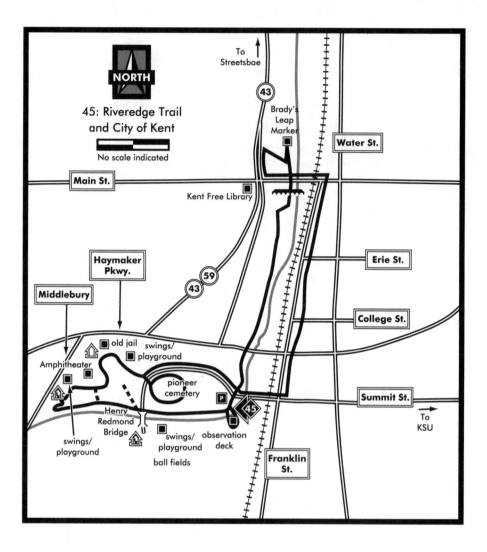

45: Riveredge Trail and City of Kent

No scale indicated

NORTH

To Streetsbae

Brady's Leap Marker

Water St.

Main St.

Kent Free Library

Haymaker Pkwy.

Erie St.

Middlebury

College St.

old jail

swings/ playground

Amphitheater

pioneer cemetery

P

45

Summit St.

To KSU

Henry Redmond Bridge

swings/ playground

swings/ playground

observation deck

Franklin St.

ball fields

deck, and you're likely to see ducks and Canada geese at this spot. Take the limestone path south (to the right) along the river, where it quickly turns into a dirt trail. As with any river path, you can expect some mud here.

Riveredge Trail is true to its name; it doesn't stray more than a few feet from the edge of the Cuyahoga River. The river was the primary reason that Kent was a popular settlement in the early 1800s. At first, the town was simply named Franklin, for the son of the original landowner. In 1805, the Haymaker family moved to Kent and built a dam to power a gristmill. As other mills popped up, the town came to be known as Franklin Mills.

What was then Franklin Mills is now a college town, full of folks with flexible schedules, so the trail sees a fare share of traffic all week long.

The trail is a mix of mostly dirt and roots, though gravel has been laid in the wettest spots. You'll cross two wooden bridges as the path follows the river

Enjoy river views and history from the boardwalk

south (downstream) and then west. On your left, a steep hill blocks the afternoon sun, making the trail cool and shady, even on summer afternoons.

About 0.25 miles into the trail, you'll pass the Harvey Redmond Bridge. It leads to the Kraemer ball fields, on your left. A small fenced-in playground and portable rest rooms are situated near the ball fields.

Cross the street and continue on the trail. A set of wooden stairs climbs up a steep hill to one of the park's many swing sets and picnic areas, but you'll want to stay on the trail going straight to enjoy the thick of the woods along the river.

The path forks again about 0.15 miles later. The rocky path to the right leads to Fred Fuller Park's main shelter and picnic area. Veer left instead, following the narrow path that winds along the riverbed. This is the least traveled portion of the Riveredge trail and also the least improved. You're likely to see deer here in any season; heron also frequent this quieter portion of the river.

Continue to the path's end, peering downstream to see an old bridge truss and remnants of the canal bed before the trail leads you sharply right, then up a steep hill. You'll emerge at the southern end of Fred Fuller, Kent's largest city park. Rest rooms are located here to the left; a small amphitheatre sits to the right.

Follow the dirt road to the right. Cars are permitted here, but traffic is light. Walk 0.2 miles past the shelter house and park office to the historic Old Jail.

The jail was built in 1869 by the order of Mayor John Thompson; though it might easily have not existed, as Mayor Thompson won the office by just two votes. Votes for Thompson totaled 145; runner-up Luther Parmelee had 143. The jail was moved to the park in 1999 and completely renovated. If you can, peek inside to see how the renovation incorporated elements of the original building.

From here, you'll head north down a steep, grassy hill. Swings, grills, and another picnic shelter sit at the bottom of the hill. Cross Stow Street, now heading west, and follow the sidewalk to the left to find Kent's Pioneer Cemetery, dating to 1810. Headstones here represent the families who figured prominently in Kent's history, including Haymaker, DePeyster, and Franklin. The cemetery gate is open from dawn until dusk.

Back on Stow Street, follow the sidewalk down to the Tannery parking lot. Cross Stow to the north to continue along the river trail. A sign here marks the entrance to "Franklin Mills Riveredge Park." Head down about 20 wooden steps, under the Haymaker

Bridge. At the bottom of the stairs, the path bends left; shallow river rapids gurgle to your right.

From wooden stairways and elevated boardwalks, you'll see some of Kent's historical industrial buildings on the left; the old downtown is on your right. From the top of a set of stairs, you'll get a good look at the Kent Dam, the oldest Masonry Dam in the State of Ohio. This area—including the Kent Dam, waterfall, and Canal Basin from the Main Street Bridge to the Stow Street Bridge—comprises the old industrial district that is listed on the National Register of Historic Places. The dam has a place in history, certainly, but its future is uncertain. The Ohio Environmental Protection Agency and the City of Kent continue to argue about the dam's impact on the river. Occasionally, water is diverted around the dam for an ecological study. It's prettiest as a waterfall; however, when the water is diverted you can really appreciate the dam's construction, circa 1836.

After crossing under the bridge, the path rises again, giving way to a relatively new brick walkway. Follow the red-brick path to the end of the line where you'll find a large rock and plaque marking the spot of Captain Brady's famous leap. Turn and retrace your steps about 0.1 miles, where the brick path veers right up a short hill.

Emerging on the eastern side of North Mantua Street, turn left. Follow the sidewalk south 0.2 miles to Main Street. The old building on the northwest corner of Mantua and Main is the Kent Free Library. It was built with Andrew Carnegie's money, on land donated by Marvin Kent more than 100 years ago.

Turning left onto Main, cross the bridge and railroad tracks into Kent's historic downtown area. Turn right, crossing Main to Franklin Street. Follow Franklin south, passing the Kent Historical Museum, which is located on the second floor of the city's original train station, built in 1875. The railroad's arrival here meant that the town would continue to grow, even as canal transportation declined. The man most responsible for bringing the new Atlantic and Great Western line to town was Marvin Kent. In 1864, the grateful citizens of Franklin Mills changed the town's name to honor him; since then, the name has stuck.

You should stick to Franklin Street until you reach Summit Street. Turn right there, going west about 0.25 miles, to reach Tannery Park, where you began.

NEARBY ACTIVITIES

Children won't want to leave Fred Fuller Park's playground equipment, and Kent's downtown offers a wide variety of things to see and do. Along this route or very close to it are several art galleries, unique shops, and restaurants for every taste. Kent State University is located 1 mile east of the Tannery Park parking lot. There, you can visit the May 4 Memorial, a somber spot recalling the day in 1970 when four students were killed during an anti-war protest. A more lighthearted campus attraction is the fashion museum—call (330) 672-3450 for hours and information.

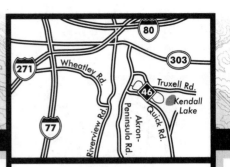

#46
Salt Run Trail

IN BRIEF

Hikers get a hilly workout while traveling through this former farm and estate of Hayward Kendall. Rolling meadows, shady creek-crossings, and layers of moss, pine needles, and ferns provide a feast for the eyes. An optional 1.2-mile loop encircles beautiful Kendall Lake, built by the Civilian Conservation Corps (CCC) in the 1930s.

DIRECTIONS

From Cleveland, take I-77 south, exiting at Wheatley Road. Head east on Wheatley to Oak Hill, turning right; then follow it as it turns left (now called Everett Road). Everett ends at Riverview Road; turn right. Turn left onto Bolantz Road, following it to Akron-Peninsula Road. Turn left (north). Turn right onto Quick Road. Pine Meadows parking lot is 0.4 miles east of Akron-Peninsula Road, off Quick Road.

DESCRIPTION

Five rolling hills come together to greet you in the Pine Meadows parking lot. There are picnic tables aplenty here, and the view is always grand. On snowy days, the hills are alive with the sounds of little folks on sleds. Fog nestles in the lower areas in the morning; on a sunny afternoon, you can see acres and acres of . . . well, pines and meadows. Frankly, the view from the parking lot is so pretty you may have to pull yourself down to

KEY AT-A-GLANCE INFORMATION

Length: 3.3 miles; optional 1.2-mile loop

Configuration: Loop

Difficulty: Moderate to difficult

Scenery: Beech-oak forest with hemlocks and pines, rolling hills, meandering creek

Exposure: Completely shaded

Traffic: Moderate

Trail surface: Dirt and clay, steeply banked in places

Hiking time: 90 minutes for Salt Run; allow 30 minutes more for Lake Trail

Season: Open all year

Access: 7 a.m.–10 p.m.

Maps: Cuyahoga Valley National Park maps available at visitors' centers in the park; the closest is Happy Days Visitor Center, on Route 303 about 2 miles east of Akron-Peninsula Road.

Facilities: First-aid station, rest rooms, and picnic tables at trailhead parking

Special comments: For additional information on this trail and Cuyahoga Valley National Park, see www.nps.gov/cuva.

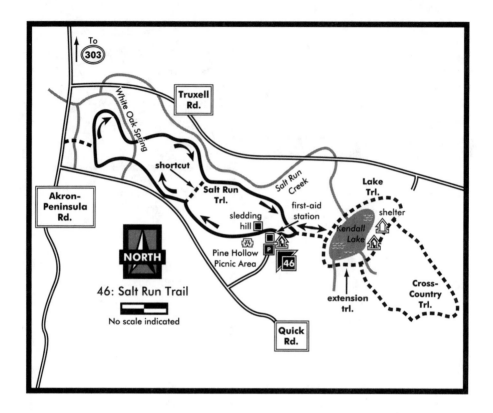

46: Salt Run Trail

No scale indicated

the lot's western end, where you'll find the trailhead. Come on. This is only the beginning.

Follow the trail signs from the western end of the parking lot, over the rolling hills, and down about ten feet to enter a dirt path. Turn left at the Salt Run sign to follow the trail clockwise. Meandering downhill, you'll soon cross a short footbridge. A shortcut to your right is best ignored—you'd miss much! Follow the trail as it bends left and heads uphill. For much of this hike, the trail rolls up and down, 10 to 30 feet at a time. The trail is rooty and uneven in places; this is a hike for sturdy boots, not sneakers.

Another curve to the left brings Quick Road into view, about 30 yards to the left of the trail. The road and the trail grow closer, then nearly together. The trail is covered with gravel for this short stretch. It's over soon—the white arrow on a trail marker beckons you off the road as the path darts back into the forest. And what a path it is—about three feet wide, it is the only level surface along the significant slope of the ravine. The ravine falls sharply to your right; you're beginning your descent into the densest part of the forest. A fork in the trail is signed—the right turn will lead you home sooner, via the short-cut trail (a loop of about 2.2 miles). Go straight instead, and you'll be rewarded with more gentle curves and steep drops, until you reach the bottom of an old field.

Enjoy the lower area of the Salt Run floodplain here, with its cool air and thick mosses; soon enough you'll be making up the difference with a series of short but steep climbs. Pine stands rise ahead of you, the flatland is below you, and you're in for another hill—this one, about a 30-foot climb.

Salt Run Trail is part of the former farm and estate of Hayward Kendall. He willed 420 acres to the state with the request that the land be used as a park, and be named for his mother, Virginia. The Civilian Conservation Corps dammed and developed Kendall Lake in the 1930s. The area was transferred to the National Park Service in 1978, becoming one of the first complete units in the National Recreation Area. Today the Pine Meadows and Salt Run area is a mix of successional forest and old meadow. You'll find a beech-oak forest, with a hearty population of grapevines and the occasional spicebush (stop and smell it! It's like lemon and nutmeg and cloves in a single leaf!). In the lower areas on the trail, you'll find a diverse population of ferns and mosses; in higher areas, where the sun can warm it a bit, you'll spot jewelweed. There's also plenty of poison ivy in these parts. The general rule to avoid contact is "leaves of three, let it be." Poison ivy, like Virginia creeper, likes to climb trees. If you are sensitive to poison ivy, and know you'll be in a dense forest, it's a good idea to wear long sleeves and pants.

As you rise up with the trail, you'll cross several long, wide footbridges. They can be extremely slippery when wet (think ice-skating in your hiking boots). Hang onto the railing as you go. Once you've landed back on the dirt trail, you'll probably notice you're surrounded by skunk cabbage.

As the path veers right to head west, you'll see a sign for the connector trail to Kendall Lake. If you follow it (left) you'll circle the lake and return to this trail in just over a mile. It's a narrow but fairly flat trail, pretty any time of year. To complete Salt Run from here, turn right. One more worthy climb awaits— punctuated by a half-dozen railroad-tie steps notched into a steep hill of clay. Take special care here when the ground is wet.

Once you've reached the top, the remainder of Salt Run is relatively flat, and you'll finish your hike in the company of tall pines and hemlocks. Their needles lay a soft carpet on the trail, welcome after the harder trekking you've seen today. Take a deep whiff of pine, and relax. You're done.

NEARBY ACTIVITIES

Of course, there's no lack of things to do here—you're in the heart of the 33,000-acre National Park. Nearby Kendall Lake is a beautiful place any time of year, so if you didn't take the extension trail to see it, consider driving over to have a look. Or, head up to Peninsula and check out Deep Lock (see p. 143).

#47
Seiberling Naturealm

IN BRIEF

This park has two distinct personalities. Inside, it's a kid playing in a mud puddle —one exhibit features bugs, another lets you pet snakes and salamanders. Outside, it's as neatly buttoned-down as a Sunday School teacher. About 300 tree and shrub varieties are displayed; many are labeled for easy identification. Two observation decks and a pair of ponds prompt quiet contemplation. Way, way in the back there's a bouncy suspension bridge. Aha! It's a kid at heart.

DIRECTIONS

F. A. Seiberling Naturealm sits on the south side of Smith Road, between Riverview Road and Sand Run Parkway. From Cleveland, take I-77 South to Ghent Road, Exit 138. Head south (left) on Ghent Road and go to the light at Smith Road. Turn left on Smith Road. After the third light at Sand Run Road, the park entrance is approximately 0.25 miles on the right.

DESCRIPTION

F.A. Seiberling founded the Goodyear Tire & Rubber Company, and if that was all he had done, you'd expect to find a park in Akron named after him. But Seiberling did much more. He served as an early member of the Board of Park Commissioners, and over the years he donated more than 400 acres to help establish the park system. In 1948,

KEY AT-A-GLANCE INFORMATION

Length: 1.5 miles (total of all park trails, 2.5 miles)

Configuration: Loop

Difficulty: Easy

Scenery: Decorative fountain, two small ponds, herb and flower gardens, ornamental and indigenous trees, a swingy suspension bridge

Exposure: About half shaded

Traffic: Moderate

Trail surface: Paved or stone paths, mulched trails

Hiking time: 45 minutes

Season: Grounds are open year-round; the Visitors Center is closed on Thanksgiving, Christmas, and New Years days

Access: Grounds are open 8 a.m. –11 p.m; Visitors Center is open Monday–Saturday, 10 a.m.–5 p.m.; Sunday, 12–5 p.m.

Maps: Available inside the visitors' center

Facilities: Rest rooms and water inside visitors center

Special comments: The nature education center and majority of the grounds are wheelchair traversible. Pets are not allowed in the park. Bicycles and other recreational equipment are also prohibited.

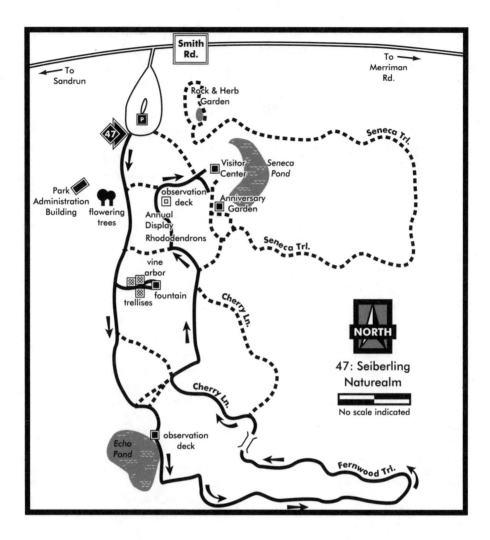

Seiberling donated the 100-acre plot on which the Naturealm now sits; it was established as a Metro Park in 1964. Today the grounds of the Naturealm offer the prettiest of plantings and well groomed trails. Meticulous planning of the arboretum and surrounding trails provides constant changes of scenery. In April and May, the crabapples are in bloom; in May and June, the rhododendrons are in bloom; richly colored perennials bloom into November.

Enter the park from the southwest corner of the parking lot. You'll head south by pines and crabapples, passing the entrance to the Volunteer Center. The decorative brick and stone–patterned path leads through the arboretum, first by the flowering, then the weeping, then by the vine trees. Less than 0.2 miles from where you start, towering white trellises lure you to a small fountain; three great blue herons (made of wrought iron) bathe in it. This is a popular place for wedding pictures, and amateur photography is encouraged. Commercial photographers, however, must obtain a special permit.

Continue on the paved trail, veering west (right) on the fork in the path just a few paces south of the fountain. You'll follow a planting of pines and deciduous trees before turning east, leaving the paved path. (*Note:* Wheelchairs and strollers can continue on the paved path, heading northeast through the middle of the park.) The wide, flat, mulched trail continues south to Echo Pond. A covered observation deck sits on the pond's north side; a park bench on the south side of the pond is tucked near a stand of cattails—an excellent place to watch for birds, butterflies, frogs, and fish.

Leave the south end of the pond and head east down a gentle incline. Turn right to follow Fernwood Trail (wooden trail markers display fern leaves). Fernwood winds its way south, then curves east through a thick deciduous forest, and, indeed, you'll find ferns here. This shady trail is furthest from the park entrance and where you're most likely to find solitude. The path straightens out at about 0.7 miles and then turns sharply to the left. From here, you wiggle your way northwest to arrive at the base of a bouncy suspension bridge.

The long, wooden bridge supported by cables spans a 45-foot deep ravine. You may find you're torn between running across it to make it swing or stopping to take in the beauty of the ravine.

Once across the bridge, you'll find your feet on Cherry Lane (trail signs marked with carving of two cherries). Turn left, and follow the path as it rises slightly to the west. Soon, the trail bends to the north where the mulch surface is replaced by pavement. The western portion of the Cherry Lane loop is as straight as the tall pines it borders. Soon, you'll come to a fork in the trail. Here you must decide to go left, taking the path through the rhododendron or to go right, through the planting of fruit and nut trees on your way to the Anniversary Garden. Either way, you'll enjoy the view, and you'll have logged about 1.5 miles when you arrive at the underground visitor center.

Inside, you'll find a creepy-crawly, hands-on educational experience. Giant hissing cockroaches and tarantulas are part of the menagerie. When a volunteer is on duty, children are often given an opportunity to pet a salamander or hold a black rat snake. Even reptile-averse grown-ups who ordinarily shy away from hands-on encounters may find themselves reaching out to the animals. If you don't want to handle the creepers or the crawlers, there's a great indoor bird-viewing area and a pond-life exhibit you have to see to believe. The pond's inhabitants (made of rubber and plastic) are built to scale, 12-times life size. Perhaps the most amazing thing about the center is that it's free to visitors. Good luck tearing yourself away before closing time.

NEARBY ACTIVITIES

The Seneca Trail is a 1.1-mile loop, starting from the Anniversary Garden on the south side of the visitors' center. Trail brochures are available inside the center and at the trailhead. About a mile south of the Naturealm down Merriman Road, you'll find the busy Merriman Valley, with a variety of restaurants and shops. You're also close to beautiful Stan Hywet Hall, 714 North Portage Path. Stan Hywet was Mr. Seiberling's home, a 65-room mansion with equally impressive grounds. There is an admission fee to tour the house and grounds; call (330) 836-5533 for details.

Special thanks to Sue Mottl for reviewing this hike description. Mottl is Chief, Department of Interpretive Programming and Environmental Education with Metro Parks Serving Summit County.

#48
Silver Springs Park

IN BRIEF

Silver Springs is an ideal destination for families who want to combine hiking, history, and hot summer fun. An historic barn and museum are located near the park's east entrance; a swimming lake sits on the western side of the park; and this trail sits right in the middle.

DIRECTIONS

From Cleveland, take State Route 8 south to Steels Corner Road. Exit heading east, then turn left (north) onto Hudson Drive. Follow Hudson Drive to Norton Road; turn right. Follow Norton about 3 miles east, crossing State Route 91 and Stow Road; then turn right onto Young Road. Park entrance is about 0.75 miles south of Norton Road, on the right (west) side of Young Road. Turn right into the park and follow the parkway west, past the barn and softball fields, about 0.5 miles to the parking lot by the trailhead.

DESCRIPTION

A bulletin board at the trailhead explains the rules—among them, bikers are strongly encouraged to wear helmets, and they must yield to hikers and joggers. The trail is a one-way directional loop. Enter it to the right and proceed in a counterclockwise direction.

Even before you find the official split marking the start of the loop, you'll encounter one of many "unofficial" trails working its way off the main loop. This

KEY AT-A-GLANCE INFORMATION

Length: 1.5 miles

Configuration: Counterclockwise loop

Difficulty: Easy

Scenery: Pine and deciduous forest

Exposure: Trail is shaded in spring and summer, when trees are full

Traffic: Moderately heavy on weekends and evenings when ball games are being played

Trail surface: Dirt trail, grass

Hiking time: 35 minutes

Season: Open all year

Access: Park closes at dark

Maps: Posted at trailhead

Facilities: Rest rooms, water, and pop machines in parking lot, east of trailhead

Special comments: No pets are allowed in this park.

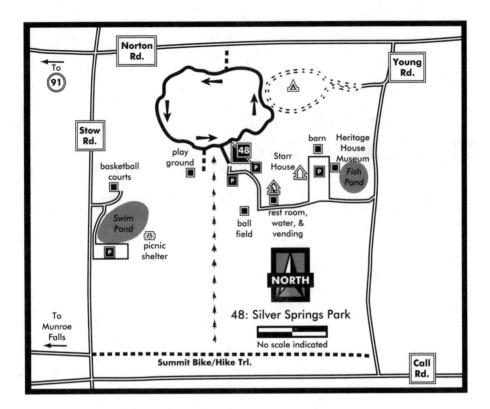

Norton Rd.

To 91

Young Rd.

Stow Rd.

barn Heritage House Museum

play ground

48

Starr House

Fish Pond

basketball courts

Swim Pond

rest room, water, & vending

ball field

picnic shelter

NORTH

To Munroe Falls

48: Silver Springs Park

No scale indicated

Summit Bike/Hike Trl.

Call Rd.

one is marked with a red arrow indicating that to follow the trail's intended path, you should go straight.

Follow the gentle incline a few paces further and to the actual beginning of the loop, where a blue directional arrow-points to the right. Here is the trail's only significant climb, up 20 feet as you list to the right. Turn around at the top of this hill and pause quietly. Look for at least two quadruple-trunked trees, and, by the time you've located them, you're likely to see and hear a woodpecker nearby as well.

About 0.25 miles into the trail, you'll probably spot the remnants of wooden fitness equipment, hearkening back to the path's past life as a par course. The remaining pieces of equipment amuse the chipmunks, who jump on them as if they were their own jungle gym.

Just about a half-mile into the trail you'll meet an unusual grouping of trees. Four maples stand on the right side of the path, one with its wrinkled, puffy face drooping your way. The tree to its right displays an oval with many rings set into it, like ripples in water carved perfectly into its side. It will be interesting to watch these trees grow over the decades; one wonders if they'll ever grow into their skins.

To this point, you've been consistently inching uphill. The low-grade climb is barely noticeable to those on foot; peddlers may feel it more readily. (The workload evens out on the back end of the loop, where they'll pedal less and brake more.)

Most of the path is hard-packed dirt, about five feet wide. The surface is relatively flat, so the only obstacles for bikers are low-lying roots, pine cones, and the occasional small rock. Nearing the 0.75-mile point, you'll cross the first of three wooden footbridges. The second one features a small ramp on each end, providing a bit of bumpy fun for bikers. Near this point you'll be able to see some of Stow's homes—they are easily visible when the trees are bare, but barely noticeable otherwise. That the city set aside this 280-acre parcel for a park and recreation area certainly pleases the residents here. (For proof, look no further than the several unmarked but well-worn paths they've created from their backyards to this trail!)

As you mark a mile, the path narrows abruptly, to just a foot or two across. (In some places, the bushes will brush your sleeve; this skinny stretch of trail may be unnerving to novice bikers.) Closing in on the last third of the trail, you'll find yourself veering mostly left, wandering amid more pines than maples. You'll also notice a few dips in the trail, and an overall downward trend. During the summer months, you may hear splashing and happy shrieks coming from the swimming lake on the park's western end.

Before closing the loop, you'll have a chance to take a wide, unmarked path to a large picnic shelter, playground area, and to the swim lake. Additional parking is available on this side of the park. Just east of that unmarked path, you'll cross the trail's third footbridge. Once across, you'll make a sharp right turn and a quick climb up five feet or so to reach the end of the loop. This time, ignore the blue arrows and turn right, down a few strides, into the parking lot where you began.

To add a mile to your hike from this point, head east through the fields to the museum and barn, located near the Young Road entrance, 0.5 miles from the trailhead. As you walk by the ball diamonds and through the grassy field heading east, you're likely to see several groundhogs. For whatever reason, the population in this park thrives; it's possible to spot as many as ten groundhogs in a single visit.

NEARBY ACTIVITIES

In addition to the barn and museum, the Stow City Players theatre is housed in this park. A municipal campground on the north side of Silver Springs Park is open to the public from April through October. Call (330) 689-2759 for information about educational programming and camping facilities.

The swim lake on the western side of the park is open to the public during most of the summer months from 11 a.m. to 7 p.m. There is an admission fee. The swim center phone number is (330) 655-2601. Enter the swim lake parking lot from Stow Road, off of Norton.

To add miles (and miles!) to your walk, hit the Summit County bike/hike trail, which runs across the park's southern edge. (See map at www.neo.rr.com/metroparks.)

#49
Spencer Lake

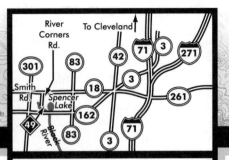

IN BRIEF

Want to get away from it all? Just 30 miles from Cleveland, Spencer Lake is probably as near to "away from it all" as you can get in that distance. Once here, chances are you won't meet another hiker on the trail.

DIRECTIONS

Take I-71 south from Cleveland to Route 18. Follow 18 west into Medina. From Medina, follow Route 3/Route 162 southwest approximately 5 miles, through the small town of Chatham, and continue west on route 162 another 4 miles to River Corners Road. Turn right (north). A sign for Spencer Lake Wildlife Area is about 0.5 miles north, directing you to turn right onto Spencer Lake Road and into the parking area.

DESCRIPTION

From the parking area on the western side of the lake, head west on the park access road (Spencer Lake Road). About 0.1 miles west of the lot, turn left into the woods, where the only marker is a blue blaze on a fence post. The wide, flat trail under the shade of tall oaks soon bends to the left, because it has to—otherwise, it would lead you right into the river.

The east branch of the Black River snakes by, about 20 feet below you and to your right. The edge of the trail is unforgiving here, but if you stay a foot

KEY AT-A-GLANCE
INFORMATION

Length: 1.5 miles (with option to follow the Buckeye Trail much farther)

Configuration: Loop

Difficulty: Easy

Scenery: Lake, river, marsh, woods, foxes, muskrats, pheasants, migratory birds

Exposure: Mostly exposed

Traffic: Light

Trail surface: Dirt and grass

Hiking time: 45 minutes

Season: Open year-round

Access: Park does not close; see special comments below

Maps: Area map available from Buckeye Trail Association or at www.dnr.state.oh.us

Facilities: Two boat ramps, two fishing/observation decks

Special comments: Spencer Lake is a popular public hunting area—hunting, fishing, and trapping are allowed by permit. This area is closed to all other activity from 8 p.m.–6 a.m., September 1–May 1; and from 10 p.m.–6 a.m., May 2–August 31. It's wise to wear bright colors and avoid early morning hours during hunting season.

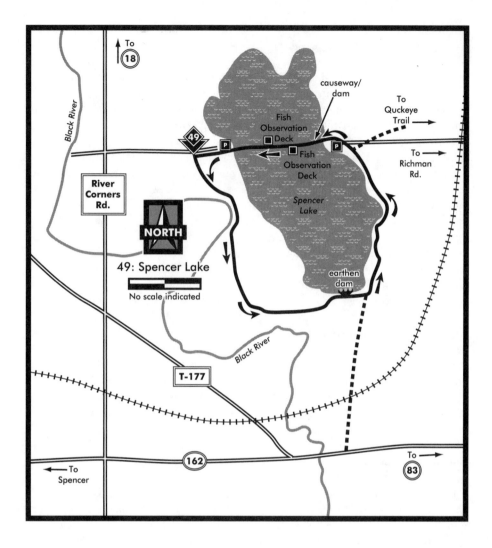

49: Spencer Lake

No scale indicated

or two back, you'll have lovely views of the shady river for the next half-mile. The view is best enjoyed while you're stopped, of course. While you're moving, you'll want to keep your eyes on the trail—you're likely to find a large log, or a whole tree, lying in your path. If you're quiet (and lucky) you may also catch a glimpse of some of the many songbirds that inhabit this area. The variety of food sources—tall oak trees, thistle, goldenrod, marshland, and nearby open fields—makes this spot very

attractive to a rich assortment of birds and mammals.

The trail bends left again, and leads you by a field and some young-growth trees—their rustle entertains you as you continue east to the dam. This area can be quite wet during spring, but the wildflowers are worth the squishing through here.

If you really don't like mud, plan to come during a dry spell or, even better, in the winter, when you're likely to see people ice fishing on the lake. Coming out of the woods and the mud, you'll pass iron-weed, goldenrod, milkweed, and other popular bird food before you land on the wide, grassy walkway to the dam.

You reach the earthen dam about 0.9 miles into the hike. The grassy path continues east 100 feet or so, and then turns right, crossing railroad tracks and ending at SR 162. Don't go there—instead, turn left, into the woods. Here the narrow path hugs the lakeshore, and then darts into the woods, heading north. You'll roll up and down a few hills, rising slowly through bramble (and wildflowers, in the spring), until you reach a spot in the woods where it seems as if you might walk right into the lake. You don't, of course, but the view here is lovely.

The path wiggles a bit through the woods, and in at least two spots you'll need to climb over fallen trees to continue your hike. In one of those places, hikers beat out a secondary path around the fallen tree; then another tree landed on that path. Philosophers on the trail might consider this a good example of man vs. nature; others may simply enjoy climbing over the tree.

About 0.5 miles from the southern dam, you'll reach the eastern parking lot and a newer, northern dam (a flood washed away the original in 1969; this dam was constructed in 1970). You'll also find the trailhead for the Buckeye Trail. Turn right if you're itching to go further. Otherwise, turn left to continue your walk here at Spencer Lake. Cross the road and walk along the well-beaten path on the north side of the dam. It's a great spot to observe ducks and other migratory birds and catch a glimpse of some of the other animals here.

This is a Wildlife Restoration Area, actively managed for sport hunting and fishing. The state acquired the land in 1956 and built dams here in the 1960s. Fish and wildlife reclamation projects have been ongoing since. Hang out, quietly, and you may catch a glimpse of the mink and muskrat populations that attract sportsmen. Grass carp have been stocked to control aquatic vegetation to improve the quality of fishing—because they are "working fish," they must be returned to the lake unharmed when caught. Bass under 15 inches must be released, too—this requirement is part of a statewide effort to see if bass length limits can improve the quality of fishing in Ohio.

To complete your hike, cross the causeway and return to the western parking lot; for a round trip of about 1.5 miles. Before you go, you may also stop at one of the two fishing/observation decks for another perspective on the lake.

NEARBY ACTIVITIES

Looking for a long day trip? You can follow the Buckeye Trail west from Spencer Lake all the way to Findley State Park, about 9 miles from here. For maps and more information about the Buckeye Trail, call (800) 881-3062. Just east of Spencer Wildlife Area, off of Route 162, you'll find two Medina County parks: Schleman Nature Preserve and Buckeye Woods. They offer trails, picnic facilities, and play equipment. To learn more about the facilities, go to www.medinacountyparks.com.

#50
Squaw Rock

IN BRIEF

A rocky ravine, gentle rapids, and a bit of a mystery are waiting for you in the Cleveland Metroparks' South Chagrin Reservation. What is the meaning behind the images Henry Church carved in Squaw Rock? Is it a collage celebrating American history, or an artistic condemnation of our government's policies of the 1800s? Go see for yourself; while you're there, you can enjoy a shady stretch of the Buckeye Trail and views of the scenic Chagrin River.

DIRECTIONS

From I-271, take Miles Road east to State Route 91 (SOM Center Road) and turn right. Follow Route 91 south about 1 mile to the park's main entrance at Hawthorn Parkway. Turn left, following Hawthorn east about 1.5 miles. The road ends at the bottom of the hill; Squaw Rock Picnic Area and parking is on your right.

DESCRIPTION

Enter the trail at the eastern edge of the parking lot, where you'll see the blue blazes of the Buckeye Trail. The path veers right and then down 72 steep and uneven limestone steps to the banks of the river and a small waterfall. Although they are shallow, after a rain the falls can be rather boisterous. As you head south and upstream, the noise tapers off to a mere gurgle. Beautiful, picturesque rock

KEY AT-A-GLANCE INFORMATION

Length: 2 miles

Configuration: Figure-8

Difficulty: Moderate; steep, uneven stairs and uphill portions of all-purpose trail are challenging

Scenery: Curious old carvings, a waterfall, rapids along the Chagrin River, deep ravine overlooks

Exposure: Almost entirely shaded

Traffic: Moderate on Squaw Rock trail; heavy on the all-purpose trail

Trail surface: Dirt trail and stone steps on the Squaw Rock loop; the all-purpose trial is paved

Hiking time: 1 hour

Season: Open all year; steps to Squaw Rock closed when icy

Access: Open from 6 a.m.–11 p.m., although some parking lots close at dusk (clearly posted)

Maps: At North Chagrin Reservation, at 3037 SOM Center Road in Willoughby, or at www.clemetparks.com

Facilities: Rest rooms at Squaw Rock parking area; public phone at the sledding hill parking lot south of Miles Road

Special comments: Good hiking boots are highly recommended for this hike.

173

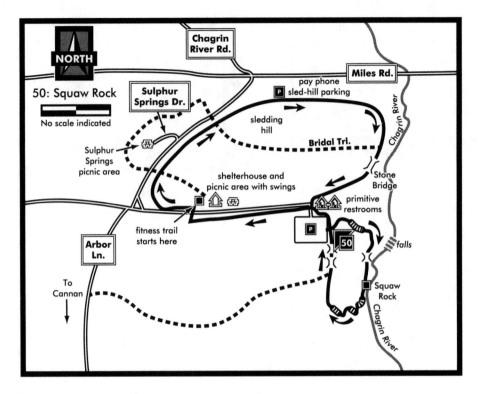

NORTH

Chagrin River Rd.

Miles Rd.

Sulphur Springs Dr.

pay phone
sled-hill parking

sledding hill

Bridal Trl.

Chagrin River

Sulphur Springs picnic area

shelterhouse and picnic area with swings

Stone Bridge

primitive restrooms

50

falls

fitness trail starts here

Squaw Rock

Arbor Ln.

To Cannan

Chagrin River

---

formations rise 25 to 30 feet above you on the right. Continue south, hugging the skinny path about 12 feet above the Chagrin River. You'll cross a stone footbridge at 0.14 miles and a wooden walkway just a few steps later, arriving at famous Squaw Rock at 0.2 miles. The rectangular sandstone rock is about ten feet high. On its south face are several carvings, including a bundle of quivers, a tomahawk, an American Indian maiden, a rattlesnake, an infant, and a bird in flight.

Henry Church carved the images in 1885. Born and raised in Chagrin Falls about 2 miles east of here, Church was a blacksmith by trade. He also enjoyed painting and sculpting. Though his art was considered unusual at the time, in 1980 (64 years after his death) his work was featured in a special exhibit at the Whitney Museum of American Art in New York City.

Church reportedly walked from his home to "Squaw Rock" every night to carve by lantern light. He quit when his neighbors found out what he was doing. On the east face of the rock are unfinished carvings of a log cabin and the US Capitol. What Church intended by the carvings is unknown, but his work lures many people to this trail.

Step back onto the path, again heading south. Climb up 63 stairs, where you'll see and hear a gentle waterfall about 12 feet high. If you're feeling adventurous, you can walk underneath it—but don't try unless you've got good balance and good boots. A bit further south, you'll climb up another long set of stone stairs.

At the top, turn right. Though you may be winded from climbing the steps, you've only covered 0.25 miles. Head north through a thick forest of hemlocks, beech, and oak trees. You'll see an alternate path that heads west from here to Arbor Lane. Go straight instead to cross two, sturdy wooden bridges. From either one, you can watch as thin tributaries bounce down to the river more than 50 feet below. The woods are thick here, so even with a faint wind, the rustling of leaves drowns out the river's sounds. Continuing north, you'll notice the blue blazes of the Buckeye Trail along this path before you return to the southeast corner of the parking lot.

(*Note:* The higher portion of this loop is flat and offers great views of the ravine. It makes a nice, easy stroll for those who aren't surefooted enough to attempt the steps and lower trail. In dry weather, the surface is hard-packed enough for most strollers.)

Cross the parking lot, turning left from its northwest corner onto the all-purpose trail that parallels Hawthorne Parkway. You'll notice you're following the blue blazes of the Buckeye Trail as the path continues uphill for nearly a quarter of a mile. The hill will get your heart thumping just in time to cross the street at Shelterhouse Picnic Area where you can try out the Parcourse fitness trail, if you wish. Various exercise stations are positioned along the trail over the next 0.5 miles.

Follow the dirt-and-gravel trail west, then north as it bends right along Sulphur Springs Drive. The Buckeye Trail turns into the woods along with the bridle trail, but you'll stay on the now paved all-purpose trail that parallels Sulphur Springs Drive. As you roll downhill on a snowy day, you'll hear howls of laughter coming from the sledding hill to your right.

Rounding the bottom of the hill, the trail curls to the east, past a small pond full of frogs and ringed with jewelweed. The path rises gently and then crosses a wide stone bridge where you can peer into the river ravine again. You'll climb up just a few more feet before returning to the northeast corner of the parking lot where you began.

NEARBY ACTIVITIES

A sledding hill sits at the north end of Sulphur Springs Drive, and additional parking is available there. Fishing is allowed at Shadow Lake, located on Hawthorn Parkway about 2 miles southeast of Route 91. South Chagrin Reservation also offers four picnic areas; the large stone "Shelterhouse" can be reserved by calling the Metroparks office at (216) 351-6300.

To visit Henry Church's hometown, the quaint Village of Chagrin Falls, you need only travel about 2 miles east on Miles Road. There's a waterfall on the western side of Main Street, and several shops and restaurants that are worth a visit.

To
90

Charles
Rd.

Strawberry Ln.

Chagrin River Rd.

Rogers Rd.

To
27

51

Wilson Mills Rd.

Mayfield Rd.

322

IN BRIEF

North Chagrin Reservation has something for everyone. The nature center's exhibits are educational and fun for all ages. Just outside, there's a bat garden. The walkways around Sanctuary Marsh are accessible to all. Bird lovers should be sure to hike the wildlife management loop. And if you like a good ghost story, gather your courage as you hike up the hills and enter the castle—if you dare!

DIRECTIONS

Exit I-271 at Wilson Mills Road. Head east about 0.5 miles, turning left (north) onto State Route 91 (SOM Center Road). Go north 4.2 miles to Sunset Lane. Turn right (east) into the park. Turn right onto Strawberry Lane (which turns into Buttermilk Falls Parkway) and follow the signs south to the Nature Center.

DESCRIPTION

Start at the Nature Center, stepping onto the paved Sanctuary Marsh Loop trail, which runs between Sunset Pond and Sanctuary Marsh. In only a few steps you'll pass the nature center's bat garden on your left—hard to miss because with its especially fragrant flowers that attract bats and other nocturnal feeders. Sanctuary Marsh Loop is perfect for strollers and wheelchairs; its boardwalk over the marsh affords a look at beaver habitat (a beaver education

KEY AT-A-GLANCE INFORMATION

Length: 5.25 miles

Configuration: Loop

Difficulty: Moderate, with difficult sections

Scenery: Waterfall, deep ravine overlooks, beaver activity, and a (possibly haunted) castle

Exposure: Mostly shaded

Traffic: Moderate to heavy

Trail surface: All-purpose trail is paved; bridle and hiking trails are hard-packed dirt.

Hiking time: 2.5 hours

Season: Open year-round

Access: Open 6 a.m.–11 p.m., some parking lots (including Squires Castle) close at dusk; lots that close early are clearly posted.

Maps: Inside the nature center or at www.clemetparks.com

Facilities: Pay phone, water, and flush toilets at nature center off Strawberry Lane; grills, water and rest rooms at each picnic area

Special comments: Got kids? Take a shorter walk (Sanctuary Marsh Loop trail to Buttermilk Falls, or the 0.6 miles Wildlife Management Loop), and then drive to the castle to tell ghost stories or have a "haunted" picnic.

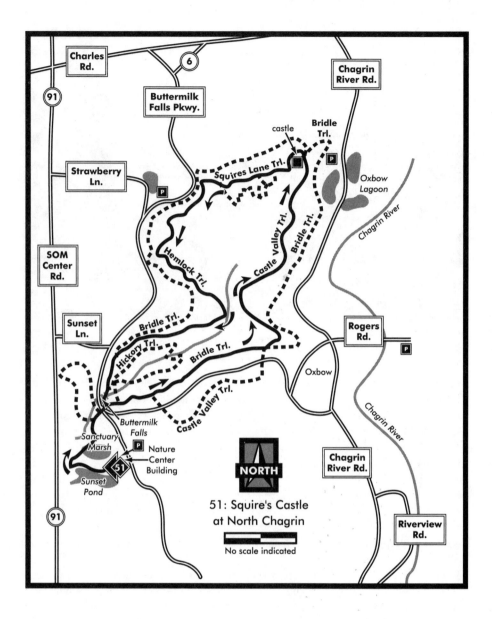

**51: Squire's Castle
at North Chagrin**

No scale indicated

exhibit inside the nature center explains what you'll see).

Head north on Sanctuary Marsh Loop, connecting with Buttermilk Falls Loop (blue trail signs). The falls overlook, on the western side of the parkway, is about 0.5 miles from your starting point. The pretty falls tumble over Cleveland Shale, which tends to fracture at right angles. The "stair steps" of Buttermilk Falls look as if they were carved by a stonemason, but were in fact cut quite naturally.

Leave the waterfalls and head east (right), crossing the parkway, where you'll find a trailhead sign pointing to the red Hickory Trail, the yellow Hemlock Trail, and the Bridle Trail. Follow

Some say Squire's "castle" is haunted

the Bridle trail right, down a hill and heading east. The trail is hilly, rising up to parallel Oxbow Lane before intersecting with Castle Valley Trail (white signs).

From here you may choose to follow either the Bridle Trail or Castle Valley Trail to the castle. They cover approximately the same distance, and connect several times. While a sturdy pair of sneakers will do on the Bridle Trail, you'll certainly want boots on the Castle Valley Trail, as it is rocky, narrow, and in places, quite steep. (*Note:* The wider, flatter Bridle Trail may be the best choice for runners; it is safer in wet or icy weather.)

For a bit of a challenge, head north (left) onto Castle Valley Trail. Hugging the side of the ravine, you'll take 38 steps down the valley and cross a little wooden footbridge into the woods. Poison ivy and jewelweed grow along the trail here. Continue to drop down into the valley, bottoming out at about 1.75

miles to cross a creek on widely-spaced sandstone steps. Rising up on the left (east) side of the trail is River Grove picnic area. The Bridle Trail is on your right.

Heading north from here, you'll spot at least three connector trails to the Bridle trail, now running parallel to Chagrin River Road. As you approach the castle, Castle Valley Trail meanders over a ridge; the Bridle Trail runs about ten feet below, level with the road.

Squire's "castle" is actually a caretaker's cottage. Feargus B. Squire, a founder of the Standard Oil Company, owned 525 acres of land here, where he planned to build a vast estate. In the 1890s, he, his wife and daughter summered in the cottage. His wife hated it and was especially fearful of wild animals. Ironically, Mr. Squire enjoyed big game hunting, traveling the world to bring home the heads and skins of exotic animals. The basement of the cottage was his trophy room. Mrs. Squire reportedly had terrible nightmares and suffered from insomnia. She often walked through the house at night, carrying a red lantern. One night, she wandered into the frightful trophy room and, screaming in terror as she hurried to leave, she tripped, breaking her neck. Some accounts say she ran into a hanging rope, strangling herself. However it happened, Mrs. Squire died that night in the country home she hated. Mr. Squire never built his estate, and the Cleveland Metroparks purchased the land in 1925. To thwart vandals, the park filled in the basement of the cottage and gutted the inside of the castle. They could not, however, stop reports of Mrs. Squire's ghost. It's said she still carries her red lantern through the cottage, and on cool dark nights, you can hear her screams from Chagrin River Road. To avoid such encounters, visit the castle in the sunshine. Even then, you'll likely have company, as the castle and surrounding picnic area are quite popular with the area's living population.

After your tour of the "castle," exit through the back door, heading west on Squire's Lane (blue signs). Squire's Lane rolls uphill as it leaves the castle behind. The trail is well marked, which is good, because it intersects several times with the purple "scenic" trail and other trails. At about 3.5 miles into the hike, Squire's Lane ends. Follow the yellow signs of Hemlock Trail, heading south along the eastern side of the all-purpose trail. Hemlock Trail is narrow and pretty, zigzagging over several tributaries to the Chagrin River. This trail offers amazing fall colors, thanks to a mighty mix of deciduous trees and evergreens. At least once along here, venture to the edge of the ravine and watch a leaf fall or a bird dive until you can no longer see it. The ravine is deep, fragrant, and peaceful. In my experience, Hemlock Trail is lightly traveled compared to the other trails here. Its beauty alone makes it worth the trip; stretches of solitude are a bonus.

Hemlock crosses the Bridle Trail before heading down 11 steep railroad-tie steps to cross a wooden footbridge over another trickle of water. Go up, then down again, twice, and you'll meet the Bridle Trail again. Briefly plod along next to the Bridle Trail, passing Sunset Lane on your right. Hemlock winds down 16 railroad-tie steps for a final foray into and out of the valley. The path widens and levels out in time to return to the trailhead across from Buttermilk Falls. If you time your trip right, returning to Sanctuary Marsh at dusk, you may get to see some beaver at work.

NEARBY ACTIVITIES

Why leave? North Chagrin Reservation and the Nature Center offer a busy schedule of activities for all ages and interests, from "Stroller Science" to "Senior Seekers" and naturalist-led hikes such as the "Romantic Moonlight" walk and the fun "Fall in the Creek Hike." You can check the schedule online at www.clemetparks.com or call (440) 473-3370 for information.

#52
Stebbins Gulch

IN BRIEF

Stebbins Gulch is a restricted natural area and a Natural History Landmark. Much of Holden Arboretum's 3,400 acres are open for visitors to explore, but not Stebbins. You'll need a reservation and a guide to see what the gulch is all about. While planning ahead is necessary for this hike, it is well worth the effort.

DIRECTIONS

From Cleveland, take I-90 east to Route 306. Follow 306 south to Kirtland-Chardon Road; turn left. Head east on Kirtland Road about 3 miles to Sperry Road and turn left. Follow Sperry Road almost 2 miles to reach the visitors parking lot on the left.

DESCRIPTION

"Three hours to go two miles!?" I was incredulous when a fellow park volunteer told me about Stebbins Gulch. I called the Holden Arboretum and signed up for the next scheduled hike.

"You're paying eight dollars to go on a hike!?" my husband asked, equally incredulous. "That's as much as a museum entrance charge," he said.

"Yep," I thought. "And you should see this museum's collection."

Driving along Kirtland-Chardon Road, glimpses of the Holden Arboretum tease you, making the journey to the entrance at Sperry Road seem longer than it really is. After turning on

KEY AT-A-GLANCE
INFORMATION

Length: 2 "alpine" miles

Configuration: Loop

Difficulty: Difficult

Scenery: Gulch, five layers of sediment, lichen, liverwort, a fossil perhaps?

Exposure: About half exposed

Traffic: Light

Trail surface: Dirt and creek bed

Hiking time: 3-plus hours

Season: Open all year

Access: Holden open Tuesday–Sunday from 10 a.m.–5 p.m.; Stebbins hike by reservation only

Maps: Not available

Facilities: Rest rooms and water at visitor's center

Special comments: Holden members get in free, visitors pay $4 admission ($2 for children ages 6–15). If this particular hike isn't for you, you're sure to find a dozen others on the arboretum's 3,400 acres. Many of the trails are easy to moderate and well marked, and free maps are available in the visitors center. Other hikes, like this one through Stebbins Gulch, require reservations and serious hiking boots. Visit www.holdenarb.org or call (440) 946-4400.

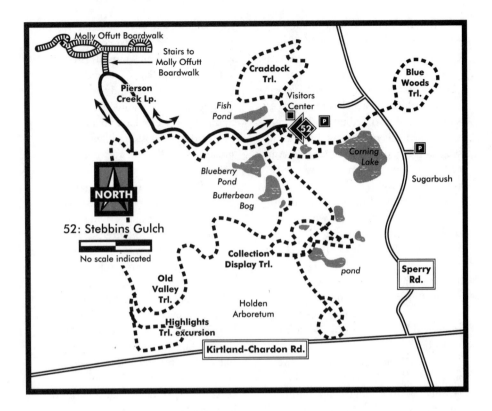

Molly Offutt Boardwalk

Stairs to
Molly Offutt
Boardwalk

Craddock
Trl.

Blue
Woods
Trl.

Pierson
Creek Lp.

Visitors
Center

Fish
Pond

Corning
Lake

Sugarbush

Blueberry
Pond

NORTH

Butterbean
Bog

52: Stebbins Gulch

No scale indicated

Collection
Display Trl.

pond

Sperry
Rd.

Old
Valley
Trl.

Holden
Arboretum

Highlights
Trl. excursion

Kirtland-Chardon Rd.

Sperry Road, you think you're almost there, but you pass the Linden collection . . . the conifer collection . . . a glimpse of the Buckeye collection . . . several ponds . . . Corning Lake. Finally, you're really there.

In 1913, engineer Albert Fairchild Holden established a trust fund in memory of his deceased daughter, Elizabeth Davis. With urging from family members, he agreed to lay the groundwork for an arboretum to honor Elizabeth. In 1931, Albert's sister and brother-in-law donated the first 100 acres. Today, Holden is one of the largest arboreta in the US, spanning more than 3,400 acres. More than 20 miles of trails and several marvelous gardens are open to members and visitors whenever Holden is open. But a few areas—too fragile to be free-for-alls, yet too educational to be completely

closed—are open only to those on scheduled hikes, conducted by Holden guides. Stebbins Gulch is such a place.

Stebbins Gulch is a bedrock ravine ecosystem. Its unique ecology is a result of the interplay among the bedrock, stream, and groundwater; on this hike, you'll get an up-close look at all three.

Our guide gathered our group in the lobby of the visitor's center. She examined our boots and checked our fortitude. "No one had open heart surgery this week? Or last?" She grinned but she wasn't kidding. It would be hard to carry someone up from the bottom of the gulch. "Treat every rock as a slippery rock," she said, "and try to step on the lowest point, to minimize the risk of slipping." Once we got to the bottom of the gulch, we'd be trudging through the stream. Finding the lowest point might mean finding your boots submerged in several inches of water. It was November. I wondered just how waterproof my boots were.

Down, down, down we went. We dropped below the beech and sugar maples, then descended through hemlocks and hardwoods. Yellow birch trees clung to the fragile hillside as we continued down, down, down. It grew noticeably cooler as we descended.

At the bottom of the hill, the ground literally falls into the creek. We watched—no, *studied*—our guide as she stepped over the side of the hill and shimmied along a crumbly ledge of shale about four inches wide with a creek three or four feet below her. Not a devastating drop, if you were to slip, but it sure would be embarrassing. We shimmied after her.

We studied the layers of shale as we shimmied. Chagrin shale—from the Devonian period, about 400 million years old—is light gray in color and full of the decayed carcasses of ancient sea life. Cleveland shale is the darker stuff. It is full of decayed plants: carriferous ferns that the dinosaurs ate, for example. Picture ferns 60 to 100 feet tall. That's what we were clinging to—decayed giant fern-trees. "Notice its darker color; do you think it has some oil in it?" our guide asked. Yes, we nodded as we clung. "That's right, it does," she responded. I wondered if the oil makes it slippery. I wondered about my boots again.

Less than a mile into the adventure, we were looking for a little blue flag. The little blue flag signalled our guide, letting her know where to dig for and find a rock containing a fossil. The fossil is worth digging for; it is a fine impression of a squid, more than ten inches long. Evidently, the squid was heading upstream before he became part of the

rock and, subsequently, a scenic stop on this hike. The stone that contains the fossil is always on the move in this streambed, hence, the blue flag. We found the squid, studied it, and left it (and the flag) where we hoped the next guide would easily find it. Then we walked up a natural staircase of Berea sandstone down which a stream flows. We didn't travel the middle of the stream constantly, but we crisscrossed it many times, looking for dry ground over here, splashing over there to see liverwort on the low-lying rocks.

Soon we came to a pretty, cascading waterfall. There was no dry ground here, so it was time to find out how well our boots gripped. Some boots gripped, others slipped. For the nongrippers, the 15-foot-long cascade became a 15-foot-long waterslide. Others of our group slipped, but not so accidentally. It looked like a lot of fun, but I didn't join in. After all, it was still November.

As we began our climb back up the loose forest floor, up through the hemlocks and beeches to the oaks, I looked at my watch. We had left the lobby (much drier) about four hours ago. Certainly, we had taken our time. We had examined fungus, took pictures of the falls, fell, and found the fossil. But was it possible we had logged less than *2 miles in 4 hours?*

Our guide smiled. "These are Alpine miles," she said.

Stebbins Gulch is worth the time, money, and wet boots. My only disappointment was that after spending so much time in the gulch, the day was over. There were so many more trails. . . and I wanted to have at them. So, consider yourself warned: Holden is addictive. A guided hike offers a good introduction to the massive property; so does a day of self-guided wandering. Either way, you'll be back.

NEARBY ACTIVITIES

Are you kidding? There are 3,400 acres right here. Twelve trails covering 20 miles require no reservation. Take the Pierson Creek Trail and Molly Offutt Boardwalk (about 2 linear miles; see map) for starters.

Eva Stephans guided our group through Stebbins Gulch. Eva is both delightful and knowledgeable of the area's geology and natural history. She also offered insights into the social history of the Kirtland/Little Mountain area—but that's another story.

Special thanks to Kelley Kornell, marketing associate, for providing additional material on Holden and Stebbins Gulch, and for reviewing this hike description for accuracy.

#53
Sunny Lake Park

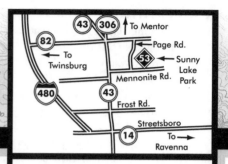

IN BRIEF

Want to soak up lazy lake views or watch great blue herons come in for long-legged landings? There are enough birds (and benches) on this lake trail to make dozens of bird-watchers happy. Green thumbs will admire the arboretum and garden on the park's south side. Looking for a more active outing? This park will please you, too—more than 2 miles of trail wrap around volleyball and bocce courts and horseshoe pits.

DIRECTIONS

From Cleveland, follow I-480 east, exiting at Frost Road. Follow Frost Road east to State Route 43; turn left. Turn right onto Mennonite Road. Follow Mennonite about 1.5 miles east to the park's main entrance on the left at 885 East Mennonite Road.

DESCRIPTION

From the shelter/office, follow the paved path east across a short wooden bridge, then begin your tour of the Bicentennial Memorial Tree Garden. It features a wide variety of trees, including flowering crab, ivory silk lilac, dawn redwood, Kentucky coffee, red buckeyes, and several varieties of oak and ash. In 1999, the Aurora Garden Club planted a garden celebrating Aurora's 200th birthday. Day lilies, overdam reed grass, autumn joy sedum, and flame grass grow there amid other decorative trees and bushes.

KEY AT-A-GLANCE INFORMATION

Length: 2.3 miles

Configuration: Loop

Difficulty: Easy

Scenery: Arboretum, natural forest, birds, a lake with jumping fish

Exposure: Mostly exposed

Traffic: Moderate

Trail surface: Mostly paved; stretches of dirt, wood-chip trails

Hiking time: 50 minutes

Season: Open all year

Access: Open from dawn–dark; if gate at main parking lot is closed, park at the Memorial Tree Garden, east of the main entrance, off Mennonite Road

Maps: Available from the City of Aurora Parks and Recreation Department, (330) 562-4333

Facilities: Rest rooms and water by main parking lot; picnic tables, shelters, and grills are scattered throughout the park.

Special comments: Six Flags Worlds of Adventure is just north of Aurora on State Route 43. During the season, it's wise to avoid the road in the late morning and early evening hours when most parkgoers are either coming or going.

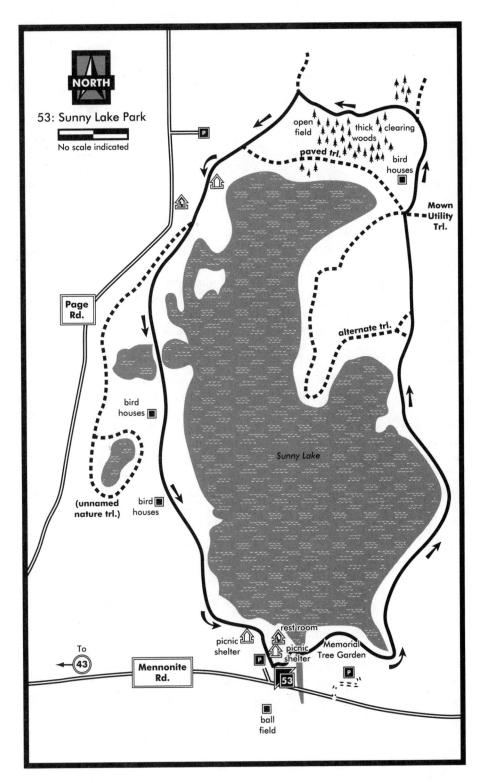

NORTH

53: Sunny Lake Park

No scale indicated

open field

thick woods

clearing

paved trl.

bird houses

Mown Utility Trl.

Page Rd.

alternate trl.

bird houses

(unnamed nature trl.)

bird houses

Sunny Lake

To 43

Mennonite Rd.

picnic shelter

rest room

picnic shelter

Memorial Tree Garden

53

ball field

The paved trail curves to the left, hugging the lake's eastern shore. In places, cattails grow so thick and tall that they obscure views of the lake. Sunny Lake is indeed sunny; most of the trail around it is exposed. That's not unusual for a lake trail. What is unusual at about this lake is that the fish jump. A lot. No matter when you walk around this lake, you'll probably notice fish jumping out of (and flopping back into) the water.

At 0.5 miles into the trail, you'll lose sight of the lake and its jumping fish. At this point, you can't see the lake for the trees. A couple of well-traveled but unmarked dirt trails on the left head through the woods toward the lake. (They're very short, and loop back to the main trail quickly, so follow them if you want.) As the woods thin out, you'll be able to see most of the lake from its mid-point. There's a lot to see.

Great blue heron sightings are almost guaranteed here. There's a rookery at Tinker's Creek State Nature Preserve, about 2 miles from here as the crow—or heron—flies. The birds often travel between the parks. Gulls and goldfinches gather here as well. At 0.75 miles into the trail, you'll come to a small clearing and several birdhouses. A mown but unmarked utility path leads east, to your right. The paved path veers left, curling down to the lakeshore. Pass both and head straight for the woods on the northern edge of the park. A hard-packed dirt trail winds through the oak and maple trees, over a couple of small hills, before leaving the woods via a short limestone path facing the Page Road parking lot. The path curves left and meets the paved trail near a small picnic shelter. As you head south from here, you can see the whole lake. Lily pads cover the water in places; this is an ideal spot to listen as frogs, birds, and bugs sing at you. The woods thicken

again as you round the lake's western edge; several park benches are placed to take advantage of the shade and the birding opportunities.

Other than mowing the trail shoulder, and the obvious care put into the Memorial Garden, Sunny Lake's trees and vegetation have been left to their own devices. The snarled brush shelters a large population of rabbits, black and gray squirrels, fat robins, noisy jays, singing spring peepers, and a few harmless garter snakes.

Returning to the main parking lot, you've logged about 2.3 miles. (Keeping to the paved path around the lake and avoiding the extension through the woods makes it a total of about 2 miles.) The two short nature trails—both of which can be quite muddy—add another 0.5 miles or so to the trip. In that time, you've probably met up with a number of dog walkers, stroller pushers, and maybe a bike or two. Sunny Lake's loop is also a popular spot at lunchtime, as workers escape the nearby industrial parks, if only for an hour.

As you complete your trip around the lake, you'll come to a bench swing just north of the main shelter. Sit and swing a spell, and keep an eye on the lake. It's jumping.

NEARBY ACTIVITIES

Sunny Lake Park's 463 acres offer plenty of activities. On the western side of the main parking lot, there are swings, volleyball and bocce courts, and four horseshoe pits. Peddle Boats and rowboats can be rented at the park office. Aurora residents can launch their own non-motorized crafts here for free; non-residents pay $8 for the privilege. Tinker's Creek State Park (see p. 190) and Tinker's Creek State Nature Preserve (see p. 187) are just about 2 miles southwest of Sunny Lake.

#54
Tinker's Creek State Nature Preserve

IN BRIEF

There may be some sibling rivalry between Tinker's Creek State Nature Preserve and her nearby and smaller sister, Tinker's Creek State Park (see p. 190), but each area compliments the other. Here you'll find a 786-acre nature preserve, with great wildlife viewing and a peaceful, quiet marshland in which to be still and enjoy a bit of solitude.

DIRECTIONS

From Cleveland, take I-480 east to the SR 91 exit. Turn right (south) on Route 91. Turn left at Old Mill Road, and head east 2.6 miles to the small parking lot on the left (north) side of the road.

DESCRIPTION

To enter the preserve and begin the hike, carefully cross Old Mill Road. A bulletin board there explains the rules of the preserve and is usually stocked with maps of the trails. The trail begins parallel to active railroad tracks, located about 300 feet to the west.

About 0.25 miles south of the trailhead sign, turn left onto Lonesome Pond Loop. The path can be quite muddy (this is a wetland, after all). Continue across the trail intersection and circle around the pond. Old-growth pines and younger deciduous trees almost completely shade the trail. In the spring and summer, an abundance of ferns and wild purple violets line the trail. The path narrows as it heads south. Not long after

(see p. 190)

KEY AT-A-GLANCE INFORMATION

Length: 2 miles

Configuration: Two loops and a short spur

Difficulty: Easy

Scenery: Seven ponds, marshlands, heron, nesting Canada geese and wood ducks, beaver, raccoons, deer, snapping turtles

Exposure: Mostly shaded

Traffic: Light

Trail surface: Dirt trail with some boardwalk

Hiking time: 1 hour for three trails and observation time at the overlook

Season: Open all year

Access: Closes at dark

Maps: At trailhead and at www.dnr.state.oh.us/parks/parkmaps/tinker.gif

Facilities: None

Special comments: Pets are not allowed in the Nature Preserve. Parking spaces are limited off Old Mill Road. There is a much larger lot at the State Park entrance, but there is no access from one park to the other except along Aurora-Hudson and Old Mill roads.

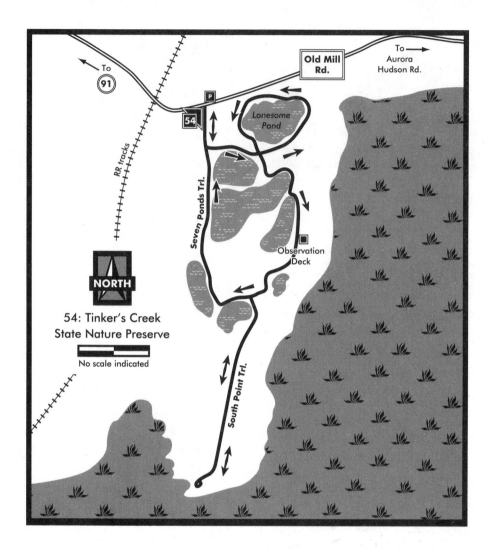

NORTH

**54: Tinker's Creek
State Nature Preserve**

No scale indicated

it narrows, the path forks—turn left (east). You'll soon step up on a wooden boardwalk. About half of this half-mile loop is boardwalk, necessary because it travels over marsh. Ohio's early pioneers liked to hunt here, but they were also wary of the squishy ground. Some referred to it as a "perilous" place, full of sinkholes and quicksand. Although the thick peat is messy, all that hikers in this area have to fear today are deerflies and mosquitoes.

You're likely to come upon deer or hear the slap of a beaver's tail as you near the pond. The boardwalk ends just about when the pond comes into sight. The marsh, full of cattails, is on your right; the pond is on your left. Lonesome Pond Loop is mostly shaded by young oak trees. Water in the pond itself is clean enough to watch crappie and turtles swimming around below the surface.

Several types of ferns dot the trail; in spring, a thick covering of mayapples appear. Their umbrella-like leaves shade the pretty white flowers. On the north side of Lonesome Pond, grass and roots have overtaken much of the trail, making for less sloppy footing, even on wet days. After circling the pond, leave it lonesome once more, and head south. A bench at the intersection of Lonesome Pond Loop and Seven Ponds Trail is a good place to contemplate what you've seen and consider your next steps.

Seven Ponds Trail heads south from here. Follow it as it weaves around the small ponds (as advertised) and leads to a wooden observation deck. The deck faces east, and from here you can see almost all of the marsh. Herons like to fly between Tinker's Creek and nearby Sunny Lake (see p. 184). It's a rare visit to either park that doesn't include a heron sighting. While this trail (and the whole preserve) sees little traffic, you may meet an avid birder or photographer here on the deck; it's popular with both species.

When you can tear yourself away from the view, follow the path around a gentle bend to the right. Soon after, the path splits. Follow the left fork south to the tip of the "peninsula" surrounded by the open marsh. Shaded by beech, oaks, and maples, this spur is especially pretty in the fall. (This spur is known as South Point Trail, although I've never seen it marked.) Return to the loop, and head west, by and between the remaining ponds.

As you head north, the trail straightens out and, for the most part, dries out as well. The railroad tracks are on your left, and the trail returns you to the intersection of Lonesome Pond Trail. With footsteps cushioned by the pine needles, you'll exit as quietly as you came in, slipping past the trailhead sign and crossing Old Mill Road. As you go, you may imagine you hear a whispered *thanks for coming* from the lonesome pond and her trails.

NEARBY ACTIVITIES

If watching the waterfowl dive and splash made you want to drop a line in the water, go around the corner to "sister" Tinker's Creek State Park. There, just off Aurora-Hudson Road, you'll find plenty of fish-friendly spots and a completely different set of trails.

#55
Tinker's Creek State Park

IN BRIEF

Meet Tinker's Creek State Park, Tinker's Creek State Nature Preserve's louder, wilder sister. Walk along boardwalks and dirt paths to explore remnants of the ice age and discover a heron rookery. The songs of catbirds and bluebirds entertain hikers as well as the family picnickers. The birdcalls are often hard to hear, however, over squeals from children on the playground.

DIRECTIONS

From Cleveland, take I-480 east to the Frost Road exit. Turn left (east) onto Frost Road, crossing over I-480, then turn left onto Aurora-Hudson Road, just east of the interstate. At dead end, turn right (still on Aurora-Hudson Road). Tinker's Creek State Park entrance is about 2 miles ahead, on the left. Park in the far lot, past the beach and ranger station, to pick up the trail.

DESCRIPTION

Start the hike on Pond Run, located at the far-western end of the parking lot. Although "Pond Run" trail isn't marked, it is easy to spot, as it cuts a wide, mulched path through short, dense growth. Within a few yards, you'll meet boardwalk because, well, simply put, otherwise you'd be in for a mud bath.

Since the Tinker's Creek area is higher than much of the surrounding area, you might ask, "Why is it so wet?" It's mushy

KEY AT-A-GLANCE INFORMATION

Length: 3.75 miles

Configuration: Three trails form a long loop; can do each separately.

Difficulty: Easy

Scenery: Herons and waterfowl, lake-loving wildflowers, 10-acre swimming/fishing lake

Exposure: About half exposed

Traffic: Busy all summer; you can find solitude here in cool weather.

Trail surface: Dirt, with boardwalks where needed

Hiking time: 90 minutes

Season: Open all year

Access: Park closes at dark

Maps: Available at ranger office and at www.dnr.state.oh.us/parks

Facilities: Playground, volleyball court, rest rooms, water, phone, and picnic areas located by the ranger office

Special comments: Pets are welcome here, on leash, but pets are not welcome at the preserve around the corner. Due to budget cuts, the beach was closed to swimming as of late 2002.

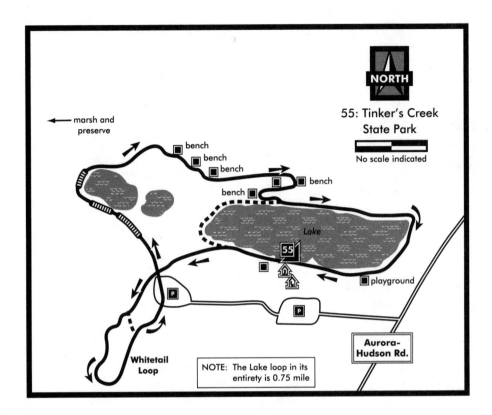

NORTH

No scale indicated

marsh and preserve

bench
bench
bench
bench
bench

Lake

55

playground

P

P

Whitetail Loop

Aurora-Hudson Rd.

NOTE: The Lake loop in its entirety is 0.75 mile

thanks to the Pleistocene, when chunks of giant glaciers broke off and dented the land. When the ice melted, it formed bodies of water or "kettle lakes." Boggy wetlands and small mounds of hills are also typical of the area. The resulting wetlands, while squishy, appeal to a variety of birds, animals, and plants. Buttonbush is especially pretty in the early spring.

When the boardwalk ends, you'll walk on grass (and it's muddy, too, most seasons). If you're quiet as you round the larger of two ponds, you may hear—or even see—beaver at work or play. A loud SLAP on the water is one beaver's way of alerting another to danger. If you hear it, you're probably too late to see the warning party, but you'll still notice signs of beaver activity in the pond. As the trail heads north and leaves the pond

behind, you see the marsh at the neighboring preserve to your left. Once a boardwalk connected the two properties, but it is submerged now, covered in several feet of mushy marsh.

Several benches dot the trail along here, and if you're a bird-watcher, this is a good place to sit still. Woodcock and snipe, and the more often-sighted catbird, like this area. Heading east, now out of sight of the pond, you'll head up a very gentle rise. The path soon loops right then turns back to the left, leading you to the grassy path around the lake. By the time you reach the lake's edge, you've logged about a mile. Follow the shoreline east then turn right along the eastern side of the lake and past tall cattails. When conditions are right, cardinal flowers also grow up above the goldenrod here.

Continue on the path as it loops by the playground and former beach area. Although this area is naturally wet thanks to glacial activity, the spring-fed lake is man-made. This was once a private swim park called "Colonial Spring Gardens." The state bought the land in 1966. It was dedicated as a state park in 1973. Head back to the trailhead, following the lake's south side, which is graced with sighing willows. Chances are you'll meet a man with a pole along the way, as this is a popular fishing spot.

Back at the parking lot trailhead, birdwatchers and wildflower lovers should press on. The southernmost loop trail here (a 1-mile jaunt with a shortcut that halves the distance) offers much. From the southwestern edge of the parking lot, follow "Whitetail Loop." Like the other trails, it is not marked, but it is easily recognized. The mostly grass trail moves south from here, but if you look up into the trees in the early spring—just as soon as you leave the lot—you'll spot the nests of great blue heron. Heron like to nest in the tops of dead, but not rotting, trees.

(Once a neighborhood begins to decay, they look for a new place to build.)

Just past the rookery, you can turn right onto a shortcut and find your way back to your car. But if you continue south in the springtime, you'll find a blooming good reason to keep walking: trillium and Virginia bluebells. You'll find them before you reach a sharp right turn on the loop, about the same time you see the backside of the private racquet club off Aurora-Hudson Road.

The trail loops back to the parking lot in, finishing up through an exposed, grassy area north of where it began.

NEARBY ACTIVITIES

Volleyball courts and horseshoe pits offer fun off the trail. You'll find a quieter place in Tinker's Creek State Nature Preserve (see p. 187), just around the corner: Take Aurora-Hudson north to Old Mill Road and turn left.

If you feel really adventurous, head for the wilds of Six Flags Worlds of Adventure, about 6 miles north of here, off Route 43 in Aurora.

IN BRIEF

The 175-acre Towner's Woods is home to an ancient American Indian mound, and to a number of creatures that require a variety of habitats: woodpeckers, owls, and deer claim the forest, while eagles like to perch high above Lake Pippen. The grassy fields along the southern perimeter of Towner's Woods provide the perfect spot for the American woodcock, or timberdoodle, to perform his mating dance. It is an impressive performance. Catch it if you can as the sun sets on an early spring evening.

DIRECTIONS

Take I–480/State Route 14 east into Streetsboro. Turn right onto State Route 43, heading south through the community of Twin Lakes. Turn left onto Ravenna Road and follow it about 2 miles east to the park entrance.

DESCRIPTION

This hike explores two distinct areas: the Towner's Woods Rail Trail and Towner's Woods Park. The trailheads to both sit on the eastern side of the parking lot. The park's wooded and hilly trails lead off to the left, but this hike begins to the right of a large park bulletin board, where you'll see the Towner's Woods Rail Trail sign. Enter that trail on an early spring evening and you just might happen upon a performance by the male American woodcock, or timberdoodle, as he tries to attract a mate.

KEY AT-A-GLANCE INFORMATION

Length: Up to 6 miles

Configuration: Interconnecting loops, out-and-back rail trail

Difficulty: Easy, with a few hills

Scenery: Fields, forests, wetlands, remnant prairie along the rail trail, lake views, a Hopewell American Indian mound

Exposure: Woodland trails mostly shaded; rail trail is exposed.

Traffic: Light to moderate

Trail surface: Dirt and grass

Hiking time: 1.5 hours or more, depending on trails selected

Season: Open year-round

Access: Dawn–dusk

Maps: Available from Portage Park District, call (330) 673-9404

Facilities: Rest rooms and water in parking lot near trailhead; there's also a sledding hill, dozens of picnic tables, two shelters, a gazebo, and benches set in all the right places.

Special comments: Lake Pippen, an important part of the City of Akron's watershed, abuts the park. The lake has long been fenced off, off-limits to all but City of Akron Water Department workers. Although the lake is closed to active recreation, the views are delightful.

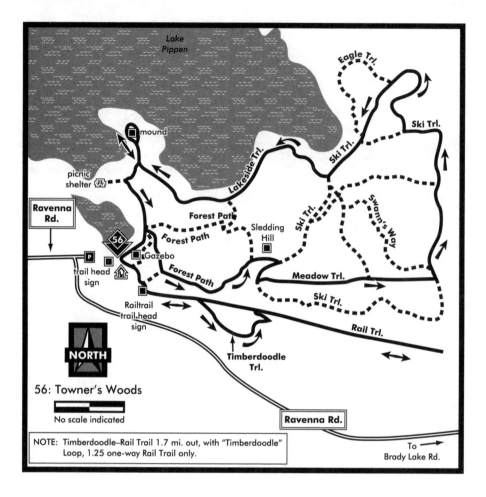

56: Towner's Woods

No scale indicated

NOTE: Timberdoodle–Rail Trail 1.7 mi. out, with "Timberdoodle" Loop, 1.25 one-way Rail Trail only.

Tall oak and hickory trees stand on your left, a railroad track lays to the right. About 100 yards into the trail, it forks. Turn right into the former farmland and stroll down the top of a gentle, grassy hill. If you've timed it right, you may encounter a timberdoodle here.

The bird has several other nicknames, like bog sucker and mud bat, which it deserves, considering its odd appearance. For starters, he's rather short and stout. He has a two-inch-long beak and big bulging eyes, both of which serve a purpose: helping him slurp up a vast amount of worms. The lower third of his beak can move independently, like a pair of tweezers, to snap up his prey below

ground. His bulging eyes allow him to watch for predators, even when his beak is completely stuck in the mud. Another unusual feature can be found on his wing. The male timberdoodle has three reed-like feathers on each wing that produces a high-pitched trilling sound when he flies high and fast. It's quite a performance.

First, he sits on the ground, producing a series of nasal-sounding beeps almost insect-like in tone. When the beeping stops, listen closely and look up. The woodcock climbs as high as ten stories, fast. It's easy to lose sight of him as he circles at the top of his flight, but you'll see him again in his trademark dive. Like a drunken kite, the timberdoodle falls fast and crooked. Back in the grass, he begins to "beep" again. It's difficult to catch the ground portion of the mating dance, but we have learned that he struts while he "beeps." On his short legs, though, and possibly dizzy from flight, he falls down often as he struts about. Hard to believe this attracts a lady.

Unfortunately, timberdoodle populations are falling as fast as their diving dance. The odd birds thrive in early successional fields. Former farmland is ideal for them—it's also ideal for shopping malls. Ironically, many parks and conservation groups who are focusing on reforestation may effectively drive the timberdoodle away. Happily, though, a stretch of prairie-type land along the southeastern side of Towner's Woods will be inviting to the timberdoodle for many more years.

The grassy loop curves to the left, rejoining the rail trail at about 0.5 miles. From here, you can continue east on the rail trail at least 1 mile (the trail will eventually connect with limestone trails leading into the city of Ravenna and beyond). Or, you can turn left onto the rail trail, returning to the parking lot and the main trailhead.

Most of the trails through Towner's Woods wind through thick forests of oak, maple, and pine to shady and strikingly beautiful views of Lake Pippen on the west. There are almost 4 miles of interconnected trails throughout the park; all are well marked. My favorite route goes like this:

Follow Forest Path, then Meadow Loop trail, past the sledding hill. Turn left (north), to join the cross-country ski trail. Follow it north, over lots of hills. Soon after the cross-country ski trail turns left, heading west toward the lake, it intersects the aptly named Lakeside

Trail. Tall oaks and pines run alongside, reaching heights of 50 feet or more. Lakeside Trail is skinny and rather sharply banked in some places. It drops down several railroad-tie steps to the lowest point in the park, just a couple of feet above the water level. Soon after, Lakeside leads you north onto a small peninsula where you'll find the Hopewell American Indian mound.

The Hopewell (and the mound) date to between 300 B.C. and A.D. 600. The mound was excavated in 1932, and 11 burials were found inside. The Hopewell culture is thought to have included worship of the dead, although admittedly, we're not quite sure what it involved. Whatever its prehistoric significance, the mound sits rather artfully on the top of a sandy knoll overlooking the lake. Long ago, it seems, the Hopewell found this spot as beautiful as we do today. Once you're done exploring the mound, head south to return to the trailhead.

NEARBY ACTIVITIES

In the middle of Towner's Woods, you'll find a sizeable sledding hill and two large picnic areas with grills. Beckwith Orchards (see p. 30) is just around the corner from Towner's Woods, and the city of Kent is about 4 miles south of here via State Route 43.

Each September, a hot-air balloon festival is held in Ravenna, just beyond the western edge of the park. Depending on the wind, you'll see the balloons for a few minutes or the better part of an hour after their evening launch. Call the Balloon-A-Fair committee at (330) 296-FAIR for details about the annual event.

Special thanks to Christine Craycroft, executive director of Portage Park District, for reviewing this section, and for providing an introduction to the timberdoodles on the trail.

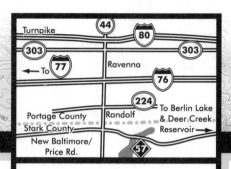

#57
Walborn Reservoir

IN BRIEF

Wander through lush, fertile landscape typical of Stark County farmland in this newly renovated park. The lake provides excellent opportunities for bird watching, and when the water is low, the bleached-white skeletons of tiny crayfish dot the lake's edge.

DIRECTIONS

From Cleveland, take I-80 east (or I-77 to I-76) to state Route 44. Follow Route 44 south to New Baltimore Road (also called Price Road here). Turn left; follow Price Road east about 3 miles to the park. The reservoir and parking lot are on the south side of Price Road.

DESCRIPTION

In northern Stark County, near Alliance, Stark County Park employees have been busy. Not only have they opened a new marina at Walborn Reservoir, but over the next few years, they will begin work on a trail connecting this park to nearby Deer Creek Reservoir. For now, visitors can explore the many trails already present here at Walborn.

From the southeastern end of the parking lot, follow the dirt and grass trail (an old service road, actually) south through young woods. The path forks to the left about 0.5 miles later—continue straight for now. You'll soon reach the shore, and be able to see the dam to your

KEY AT-A-GLANCE INFORMATION

Length: 1.8 miles

Configuration: Figure-8 with parking in the middle (do either side as separate loop if you choose)

Difficulty: Easy

Scenery: Blue birds, wildflowers, osprey, eagles, loons

Exposure: Mostly shaded

Traffic: Moderately busy, especially on weekends

Trail surface: Dirt and grass

Hiking time: 1 hour

Season: Park open year-round; marina open April–September

Access: Dawn–dusk

Maps: Posted at sign kiosk in park and online at www.starkparks.com

Facilities: Rest rooms, water, concession, and pay phone at marina

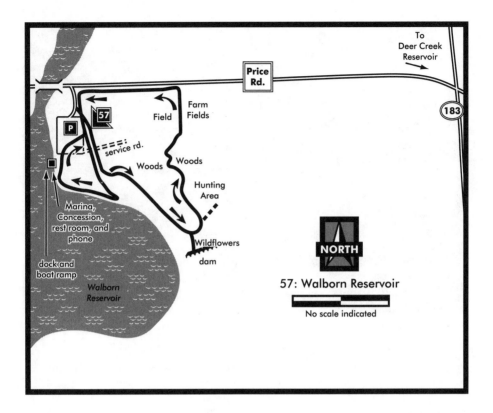

57: Walborn Reservoir

No scale indicated

left. Turn right, following the shore clockwise, and listen. Few things are as peaceful and calming as water lapping gently on a shore. The going is relatively easy, as long as you don't mind a bit of slogging through the sandy soil.

While visiting here in the summer, you'll probably see bright-yellow cloudless sulphur butterflies along this stretch. From spring through fall, keep an eye out for heron, a pair of bald eagles, and the occasional osprey, especially in August and September when the low water beckons waterfowl with tasty surprises. The Ohio Department of Natural Resources (ODNR) has worked to repopulate this area with ospreys, and their efforts are paying off. An osprey may resemble a gull while circling overhead. If you notice the bird hovering, then diving feet first into the water for a fish, you've spotted an osprey.

As you make your way along the shore, you'll find yourself crawling over fallen tree branches and creeping over the carcasses of expired crayfish. Ohio has about 20 species of crayfish. Many varieties burrow in the mud and are active only at night. That's fine with the owls, which like to eat the little crustaceans. Live crayfish also make good bait, but if you do decide to wet a line in the lake, it's important to use only native species. The bait that swims away can establish itself in the new habitat, and some non-native species, like the rusty crayfish, are so aggressive they can wipe out native varieties and wreak havoc on a delicate ecosystem.

About half-way around the shore, you'll have to make a sharp right-hand

Watch for osprey here

turn to stay dry. The trees here hug the bank. They planted their roots half in water, half in soil, so when the water is low, some of the roots appear to have grown into thin air. Also, when the water is low, especially along the western shore, you'll appreciate displays of drift-wood and rock art. Over the years, water and wind mold unique shapes and etch unusual patterns in both mediums. The pieces are displayed against a background of variegated dirt and clay.

Take a flat rock and skip it into the lapping water before you return to the marina, at about 0.7 miles. Follow the new boardwalk around the dock, then cut across the parking lot (northeast) to return to your starting point.

This time, when you follow the wide, flat trail south, take the fork to the left. You'll go up a slight hill and find yourself amid tall scotch pines. The wide path is covered with equal parts grass and pine needles, making the footing softer than the beach portion

of the hike. Soon, you'll emerge from the trees, rolling down a hill to turn sharply right.

This spot behind and below the dam offers a thicket of aster, goldenrod, and thistle, and it is popular with blue birds. Walk a few hundred feet into the thick of things, and see if you can spot one of the small, sweet-songed birds here. Then, turn around and continue on the trail as it rises slightly to the east along a shady, grassy path.

As you walk uphill, you'll reach a Y in the trail. Take the trail to the left and enter a thick wood of young walnuts and maples. The path bends left and leads up a hill through an ODNR public hunting area.

As you continue up a gentle incline, the woods thin out and eventually the path emerges to bisect a farm field. Where the trail dead-ends at Price Road, turn left and (carefully) follow the wide grassy berm west along Price to return to the park entrance and parking lot.

NEARBY ACTIVITIES:

There's a 6-horsepower limit on the reservoir, so this is a good place to bring small sailboats, canoes, and kayaks. Fishing is good here, year-round; bass is a common catch.

For more hiking and boating nearby, follow Price Road east about 3 miles to Deer Creek Reservoir, another Stark County Park that saw major improvements in 2001–2002. For information about interpretive programs, or about the status of connecting trails, go to www.starkparks.com or call (330) 477-3552.

Special thanks to Dan Kunz, Natural Resources Manager, Stark Parks for reviewing this hike description.

#58
West Branch State Park

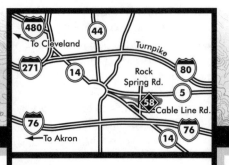

To Cleveland
Turnpike
Rock Spring Rd.
Cable Line Rd.
To Akron
480
44
271
14
80
5
#58
76
76
14

IN BRIEF

Like a lazy roller coaster, this hike follows gentle ups-and-downs on the south side of West Branch reservoir. You'll see little traffic, and the pretty woodlands and lake views combine to make this a pleasant trek.

DIRECTIONS

Take State Route 14 south to State Route 5. Follow Route 5 about 5 miles east of Ravenna to Rock Spring Road. Turn right on Rock Spring Road and go about 2 miles to Cable Line Road. Turn left, following signs to the boat ramp parking lot.

DESCRIPTION

The trails on the south side of West Branch Reservoir's boat launch area are marked for snowmobiles and mountain bikes. They also make delightful hiking paths. While the boat launch ramp is crowded on warm weekends, the trails see little traffic. Start your hike at the south side of the parking lot, entering the trails behind the bulletin board where park notices and a map are posted. You'll head up a short hill and turn left to follow the main "Cable Line" trail east toward the reservoir.

This partially paved road rolls along under the remainder of a beech-maple forest that once stretched from Mansfield to Pennsylvania. As the path rolls upward, the pavement holds its own, but by the

KEY AT-A-GLANCE INFORMATION

Length: 2–7 miles

Configuration: Out-and-back with optional loops off the main trail

Difficulty: Moderate

Scenery: Heavily wooded beech-maple forest, a few stands of pine, lake views, overlook

Exposure: Mostly shaded

Traffic: Very light (except after a snowfall!)

Trail surface: Main trail partly paved, loops are dirt

Hiking time: 1–3 hours, depending on the loops you choose

Season: Open year-round

Access: 6 a.m.–11 p.m.

Maps: Posted at the trailhead and available at the park office, 5708 Esworthy Road

Facilities: Primitive rest rooms, pay phone, picnic shelter, and grills by boat ramp

Special Comments: All bike/snowmobile trails lie within an Ohio Department of Natural Resources (ODNR) public hunting area. Small game is in season mid-August–mid-April. Wear bright colors when on the trails. For more information, see www.dnr.state.oh.us/parks.

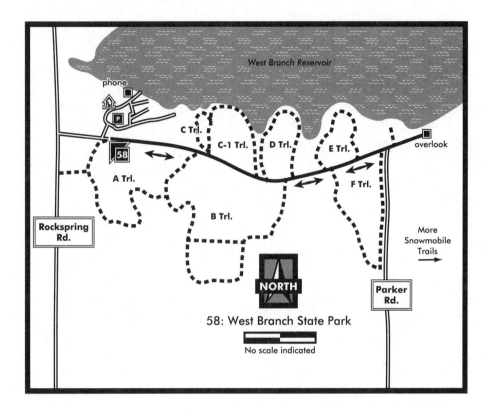

58: West Branch State Park

No scale indicated

bottom of the hill, it has lost ground to the encroaching grass. And so it goes. The battle between grass and asphalt continues all along the path, over 5 distinct hills, each offering at least a 20-foot climb. The grass has taken most of the low areas; the pavement still holds the tops of the hills. In between battles, on both sides of the path, small streams snake their way through the woods on their way to the reservoir.

The path rolls up to Porter Road, and while the street sign is gone, you'll recognize it by the circular turnaround, where there's room for several cars to park. This area, too, is zoned as a public hunting area; however, most folks here are armed with fishing poles. Cross Porter Road and continue east. You can see the reservoir from here, and a culvert wall on your left serves as a make-do

bench. (On early spring evenings, this is a good seat from which to listen to the chorus of spring peepers.) About 0.25 miles east of here, the trail dead-ends into a lovely overlook (and a popular fishing spot) on the water's edge. After admiring the view, turn back and head west.

Returning directly to the trailhead will give you a 2-mile hike. However, if you plan to follow the snowmobile trails on the way back, you have a lot to look forward to. The park map labels them alphabetically, but the trails themselves lack signs. The four short loops on the north side of Cable Line Trail wind through shady beech-maple and small stands of pine. Each loop bumps along to reach the water's edge, then turns south again, looping back to the main trail. Short wooden bridges carry you across the many twisting tributaries winding their way to the reservoir. On the south side of Cable Line, two longer loops ("A" and "B," about 1 mile each, and "F," about 0.9 miles) are more exposed than the northern paths, and just as hilly. If you follow the main trail and all the loops here, you'll have covered just over 7 miles.

NEARBY ACTIVITIES

West Branch State Park offers a variety of wet and dry activities for folks of all ages and interests. Picnic shelters can be reserved for a fee. A 700-foot swimming beach, complete with changing facilities and concessions is located on the southeastern side of the reservoir (admission is free). The marina rents boats ranging from canoes and rowboats to ski boats and Waverunners. The marina also offers a 90-minute pontoon boat cruise that highlights park features, including the dam that was completed by the Army Corps of Engineers in 1965. (In case you were wondering—the west branch of the Mahoning River was dammed to create the reservoir, so there's nothing cryptic about the park's name.)

In addition to the snowmobile/bike trails, an 8-mile segment of the Buckeye Trail loops through the park's eastern end. Add to that about 20 miles of nature and bridle trails, and there's enough day hiking here to keep you, and your boots, busy for a month. The park's campground was enlarged and remodeled in 2001. Call the park office at (330) 296-3239 for more information.

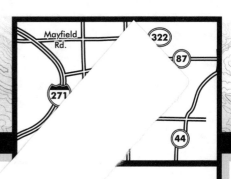

#59
The West Woods

IN BRIEF

The West Woods, in Russell and New-
bury Townships, is Geauga County's
newest park. It spans 900 acres an
ters several dwindling species.
a small cave, explore the are
and—adjacent to the par
the world's largest geoc

DIRECTIONS

From I-271, follow Route 422 east to
Route 306. Take Route 306 north to
Route 87. Turn right onto Route 87.
The West Woods is on the south side of
Route 87, 2 miles east of Route 306.

DESCRIPTION

(Note: The West Woods Nature Center
opened officially in the fall of 2002, after
this book went to print. For that reason,
this trail description starts from the
northernmost parking lot.)

When the nature center opens, additional parking will be available by the
nature center, and you may begin hiking
from there.

Start at Pioneer Bridle Trail, from the
southwest end of the parking lot. Step
onto the wide dirt trail, carpeted with
pine needles. Fifty steps or so later, the
trail dips and bends sharply to the right.
Turn and follow it downhill as it winds
through the dense woods.

As the trail sidewinds to parallel route
87, you'll notice lots of chain ferns. The
path narrows as it heads west. For a short

ANCE
TION
ı: 4.5 miles

nfiguration: Two loops

Difficulty: Moderate

Scenery: Forest, wildflowers,
pristine Silver Creek, remarkable
variety of bugs and butterflies

Exposure: Mostly shaded

Traffic: Light

Trail surface: Hard-packed dirt,
gravel

Hiking time: 1 hour 40 minutes

Season: Open year-round

Access: 6 a.m.–11 p.m.

Maps: Available inside nature
center

Facilities: Emergency phone, rest
rooms and water at nature center;
two picnic shelters

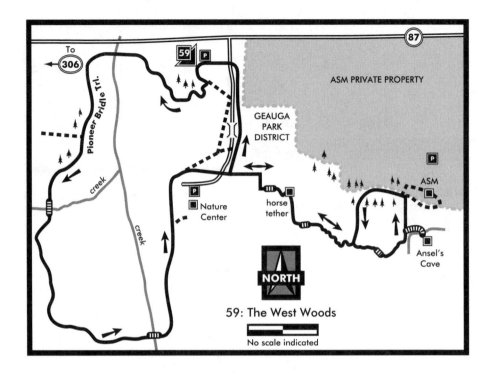

ASM PRIVATE PROPERTY

GEAUGA
PARK
DISTRICT

Nature
Center

horse
tether

ASM

Ansel's
Cave

NORTH

59: The West Woods

No scale indicated

time, you walk very close to the road,
but then the shady path widens and
drops down a short, steep hill, below the
traffic where it's a much quieter world.
On your left is a small creek, and during
the summer, the surrounding Joe Pye
weed, tall thistles, ragweed, and Queen
Anne's lace create a haven for birds, butterflies, and a crowd of dragonflies.

Before you've logged a mile, you'll
cross the creek and turn left, (south),
leaving Route 87 traffic behind for good
to enter a sweet-smelling pine forest.
The path can be muddy here, but where
it is at its stickiest, walk-arounds have
been worn for you. Remember that this
is a bridle trail, so yield to those on
horseback.

You'll soon reach an unmarked path
heading right (west) off the trail (it
leads to Route 306). Stay on the main
path, eventually crossing a wide, wood-
en footbridge where the creek is wider
than before.

As the trail wiggles through the forest
it continues to climb slowly. You move,
gradually, from a thick stand of thin trees
to an area of older growth. Under the
taller trees, you'll find mulberry bush,
and in the summer you'll spot angel
wings and jewelweed along the way.
Before you reach the back of the nature
center, you'll roll up and then down a
small hill, arriving at the West Woods
Nature Center and two picnic shelters.
Stop in at the nature center for hands-on
lessons about the geology, hydrology, and
ecology of Geauga County.

From the nature center, you can continue north on a wide path, next to the
park road, and return to the north parking area to complete the first loop of
your hike. To continue, cross the road
and follow the trail leading east to
Ansel's Cave.

The hard-packed, dirt-and-gravel trail
eases up a gentle rise; several benches
along the way offer rest. Continuing

Entering what remains of Ansel's Cave

along the edge of a 15- to 20-foot deep ravine, you'll cross over a short wooden footbridge, passing increasingly larger outcroppings of Sharon conglomerate sandstone infused with small, smooth pebbles.

The trail snakes a bit, but heads generally east and up. After a few minutes of steady uphill action, you (and the path) will reach the top of a large shale formation. From here you'll have a good look at the ravine, now 20 to 25 feet below. You're surrounded by maples and probably ready for a bit of a break. You've got it—ahead, you'll begin your descent with the aid of a wooden stairway, and then another. At the bottom of the second stairway, you'll see the rock formations for which the trail is named.

In the early 1800s, the cave was the home of Ansel Savage—whether he was a hermit, as some rather romantic accounts contend, is not certain. What hermit pursues political office? Savage served as a clerk, treasurer, and trustee of Russell

Township between 1830 and 1833. Although he drops off the local historical records in 1834, lore about the cave continues. The cave was a wolf den for some time into the 1840s; it's also said that a band of counterfeiters both hid out and worked inside the cave.

Following the boardwalk alongside a crooked creek bed, you may wonder, "what cave?" A waterfall and what's left of the cave stands about 75 feet off the trail to your right. Water and erosion caused the cave to cave in; the back entrance is also blocked. So while what's here is only the cave's "remains," what remains is lovely. An assortment of graffiti remains here, too; some of it dates back to 1877. (Read it, but please, don't add to it.)

Once you've had a good look around, turn and continue up the dirt trail. A series of S-shaped curves will lead you in a semi-circle that loops back to the main trail under tall black walnut and white pines. But at the top of the rise, just west of the cave, you can't help but notice another striking formation: the geodesic dome at Materials Park.

Materials Park is the world headquarters of ASM International. ASM (formerly the American Society of Metals) is an international society for materials engineers and scientists. ASM's Geodesic Dome is the largest of its kind in the world. Designed by ASM member Buckminster Fuller, it stands 103 feet high, is 274 feet in diameter at its base, and weighs 80 tons. It contains 13 miles of aluminum tubing and rods; foundations for the dome pylons extend 77 feet below ground.

Although Materials Park is private property, ASM allows visitors to walk under the dome during daylight hours. Under the giant structure, you'll find a fascinating garden of trees, shrubs, and more than 60 specimens of raw mineral ores—all labeled. A memorial to one of ASM's founders, William Hunt Eisenman, is there too, with a quote he cited:

Make no little plans;
They have no magic to stir one's blood
Make big plans;
Aim high in hope and work
Remembering that a noble, logical diagram
Once recorded will never die.

Eisenman donated 100 acres of farmland to ASM and laid the plans for its headquarters here. Although he died before the building was complete (in 1959), his request that we "make no little plans" has been realized, perhaps in ways even he did not imagine.

To complete The West Woods, the Geauga Park District purchased more than 500 acres from ASM. Obviously it was no "little plan" that created this park. Land donations, purchases, and careful planning have created this sizeable spread.

The West Woods' mature forests are home to barred owls, flycatchers, thrush, vireo, and several threatened plant species. The butternut tree, closed gentian, blunt mountain mint wildflowers, and tall manna grass all live here. The Ohio Department of Natural Resources Wildlife Division selected Silver Creek's tributaries as key spots to reintroduce the native brook trout, considered a threatened species. It's clear that the West Woods is a result of the "big plans" that Eisenman revered; it is also proof of the "magic" those plans can make.

If you choose to walk under and around the dome, remember that this is private property, and you are there upon your honor. Then return to the trail, which loops back into itself before returning to the park road. A wide, mulched trail alongside the road leads you back to the north parking lot where you began.

Special thanks to Paige Hosier, Geauga Park District marketing department, for providing historical documents on the cave and for reviewing this description—with help from Dan Best and others—even before the West Woods' official opening.

#60
Whipp's Ledges

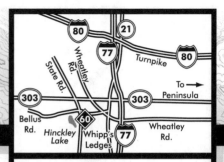

IN BRIEF

If you like to climb and gawk at great distances, Whipp's Ledges is for you. If buzzards are your bag, you'll want to visit this Medina County outpost of the Cleveland Metroparks in March. Visit anytime to enjoy the 90-acre lake.

DIRECTIONS

Hinckley Reservation is located in Hinckley Township, just south of Route 303. From Cleveland, take I-77 to the Route 21 exit and go south to Route 303. Turn right, going west about 3 miles to State Road. Turn left. Whipp's Ledges parking lot is about 1 mile south of Route 303, on the left (east) side of State Road.

DESCRIPTION

Hinckley Reservation has a fantastic reputation as "The Home of the Buzzards." The buzzards are actually turkey vultures, who return to roost each year, quite predictably, in mid-March. Hinckley understandably celebrates the buzzards' annual homecoming. But all the fuss about the raptors shouldn't suggest that buzzards are the only ones who might be attracted to the park year after year. Hinckley Reservation is full of reasons to return—for those who are driving as well as flying.

Whipp's Ledges is one good reason. Start your steep climb from the eastern end of the parking lot. You'll

KEY AT-A-GLANCE INFORMATION

Length: 0.5 miles (with option to do many miles more)

Configuration: Loop

Difficulty: Short but difficult

Scenery: Giant rock boulders and mini-caves of Sharon conglomerate, a spectacular view from the top

Exposure: Mostly shaded

Traffic: Moderate to heavy traffic

Trail surface: Dirt and rocks

Hiking time: 30 minutes, plus gawking time

Season: Open all year

Access: Cleveland Metroparks Reservations are open 6 a.m.–11 p.m. except where otherwise posted

Maps: Available at ranger station on Bellus Road and posted at the Boathouse

Facilities: Rest rooms, picnic shelter, and grills

Special comments: Here, as at Nelson's Ledges, you need to be cautious while climbing. Hang onto your children and dogs. To be blunt, a drop off the edge of one of these ledges could prove fatal. With reasonable care, you'll enjoy the hike and the views tremendously.

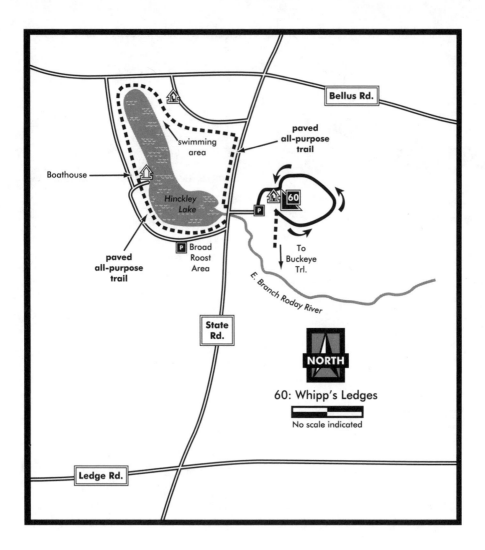

60: Whipp's Ledges

NORTH

No scale indicated

huff-and-puff from the get-go, and the fact that you'll have some roots and a few stone stairs to aid your climb is a mixed blessing. These steps—from root to root and from step to step—require serious knee lifting. Keep going; the view is worth the climb.

A sign for the Buckeye Trail points right (southeast) but your trek continues to the northeast. Don't worry that your path isn't marked; your destination is impossible to miss. The ledges loom ahead of you almost from the moment

you enter the trail. Up you go, huffing and puffing and rising along with the giant Sharon conglomerate outcroppings. Your footing may be slippery, as the ground is sandy and pocked with "lucky stones," small milky-white quartz pebbles that have fallen out of the larger conglomerate rock. Giant boulders—100 feet tall—loom straight ahead.

The trail bends to the left. Look at the massive stones on your right. Notice how the lichen grows in the indentations or pock-marks of the Sharon

Frequent visitors at the boat house

conglomerate, making an interesting play of light on the smoky dark rock.

Soon the massive stones to your left, 10 to 20 feet off the path at one point, begin to merge with those on your right, until you are squeezed into making a decision: either crawl through a narrow tunnel or sidestep to the right, climbing up and on top of the boulders. Whether you tunnel through or crawl up, just don't miss the view from the top of the ledges—you'll stand about 350 feet above Hinckley Lake, and, looking west, you'll have a fantastic view of the valley.

As you ease down from the big rocks, you'll probably need to use your hands as well as your feet to steady your descent. Loose gravel and leaf debris on top of the sandy soil makes for slippery going, in both wet and dry conditions. The trail bottoms out just north of where you began, but before you complete this short loop, you'll walk through a 4-to-6 foot wide "hallway" created by

2 massive rocks, each about 20 feet tall. Though it's not a cave, you may feel quite boxed in.

From here, the path winds west a bit, then veers to the left to find its way back to the picnic shelter and the parking lot.

Although you've reached the end of this short trail, plenty of Hinckley Reservation remains to be investigated. The reservation covers 2,000 acres. Consider visiting Whorden's Ledges to see the stone carvings there, or head off for the lake. You'll find boaters there in summer, skaters in the winter, and ducks and other wildlife year-round.

NEARBY ACTIVITIES

Want more miles? Hit the all-purpose trail here for a 3- to 4-mile trek around Hinckley Lake. You can rent pedal boats, rowboats, canoes, kayaks, and even a pontoon boat by the hour at the boathouse. A swimming area on the north side of the lake can be reached off Bellus or State Road.

Appendices

Appendix A—Outdoor Shops

Appalachian Outfitters
60 Kendall Park Road
Peninsula; (330) 655-5444

Gander Mountain
2695 Creekside Drive
Twinsburg; (330) 405-2999

5244 Cobblestone Road
Elyria; (440) 934-8222

9620 Diamond Centre Drive
Mentor; (440) 639-8545

Newman Outfitters
6025 Kruse Drive
Solon; (440) 248-7000

20180 Van Aken Boulevard
Shaker Heights; (216) 283-8500

Appendix B—Places to Buy Maps

CUYAHOGA VALLEY NATIONAL PARK

Canal Visitor Center
Independence,
(216) 524-1497 or (800) 445-9667

Happy Days Visitor Center
Peninsula,
(330) 650-4636 or (800) 257-9477

EARTHWORDS NATURE SHOPS OF CLEVELAND METROPARKS

North Chagrin Reservation
3037 SOM Center Road
Willoughby Hills; (440) 449-0511

Ohio & Erie Canal Reservation
4524 E. 49th Street
Cuyahoga Heights; (216) 206-1003

Rocky River Reservation
24000 Valley Parkway
North Olmsted; (440) 734-7576

F. A. Seiberling Naturealm, Metroparks Serving Summit County
1828 Smith Road, Akron; (330) 867-5511

Appendix C—Hiking Clubs and Events

Akron Bicycle Club
(hikes off-season)
www.akronbike.org

Cleveland Hiking Club
www.community.Cleveland.com/
  cc/chclub
(440) 449-2588

Portage Trail Walkers
(330) 673-6896

Appendix D—Bibliography

Abercrombie, Jay, *Walks and Rambles in Ohio's Western Reserve*. Woodstock, VT: Backcountry Publications, 1996.

Bartush, William W., *Lake View Cemetery Historical Trail*. Eagle Scout project, Troop 656, Cleveland Heights, OH (undated).

Beasley, Bob, "New Bike Trail Puts Cuyahoga Falls on Line," *Falls News-Press* (Stow, OH), 24 September 1995.

Bobel, Pat, *The Nature of the Towpath*. Akron, Ohio: Cuyahoga Valley Trails Council, Inc., 1998.

Corbett, Peter, "Pathfinders: Walking Medieval Labyrinths in a Modern World." *Grace Cathedral* enrichment features, 11 November 1998.

Cuyahoga Valley Trails Council, *Cuyahoga Valley National Recreation Area Trail Guide Handbook*. Akron, OH: Cuyahoga Valley Trails Council, 1996.

Directory of Ohio's State Nature Preserves. Columbus, OH: Ohio Department of Natural Resources, 1998–2000.

Gross, W.H. (Chip), *Ohio Wildlife Viewing Guide*. Helena, MT: Falcon Publishing, 1996.

Hallowell, Anna C. and Barbara G., *Fern Finder*. Rochester, NY: Study Nature Guild, 1981.

Hannibal, Joseph T. and Schmidt, Mark T., "Rocks of Ages." *Earth Science,* Spring 1998.

Hoskins, Patience Cameron, *Cleveland On Foot*. Cleveland, OH: Gray and Company, 2001.

Latimer, Jonathan P., and Nolting, Karen Stray, *Backyard Birds* (Peterson Field Guides for Young Naturalists) Boston, MA: Houghton Mifflin Company, 1999.

Leedy, Jr., Walter C., "Cleveland's Terminal Tower—The Van Sweringens" *Afterthought,* (Cleveland State University) 28 July 1997.

Manner, Barbara M. and Corbett, Robert G., *Environmental Atlas of the Cuyahoga Valley National Recreation Area*. Monroeville, PA: Surprise Valley Publications, 1990.

Ohio & Erie Canal Corridor Coalition, *Towpath Companion*. Akron, OH: Ohio &Erie Canal Corridor Coalition, 2001.

Path Finder—A Guide to Cleveland Metroparks. Cleveland, OH: Cleveland Metroparks (undated).

"Peninsula Village Architectural Tour," Peninsula Area Chamber of Commerce, Peninsula, OH (undated).

Sacha, Linda Hoy, "Area Cemeteries Rich in Historic Milestones of City," *Sun Newspapers,* 4 June 1998.

Waters, Sally, *25 Bicycle Tours in Ohio's Western Reserve*. Woodstock, VT: Countryman Press, 1991.

Watts, May Theilgaard, *Tree Finder.* Rochester, NY: Nature Study Guild, 1998.

Wright, Caryl, "Eccentric Russell 'caveman' was no hermit," *Russell Historical Society Newsletter,* Vol. I Issue 9 March 19, 1990

Zim, Herbert S. (PhD) and Cottam, Clarence, (PhD), *Insects.* New York, NY: Golden Books, 1997.

OTHER RESOURCES

Cleveland Metroparks
www.clemetparks.com

Cuyahoga Valley National Park
www.dayinthevalley.com

Geauga County Parks
www.geaugalink.com/parksfrm.html

Lake County Parks
www.lakemetroparks.com

Lorain County Metroparks
www.loraincountymetroparks.com

Medina County Historical Society
www.rootsweb.com/~ohmedina/mchistor.htm

Medina County Metroparks
www.medinacountyparks.com

Metroparks serving Summit County
www.neo.rr.com/metroparks/home.html

Ohio Outdoor Sculpture Inventory (OOSI)
www.oosi.org

Ohio Department of Natural Resources, Ohio State Parks
www.ohiodnr.com

Portage County Historical Society
www.history.portage.oh.us

Stark County Parks District
www.starkparks.org

Summit County Historical Society
www.neo.lrun.com/summit_county_historical_society

Index

About the Author

Diane Stresing

Diane Stresing grew up in Columbus, moved to the Cleveland area in 1989, and currently lives in Kent. A genuine Buckeye, Diane received a BA in Journalism from The Ohio State University. Although her byline can be found in a wide variety of national trade and consumer magazines, she's also published close to home, in *The Cleveland Plain Dealer, The Record Courier, FOCUS,* and *North Coast Sports.* When she's not writing, Diane volunteers with the National Park Service and stumps for local park issues.